Do It Green! MAGAZINE

MINNESOTA'S ONLY COMPREHENSIVE COMMUNITY GUIDE TO GREEN AND SUSTAINABLE LIVING

Sixth Edition, First Printing, November 2010
Produced & Published by Do It Green! Minnesota
100% Volunteer-Powered

Minneapolis, Minnesota
612-345-7973
U.S.A.
email: info@doitgreen.org • www.doitgreen.org
© 2011

CREATED BY THE COMMUNITY
FOR THE COMMUNITY

Then & Now
How Far Have We Really Come?

By **AMI VOELTZ** and **SARA GROCHOWSKI**

Welcome to the Sixth Edition of *Do It Green! Magazine.* Over the last couple of decades, much has changed in the green world while much has remained the same. In several areas, we have moved forward and others have faced retreat. In 1993, old growth forests were protected by a presidential executive order; however, only three years later logging of these old growth forests began again in the West. A Gallup poll that ran in 2010 showed that Americans more than ever believe the seriousness of environmental issues are "greatly exaggerated." Believe it or not, some people still think that climate change is the "hoax of the century." An overwhelming set of facts and circumstances can create an illusion that *nothing* has changed in the green world and nothing ever will.

The mission of Do It Green! Minnesota is to educate Minnesotans about green and sustainable living while promoting healthy local communities. In carrying out this mission the last ten years, we have met thousands of people along the way and taken part in hundreds of events that remind us every day that the world of sustainability is in fact alive and truly moving forward.

The first Living Green Expo here in Minnesota was held in 2002 and was considered one of the first well-coordinated green living events in the region and certainly the largest. One reporter commented that the first Living Green Expo "brought back-to-the earth old hippy types, local farmers and makers of goods from handmade clothes to edible pesticides for the lawn." This may be true; however, the expo and the Minnesota green movement has now attracted all walks of life. Examples include: those working on solar batteries in their back sheds, politicians introducing green initiatives, neighbors learning how to garden sustainably, families taking energy challenges at home, churches coming together to educate their communities, youth starting Earth clubs at their school, and community leaders organizing educational events.

Raising interest and action about sustainability is not just seen at large expos, conferences and organization meetings, but is also seen at the individual level. For example, the demand for Community Supported Agriculture (CSA) is ever growing that most farms sell out shares well before the actual planting season. The number of local farmers' markets continues to grow year after year. Furthermore, more people are taking their own action and planting gardens at home. In addition, consumers are now demanding to know what exactly their clothing materials are made from and are paying close attention to labels on products before actually purchasing them.

We emphasized in our last edition of *Do It Green! Magazine* that green living is not a modern concept—practices of growing your own food, buying only what you need and treading lightly on the earth are deeply rooted in our history and culture. Despite any evidence to the contrary, we are indeed moving ahead! **AND YES, THERE IS STILL SO MUCH MORE WORK TO DO!**

Change starts with commitment, whether it is the decision to plant native flowers, turn down the temperature on the thermostat two degrees or install a geothermal heating and cooling system. *Every* action large or small makes a difference!

We hope you enjoy your copy of the 2011 edition of *Do It Green! Magazine.* The theme of this edition, Then & Now, highlights how things used to be and how things have changed in the green and sustainability movement here in Minnesota the last 20 years. You will find very interesting articles, thoughts and ideas. We hope that you get through each and every article and share the information in this guide with others in your community. We invite you to contact us with any comments or suggestions you have at info@doitgreen.org or call us anytime at 612-345-7973. If there is a topic you think we should cover, let us know or offer to write it for our 2012 edition!

OUR PROGRAMS...

I n addition to publishing this guidebook, Do It Green! Minnesota has undertaken a series of projects in 2010 to help educate Minnesotans on living more sustainably, fostering healthy and sustainable communities, and living green and simply:

DO IT GREEN! RESOURCE CENTER

Do It Green! Minnesota launched our brand new resource center at the Midtown Global Market on Earth Day this year. We now host a 400 square foot resource center with educational displays, books, videos and eco kits available for check-out, workshops, and experts available to answer your questions. Stop by to visit us!

THE RAIN DROP PROJECT

Do It Green! Minnesota began our newest program called The Rain Drop Project in 2010. The project's mission is to educate residents about water conservation through educational materials such as a home water audit checklist which was distributed to over 700 families that purchased a rain barrel this year. In addition, our Rain Drop Team researched and put together a plan to launch 15 rain barrel education sites in the Mississippi Watershed.

DO IT GREEN! WORKSHOP SERIES

In 2010, Do It Green! Minnesota hosted over 30 hands-on workshops throughout the Twin Cities region on topics such as backyard beekeeping, gardening, harvesting, canning & preserving, homemade baby food, sewing, our footprint and more.

FIFTH ANNUAL GREEN GIFTS FAIR

As we go to print, we are planning our largest Green Gifts Fair event yet with over 70 local green artists, vendors, hands-on demos and educational tables. At our stage we will have an eco fashion show, holiday music, and local chef cook off. We expect a larger crowd than last year's event, which totaled over 5,500 visitors at the Midtown Global Market.

1990

The 20th annual Earth Day, considered the start of the environmental movement, is celebrated around the world.

Amendments to the Clean Air Act strengthen sulfate and nitrate emissions limits from electric power plants, addressing the problem of acid rain.

Nearly 100 countries agree to the London Protocols addressing atmospheric ozone.

A high-speed rail line linking Chicago and the Twin Cities is proposed, to public acclaim.

1991

Oilfield sabotage in Kuwait causes disastrous fires and spills of over a million gallons.

The Minnesota Legislature limits mercury levels in batteries.

Violation of the federal carbon monoxide standard prompts vehicle inspections.

A pipeline rupture near Grand Rapids spills 1.7 million gallons of crude oil. The Legislature enacts the 'Spill Bill' in response.

1992

The Rio de Janeiro Earth Summit leads to climate resolutions such as the Kyoto Protocols.

U.N. bans drift net fishing to preserve dwindling global fish stocks for the future.

The Minnesota Land Recycling Act is enacted to speed cleanup of brownfields.

The Mall of America opens.

1996

BSE ("mad cow" disease) in European cows is linked to humans, Poor practices and mobility cause a major international health crisis and distrust of meat products.

Logging of old-growth forests resumes in the West.

The Grand Staircase-Escalante National Monument becomes first in a series created during the '90s. The 8 million conserved acres represents more land set aside than any effort since Theodore Roosevelt.

Minnesota joins neighbor states in creating the Midwest Regional Rail Initiative for developing integrated passenger rail systems.

1997

President Clinton signs an order designed to protect children from environmental risks to their health.

The Kyoto meeting of the Conference of Parties to the U.N. Climate Change Convention leads to agreements to reduce greenhouse gas emissions. The Kyoto agreement is rejected by U.S. Congress despite adoption by over 100 nations.

Minnesota experiences massive floods along the Red and Minnesota Rivers. The 500-year flooding causes hundreds of millions in damage.

1998

Recorded temperatures rank as second warmest year on record, with only 1934 a statistically insignificant fraction higher.

Federal transportation bill includes over $100 million in funding for MN light rail transportation projects.

The Minnesota Pollution Control Agency fines Koch Refining a record $6.9 million for air, water and hazardous waste violations.

2003

Coal mining by mountaintop removal, the most harmful method of mining coal, clears federal legal hurdles.

2004

The Kyoto Treaty goes into effect despite U.S. legislative inaction.

The second Report Card on Environmental Literacy is published by Hamline University. It finds slight improvements in Minnesotans' understanding of environmental issues, but room for a great deal more.

Vehicle inspections and tighter controls lead to a 70% drop in Minnesota mercury levels since 1990.

2005

Energy Policy Act provides incentives for new non-polluting energy technologies.

Atmospheric CO_2 concentrations top 380 ppm (parts per million).

NASA reports the warmest year on record, topping all previous records since the beginning of modern temperature records.

The seminal book *Last Child in the Woods* is published, a cautionary tale about the trend pulling children away from nature and a call to reintroduce them for healthy development.

2006

Hurricane Katrina results in huge loss of life and enduring environmental crises.

NASA concludes that temperatures are highest in 12,000 years.

World population hits 6.5 billion.

Minnesota again leads the nation in proposing daily total limits on mercury in our waters.

Polar ozone holes reach maximum size at over 10.5 million square miles.

Forest lands under state care, nearly 5 million acres, are certified as sustainably managed by the Forest Stewardship Council and Sustainable Forestry Initiative.

2009

G8 industrialized nations agree to cut greenhouse gas emissions by 50% by 2050.

The second-warmest recorded year is logged, beaten only by 2005 and joining several recent years in a near-tie for second highest annual temperature. The U.N. weather agency ranks the decade 2000-2009 as the warmest on record.

The Trumpeter Swan re-introduction program, spearheaded by the Three Rivers Parks District, culminates in success. Begun in 1966, one of the nation's longest wildlife programs has led to an increase from zero wild birds to a self-sustaining population of over 3500.

Twin Cities' environmental education reaches 40. Since the inception of the Lowry Nature Center in 1969, metro programs have served untold thousands.

MINNESOTA AND ABROAD

Timeline by
JEFF BARTLETT
DO IT GREEN! MINNESOTA

1993

The Interior Department sets up the National Biological Survey, aimed at assessing and understanding diversity and ecosystems.

Old growth forests gain protection by presidential executive order.

1994

The Minnesota Office of Environmental Assistance is established to manage and educate about waste and other environmental issues.

Students discover severely deformed frogs in rural Minnesota. Research begins on environmental factors affecting amphibian development.

Minnesota's new Landfill Cleanup Act creates the Closed Landfill program, improving care and monitoring.

1995

Conservation groups and the World Bank partner to establish plans to create over 150 marine wildlife reserves.

The Cedar Lake Trail, dubbed the nation's first "bike freeway," is inaugurated in Minneapolis.

1999

World human population reaches the 6 billion mark, twelve years after its 5 billion global milestone.

Minnesota's average high temperatures for the decade rise to near 55 degrees Fahrenheit.

2000

Nuclear reactors at Chernobyl, Ukraine, the site of the world's worst human-caused environmental disaster, are finally shut down.

CFCs and other ozone-depleting chemicals reach record maximum levels.

2001

The first comprehensive published satellite survey shows widespread shrinking of glaciers.

The U.N. publishes the third major report of the Intergovernmental Panel on Climate Change underlining the robust link between climate change and human activity.

2002

The Center for Global Environmental Education at Hamline University releases its first Minnesota Report Card on Environmental Literacy, showing a range of positive behaviors but disparity in environmental knowledge among Minnesotans.

Minnesota enacts legislation limiting the use of phosphorus in fertilizers, protecting waterways and wetlands.

The Food, Drug and Cosmetic Act sets limits on toxins such as pesticides in foods.

The Minnesota Pollution Control Agency organizes and co-sponsors the first Living Green Expo.

2007

Minnesota signs the Great Lakes Compact, joining other states in improved management practices. The Supreme Court rules that CO_2 is a greenhouse gas and must be regulated under the Clean Air Act.

The Minnesota Forest Legacy Partnership launches projects conserving over 50,000 northern Minnesota forestlands.

Wind energy capacity crosses the 100-gigawatt threshold, more than doubling in three years.

The Three Rivers Park District turns 50. Its mission to promote environmental stewardship through recreation and education spans 27,000 acres of natural resources-based parks.

Minnesota's Next Generation Energy Act mandates an 80% drop in greenhouse emissions by 2050, and sets a utility company minimum of 25% renewable sources.

2008

The Tennessee Valley Authority ash spill dumps over a billion gallons of toxic sludge in Tennessee.

The U.S. greatly accelerates its wind energy capabilities, increasing capacity by 50% in about a year's time.

Minnesota's Clean Water, Land and Legacy Amendment dedicates tax money to create funds for parks, conservation and environmental projects.

Minnesota implements an incremental gasoline tax to help pay for public transportation and other projects.

Minneapolis Public Schools begin use of green cleaning products in all school buildings.

2010

Despite increased activism, a Gallup poll shows more Americans than ever believe that environmental problems are "greatly exaggerated."

The Deepwater Horizon oil spill becomes the leading marine environmental disaster in human history.

Minnesota's "Complete Streets" policy directs that new roadway designs consider public transportation, pedestrians, and other alternatives.

Minneapolis becomes the nation's most bike-friendly city according to Bicycling Magazine. The public bikeshare program Nice Ride Minnesota is launched, a great leap forward for pedal power in the Twin Cities.

Monthly atmospheric CO_2 hits 390 ppm, higher than any measured in the past 20 million years.

A coalition of Minnesota nonprofits introduces landmark legislation requiring green cleaning products in the state's public buildings.

Table of Contents

THE DO IT GREEN! DIRECTORY

FOOD

GOODS & SERVICES

HOME

TRANSPORTATION

GARDENING

ENERGY

Mission Statement

The purpose of *Do It Green! Minnesota* is to educate Minnesotans about green and sustainable living and promote building healthy, local communities through:

- The printed guidebook *Do It Green! Magazine* and web site www.doitgreen.org
- Community workshops and skillshares
- A resource center for educational tours and research

Do It Green! Minnesota will ensure that people of all incomes will have access to our publication and activities, and we will serve as a model for other cities and states nationwide. This guide can be found at most libraries, schools, and retail locations throughout Greater Minnesota. If you would like a guide donated to your organization, please contact us at info@doitgreen.org.

Our Organization

Do It Green! Minnesota consists of a core Do It Green! Team of 15 people and over 100 other volunteers. Other organizational activities include e-newsletter, hands-on workshops, resource center in the Midtown Global Market in Minneapolis and information tabling.

Publication Manifesto

During the entire production of this publication, the Do It Green! Team made every decision based upon what is best for the environment. Many of us bike, bus or walk for transportation, we use backsides of paper, re-claimed materials and email correspondence as much as possible. The publication itself is printed with soy ink on 100% post-consumer paper from an ethical company that offers recycled papers. We chose an ecologically-minded Great Printer and used digital imaging that allowed us to electronically send our file directly to the printing press. In addition, the binding is made with non-toxic, water-based glues. Last, but not least, the design of the pages and size of the book ensured the least amount of paper waste possible.

Design Manifesto

The main goal of *Do It Green! Minnesota* is to promote sustainability. A large part of this goal includes supporting local, small "industries." These industries are not merely businesses but are often individuals supporting themselves and preserving their autonomy. The resulting attitude is a D.I.Y. (do-it-yourself) mind-set, breaking the cycle of dependence on corporations, technology and governmental policies.

Do It Green! Minnesota walks a fine line between these two worlds; in many ways we are selling a product—a product of thoughts and ideas. We have the frustrating task of competing with mainstream, commercialized culture and media. As a result, the overall design of the *Do It Green! Magazine* will portray a genuine interest in the hand-made instead of the computer-generated/technology-driven design. Whenever possible, the publication will include hand drawn lettering, illustrations, and diagrams. This often means accepting imperfections (or better yet, relishing them) and reassessing how society views "good design." Overall, we expect the design of the *Do It Green! Magazine* to reflect the idea that art and design are not tools to sell and make money but rather expressive instruments inherent in the human species.

Do It Green! Magazine Team

The Do It Green! Magazine Team members donated their time to this publication on top of holding other full-time jobs or attending school:

Ami Voeltz-Schakel, *Editor-in-Chiefette*
Sara Grochowski, *Editor-in-Chiefette*
Katrina Edenfeld, Jennifer Harmening, *Category Editors*
Michael Kooiman, *Publication & Ads Designer*
Katie Daisy, *Cover Illustrator*
Katharine Nee, *Minnesota GREEN PAGES Directory*

Do It Green! Team Writers
Jeff Bartlett, Karna Barquist, Katrina Edenfeld, Sara Grochowski, Alena Hyams, Eva Lewandowski & Katharine Nee, in addition to the many writers who have contributed articles in this guidebook.

Proofreaders
Hagdis Tschunko, Eva Lewandowski, Jocelyn Anderson, Erin Bowley, Jeff Bartlett, Alena Hyams

Authors

There are over 100 different authors' voices in the articles of this publication. Many of the articles were written for *Do It Green! Magazine* and others were reprinted from other publications or web sites. Most of the authors are Minnesotans who wanted to share the information they feel is important for you to know. Their names are listed with the article(s) they wrote and can also be found in the table of contents.

Follow us on **twitter** at DoItGreenMN

Become a fan of Do It Green! Minnesota on **facebook**

Join the Do It Green! U of M Chapter on **facebook**

THE 2011 MINNESOTA DO IT GREEN! DIRECTORY

The organizations and businesses that appear in the 2011 Do It Green! Directory have passed sustainability criteria created by the Do It Green! Minnesota Team. The Team reviews each application by the criteria listed at doitgreen.org.

Please let these businesses know you found them in the Do It Green! Directory!

Get your business or organization listed in the 2012 Do It Green! Directory today! Go to doitgreen.org and fill out a short application online or call 612-345-7973 to request an application to be mailed to you.

FOOD

Barbette
1600 West Lake Street
Minneapolis, MN
612-827-5710
www.barbette.com

Barbette uses local and organic ingredients as much as possible, presenting beautiful food in a casual, eclectic, bistro atmosphere. Open seven days a week at 8 am for brunch, lunch, dinner and late night.

Bryant Lake Bowl
810 West Lake Street
Minneapolis, MN
612-825-3737
www.bryantlakebowl.com

Bryant Lake Bowl is a restaurant, cabaret theater, and bowling alley. BLB strives to present locally sourced and organic ingredients on the menu, moving toward making the business as sustainable and earth-friendly as possible for many years now.

Peace Coffee
2801 21st Ave. S. Suite 130
Minneapolis, MN
612-870-3440
www.peacecoffee.com

Proudly roasting, pedaling & brewing outstanding 100% Fair Trade, Organic & Shade Grown coffee in the Twin Cities for 13 years. Commit to Your Beans & Your Bike!

Red Stag Supperclub
509 1st Avenue NE
Minneapolis, MN
612-767-7766
www.redstagsupperclub.com

MN's 1st LEED Certified restaurant featuring a contemporized supperclub menu focused on locally farmed and organic ingredients. Open for lunch, dinner, late night, and brunch on the weekends.

Whole Foods Co-op
610 E 4th Street
Duluth, MN
218-728-0884
www.wholefoods.coop

Halfway between the Twin Cities and Grand Marais! Whole Foods Co-op is a full service natural foods grocer focusing on natural, organic and local foods.

GOODS & SERVICES

Bag-E-Wash Co., LLC
612-532-1407
www.Bag-E-Wash.com

Bag-E-Wash is a dishwasher accessory that allows consumers to effectively wash and dry their zipper-style food storage bags in the dishwasher. We also sell Bag Dryers, Reusable Produce Bags, Grocery Totes and Bio Fresh Bags. Don't throw them away. Reuse them!

Chinook Book— The Original Blue Sky Guide

612-455-8380
www.chinookbook.net

Chinook Book is your resource guide for the Twin Cities, offering the best of what's green and local with coupon savings of over $3000, neighborhood maps and interactive features.

Bright Sun Candles

651-485-6947
www.BrightSunCandles.com

Bright Sun Candles are all-natural soy wax candles. We hand-pour our candles in recyclable tins and recycled wine bottles in Saint Paul, MN. Our candles are crafted with high-quality soy wax, therapeutic-grade essential oils, metal-free wicks and no dyes. Soy candles burn twice as long as paraffin and emit less soot. Soy wax is also a sustainable resource, unlike paraffin, which is derived from petroleum.

Bryn Mawr Soap Company

Minneapolis, MN
612-374-3613
www.brynmawrsoap.com

Producing handmade natural soaps (no artificial scenting or additives) that have a wonderful lather, and are long-lasting. Available at most Twin Cities area co-ops and natural food stores.

CONTEMPL8 T-SHIRTS

Minneapolis, MN
612-870-7000
www.CONTEMPL8.net

Providing Eco-friendly, Water-Based T-Shirt Printing since 2001. We print your design on t-shirts, hoodies, onesies and more. We specialize in sweatshop free and organic shirts. We ONLY use water-based ink, and that is all we have ever used. We also use 100% wind power. We are located in Minneapolis, and we are independent, socially responsible, sustainable and affordable.

Do It Green! Magazine

Minneapolis, MN
612-345-7973
www.doitgreen.org

Minnesota's only comprehensive community guidebook to sustainable living. Magazines can be found at your local library, bookstore, or food co-op.

Green Career Tracks

Minneapolis, MN
612-822-0288
www.greencareertracks.com

Career guidance to help you pursue green career opportunities that support a sustainable world. Services include career coaching, skills assessment, resume development, market research, search strategy. Free half-hour consultation.

Handmade Tile Association

34 13th Ave NE
Minneapolis, MN
612-781-6409
www.handmadetileassociation.org

The HTA publishes an annual directory of local and national tile and mosaic artists and resources. The directory represents local handmade tile and mosaic artists from whom you can commission kitchen backsplashes, fireplaces, bathrooms and art for almost any application. Find out information on the annual MN Tile Festival.

Lifeworks Services Inc.

1355 So. Frontage Street Suite 101
Hastings, MN
651-268-2852
www.lifeworks.org

Fire starters made from 100% recycled product by people with disabilities.

Minnesota's Own Calendars

Minneapolis, MN
612-968-0708
www.mncalendars.com

Beautiful, fun and informative calendars that reflect the unique culture of Minnesota. Produced with bio-based inks, 10% PCW paper and 0% print production waste. Made in Minnesota — the design, images, printing and even the paper they're printed on!

HOUSE & HOME

Amazon Environmental, Inc.

7180 West Commerce Circle
Fridley, MN
763-572-0800
www.AmazonPaint.com

Amazon Environmental, Inc. sells 12 colors of recycled latex paint. Amazon Select paint is very inexpensive and regularly passes the Master Painter's Institute's quality tests. Our paint is made of at least 98% post-consumer products and carries the Green Seal certification for environmental standards.

Better Homes & Garbage

Uptown, Minneapolis
612-644-9412
www.BHandGarbage.com

Better Homes & Garbage collects and salvages quality reusable building materials and offers them for sale to the public. Browse inventory on line at www.BHandGarbage.com. Shopping "by appointment only" in Uptown Minneapolis.

Bob Alf Construction

1657 Marshall Avenue
St. Paul, MN
651-206-1937
www.bobalfconstruction.com

Bob Alf Construction is an innovator in sustainable residential building and remodeling services. In addition to traditional contracting, BAC offers Construction Coaching for those Do-It-Yourselfers who need some help with building science, construction skills or green strategies.

Borden Window

936 Beech Street
St. Paul, MN
651-338-7163
www.bordenwindow.com

Keep your old windows, make them work like new. We turn old drafty windows into energy efficient tilt-in windows. The best alternative to new windows.

EcoDEEP

2199 Pinehurst Ave.
St Paul, MN
612-788-8641
www.ecodeep.com

EcoDEEP is an architecture, design and green building consulting firm specializing in new and remodeled construction for residential and commercial projects, energy efficient practices, carbon reduction and high performance solutions for people who care. Our work promises that good design and environmental betterment are inherently interdependent and that high performance, sustainably designed buildings must be simple, economical and equitable. To learn more about EcoDEEP, and to view photos of our work please explore our website.

ENERGY

Center for Energy and Environment
212 3rd Ave N, Suite 560
Mpls, MN 55401
612-335-5858
www.mncee.org

A nonprofit organization that promotes the responsible use of natural and economic resources. CEE offers a full spectrum of energy, environmental and building rehabilitation services designed to improve the lives of business owners, homeowners and tenants. Often these services are provided through partnerships with neighborhood organizations, government agencies and businesses.

Metro Clean Energy Resource Team (CERT)
2801 21st Avenue South
Minneapolis, MN 55407
612-278-7100
www.CleanEnergyResourceTeams.org

Connecting communities to resources to plan and implement local energy projects.

Skally Management – Live Green Apartments
622 Grand Ave, #101
St Paul, MN
651-263-4080
www.LiveGreenApts.com

At Skally Management we are a family-owned and operated real estate management company that practices Eco-Management: sustainable, responsible real estate management designed to have a positive impact on our local environment and community.

GARDENING

All Organic Garden Care
St Paul, MN
651-235-2505
allorganicgardencare@yahoo.com

All Organic Garden Care provides environmentally responsible garden care using only non-toxic organic products.

Diamond Cut Lawn Care
3109 W 50th Street, # 132
Minneapolis, MN
952-929-2000
www.diamondcutlawncare.com

Diamond Cut Lawn Care provides a completely organic fertilization and weed control program that is safe for people, pets and the environment. Diamond Cut also provides full service environmentally sound lawn care.

Recycling Association of Minnesota (RAM)
PO Box 14497
St. Paul, MN
651- 641-4560
www.recycleminnesota.org

RAM is committed to promoting resource conservation through waste prevention, reuse, recycling, composting and purchasing practices in Minnesota. We provide outreach activities, conferences, forums, educational kits and more.

Rethink Recycling
www.RethinkRecycling.com

RethinkRecycling.com is your go-to guide for waste & recycling in the Twin Cities. Rethink Recycling helps citizens living in the six-county Twin Cities metro area understand the urgent need to make environmentally responsible purchasing and disposal decisions in their daily lives.

simplyneutral
18055 96th St SE
Becker, MN
320-309-5496
www.simplyneutral.com

Natural, non-toxic cleaners that are gentle enough for people with asthma, allergies, eczema, and multiple chemical sensitivities—yet strong enough to handle your toughest household dirt. Biodegradable and sustainably packaged.

Morr Construction
3600 North Lexington Avenue, Suite 209.
Shoreview, MN
651-633-0139
www.morrconstruction.com

From remodeling and additions to new homes, Morr Construction is dedicated to building sustainably. We bring energy efficiency, green materials, and overall health and comfort to any project. We are building a better way to live.

Natural Built Home
4020 Minnehaha Avenue
Minneapolis, MN
612-605-7999
www.naturalbuilthome.com

Natural Built Home has the largest selection of eco-friendly building materials in Minnesota. Our showroom is filled with eco-friendly flooring, counter tops, non-toxic paint, tile, cabinetry, insulation, dual-flush toilets and more. We also offer installation services for many of our products. Whether you are painting a nursery or building a new home, Natural Built Home will help make your green home dreams come true.

Otogawa-Anschel Design-Build, LLC
1214 42nd Avenue N
Minneapolis, MN
612-789-7070
www.otogawa-anschel.com

A small, award-winning firm devoted to green building and remodeling for urban living. Visit us online to learn more about our company, green build philosophy, and to view photos of our work.

Green Clean Solutions
320-266-5906
www.gogreencleansolutions.com

Aromatherapeutic Cleaning Products promoting a healthy planet and a healthier you. Green Clean Solutions are hand crafted in Clear Lake, MN using certified organic plant based ingredients and pure essential oils.

LULU Painting
Minneapolis, MN
612-275-6744
www.lulupainting.com

Proud to be one of the Twin Cities' leading eco-friendly painting companies. We use VOC-free paints, Recycle, and Re-use materials and products in local homes and businesses. Make yourself at home with LULU Painting!

Moss Envy (formerly Twin Cities Green)
3056 Excelsior Blvd,
Minneapolis, MN
612-374-4581
www.mossenvy.com

The local leader in selling eco-conscious goods for your home and life. Discover sustainable furniture, decor, home goods, gifts, jewelry, baby gear, mattresses, building supplies, and more at Moss Envy.

COMMUNITY

Northland Bioneers Conference
612-388-2542
www.nbconference.org

This regional version of the Bioneers national conference in CA features the Bioneers plenary speakers presented via DVD and workshops with regional experts. Conference participants also experience topic dialogues, networking opportunities, and interact with 30+ exhibitors. Watch for the 6th Annual Conference in 2011.

TRANSPORTATION

Metro Transit
560 Sixth Avenue North
Minneapolis, MN
612-373-3333
www.metrotransit.org

The transportation resource for the Twin Cities, offering an integrated network of buses and trains as well as resources for those who carpool, vanpool, walk or bicycle.

ENVIRONMENT

The Green Institute
2801 21st Avenue South
Minneapolis, MN 55407
612-278-7100
www.greeninstitute.org

The Green Institute is a non-profit focused on projects and practical innovations that simultaneously improve our community and the environment.

BUSINESS

Bolger Vision Beyond Print
3301 Como Avenue SE
Minneapolis, MN
651-645-6311
www.bolgerinc.com

Provides a full spectrum of integrated services and solutions to help our customers excel at communicating with their audience including commercial printing, print on demand/variable print, display, technology solutions, mailing and real time fulfillment.

MEDIA

Mykey3000 Graphic Design
Mike Kooiman
612-281-9247
www.mykey3000.com

Offering one-of-a-kind solutions for your project. Illustration, graphic design and web services. Visit my web site for a full portfolio.

Do It Green! Minnesota
Minneapolis, MN
612-345-7973
www.doitgreen.org

Minnesota's only comprehensive community guidebook to sustainable living. Check out the 2011 edition at your local food co-op or bookstore featuring articles, tips, resources and stories on Living Green, Living Simply.

Edible Twin Cities
2136 Ford Parkway, #292
St Paul, MN
612-229-0498
www.edibletwincities.net

A free, quarterly publication that celebrates local food artisans, farmers, chefs, and retailers. Free at over 200 locations throughout the metro area, or subscribe online for $28 to have it delivered.

EDUCATION

Dakota Valley Recycling
13713 Frontier Court
Burnsville, MN
952-895-4559
www.DakotaValleyRecycling.org

The shared recycling department for the Cities of Apple Valley, Eagan and Burnsville. DVR connects residents and businesses to recycling, composting and disposal information. Home of the ARROW program, recognizing area businesses for their environmentally responsible choices.

Hennepin County Environmental Services
417 N. 5th Street, Suite 200
Minneapolis, MN
612-348-3777
www.hennepin.us/environment

Information on how to reduce waste, recycle more, and properly dispose of hazardous items. The county also offers information on energy conservation, protecting water resources and education resources and grants that are available.

Minnesota Pollution Control Agency
520 Lafayette Road N
St Paul, MN
651-296-6300
www.livinggreen.org or
www.pca.state.mn.us/education

The Minnesota Pollution Control Agency provides educational resources for people trying to reduce their environmental impact in Minnesota and education resources for teachers and environmental educators.

Sewtropolis
5 West Diamond Lake Road
Minneapolis, MN
612-827-9550
www.sewtropolis.com

Sewtropolis is a DIY sewing studio and fabric store located in South Minneapolis. We have a large, spacious sewing studio equipped with everything a sewer may need, including the sewing machine. We offer fabric and patterns from such designers as Amy Butler, Heather Baily, Kokka, Oliver + S and more. Beginning sewing classes offered for adults, teens and children.

2011-2012 DO IT GREEN! DIRECTORY

MEMBERSHIPS FOR GREEN BUSINESSES & ORGANIZATIONS

Do It Green! Directory, in print
(it's in your hands!)

Do It Green! Directory,
online sample listings

How do I get my business or organization listed in the Do It Green! Directory?

All businesses and organizations must first apply to become a member by completing the online application at: **doitgreen.org/greenpages**.

Who is eligible to be in the Do It Green! Directory

Our board will evaluate your online application using the guiding criteria listed on this page. Applicants must meet two or more of the following criteria. We will notify you by email within two weeks if your business has been accepted.

Upon acceptance of your application, your listing will be posted online and your print listing will launch in November 2012 at the 6th Annual Green Gift Fair and will be distributed on magazine racks at over 75 locations in Greater Minnesota.

All directory members must meet two or more of the following criteria:
• local/regionally produced
• energy efficient/renewable energy
• less toxic
• durable/reused
• recycled content
• plant-based
• reduced packaging
• conserves/protects water
• organically grown/sustainably produced
• socially responsible
• builds strong communities

Do It Green! Directory/ Do It Green! Minnesota Users
• www.doitgreen.org green living database averages 10,000 hits/day.
• 17,000 *Do It Green! Magazines* have been sold and donated since 2001 at over 75 retail locations.
• Users are ages 20–45, progressive thinkers, environmentally-conscious, mostly Twin Cities Metro area residents (including suburbs) and Duluth residents.
• **For additional profile information visit doitgreen.org/greenpages**

TURN THE PAGE FOR SIGN-UP INFO!

INDIVIDUAL MEMBERSHIPS

IF YOU SUPPORT OR ENJOY OUR PROGRAMS

BECOME A DO IT GREEN! MINNESOTA MEMBER ...

OR GIVE A MEMBERSHIP AS A GIFT!

Sign up today!

- ☑ YES! I want to become a member of Do It Green! Minnesota
- ☑ YES! I would like to give a membership as a gift to:

_____

_____

Check membership level...

- ☑ Individual $30 ($20 Student)
- ☑ Family $75
- ☑ Supporter $250
- ☑ Lifetime $500

Name _____

Email _____

Phone _____

Address _____

City/State/Zip _____

_____

Submit your membership form online at **doitgreen.org/memberships**, call us at 612-345-7973 or mail to:

DO IT GREEN! MINNESOTA
Midtown Global Market
920 East Lake St., Suite G11
Minneapolis, MN 55407

2011-2012 DO IT GREEN! DIRECTORY

Basic Web Listing ($35)

- ✿ Do It Green! Directory listing online at www.doitgreen.org *(Usage 10,000 hits/day)*
- ✿ Receive the Monthly Do It Green! and Eco Business Tools E-Newsletters *(Sent to 5,000+ groups or individuals)*
- ✿ Do It Green! Directory 2011–2012 Membership Decal

Green Listing ($150)

- ✿ Basic Web Listing ($35 value plus...)
- ✿ Do It Green! Directory print listing in 2011–2012 Annual *Do It Green! Magazine (Distribution: 5,500)*
- ✿ Option to buy ad space in the 2011–2012 Annual *Do It Green! Magazine*
- ✿ Option to sponsor a monthly Do It Green! E-Newsletter
- ✿ Welcome packet with green business information

Greener Listing ($300)

- ✿ Basic Web & Green Listing ($472 value, plus...)
- ✿ Banner ad in the 2011 Do It Green! Monthly E-Newsletter *(Sent to: 5,000+/ $200 value)*
- ✿ Half price on booth at the 2011 November Green Gifts Fair *($87 value)*
- ✿ Option to buy ad space in the 2012 Annual *Do It Green! Magazine*
- ✿ Option to buy coupon space and a banner ad in an issue of the Do It Green! Monthly E-Newsletter for an additional $50.

Greenest Listing ($500)

- ✿ Basic Web, Green & Greener Listing ($1185 value, plus...)
- ✿ One box ad in the 2012 Annual *Do It Green! Magazine* (Circulation: 6,500, $200 value)

- ✿ One-year membership to Minnesota Waste Wise. Includes a waste audit or newsletter ad in Waste NOTes year-round Technical Assistance. *($200 value)*
- ✿ Prominently placed booth at the 2011 November Green Gifts Fair *($300 value)*

All Green Social Media Listing ($400) NEW!

⭐ This listing option utilizes all online social media networking that will not create paper waste.

- ✿ Do It Green! Directory listing online at www.doitgreen.org *(Usage 10,000 hits/day)*
- ✿ Banner ad in the 2011 Do It Green! Monthly E-Newsletter *(Sent to 5,000+ groups or individuals)*. Your coupon listed at the bottom of the same E-Newsletter issue. *($250 value)*
- ✿ Quarterly posts on the Do It Green! Minnesota Facebook page and will repost members' posts *(350 fans)*
- ✿ Quarterly Tweets to Do It Green! Twitter followers and will follow and re-tweet any member posts *(400 followers)*
- ✿ Both Facebook and Twitter posts can either be the basic contact info for your business and a link to your website, or information about a promotion you are running at that time and a link to your website.

Exclusive Sponsorship

⭐ Contact Katharine Nee or Ami Voeltz to discuss the Exclusive Sponsorship option. Sponsorships are limited to eight businesses/organizations. Sponsorships begin with a full page ad and an active link and logo on our home page for a year.

All directory listings and advertisers must first submit a Do It Green! Directory online application at **doitgreen.org/greenpages**.

ADVERTISING ADD-ONS:

For specific details for Add-Ons visit www.doitgreen.org/greenpages

- ★ BASIC BOX PRINT AD (⅑ page): $200
- ★ FEATURE PRINT AD (⅓ page): $425
- ★ E-NEWSLETTER COUPON AND SPONSORSHIP $250
- ★ DISPLAY/PRESENTATION at the Do It Green! Resource Center $250
- ★ FACEBOOK/TWITTER ADD-ON $100
- ★ BUSINESS-TO-GREEN BUSINESS AD $50

Home Water Audit Checklist

Published by Do It Green! Minnesota <DoItGreen.org>.
Excerpts reprinted from www.21acres.org.

This home audit helps you identify things that you can do RIGHT NOW to help reduce water use in your home and to keep our waters clean and safe.

Reduce Your Personal Water Impact at Home:

Kitchen

[×] When washing dishes by hand, don't let the water run between rinsings. Fill one sink or tub with wash water and the other with rinse water.

[×] Don't rinse your dishes before placing them in the dishwasher. This saves the planet 6,500 gallons of water per year and you $30 per year.

[×] Only run your dishwasher when it is completely full.

[×] When you are washing your hands, don't let the water run while you lather.

[×] When boiling water for cooking, use a measure cup to ensure you are not using more water than is necessary to prepare the dish. Also be sure to cover the pot to save energy too!

[×] Wash your fruits and vegetables in a pan of water instead of running water from the tap.

[×] Collect the water you use for rinsing fruits and vegetables, and then reuse it to water houseplants.

[×] Don't use running water to thaw food. Defrost food in the refrigerator for water efficiency and food safety.

[×] Avoid highly processed beverages like soft drinks. They can require up to twice as much water during production as is found in the end product.

[×] Soak pots and pans instead of letting the water run while you scrape them clean.

[×] For cold drinks, keep a pitcher of water in the refrigerator instead of running the tap. This way, every drop goes down you and not the drain.

[×] Designate one glass for your drinking water each day or refill a water bottle. This will cut down on the number of glasses to wash.

[×] Use the garbage disposal sparingly. Compost vegetable food waste instead and save gallons every time.

Bath

[×] Take showers (10-15 gallons of water used) rather than baths (30 or more gallons used) for one person.

[×] Give your young children baths one after the other, rather than drawing separate baths for them.

[×] Shorten your shower by a minute or two and you'll save up to 150 gallons per month. Try using an egg timer to shorten your shower.

[×] When running a bath, plug the tub before turning the water on, and then adjust the temperature as the tub fills up.

[×] Turn off the water while brushing your teeth and save up to 240 gallons a month.

[×] Turn off the water while you wash your hair to save up to 150 gallons a month.

[×] Turn off the water while you shave and save up to 300 gallons a month.

[×] Keep a bucket in the shower to catch water as it warms up or runs. Use this water to flush toilets or water plants.

[×] Replace your showerhead easily and inexpensively with a water-efficient model, and save up to 750 gallons a month.

[×] Repair leaky faucets or toilets. A single dripping hot water faucet can waste up to 200 gallons of water a month.

[×] Put food coloring in your toilet tank. If it seeps into the toilet bowl without flushing, you have a leak. Fix it to save up to 1,000 gallons a month.

[×] Upgrade older toilets with water efficient and dual flush models.

Laundry and Appliances

[×] Run your clothes washer only when it is full. You can save up to 1,000 gallons a month.

[×] Rather than using a humidifier, put moisture in the air by hanging your clothes inside to dry (and save energy too!).

[×] Front load washing machines can save as much as 40 cents per load.

[×] When buying new appliances, consider those that offer cycle and load size adjustments. They're more water and energy efficient.

[×] When upgrading appliances replace water cooled refrigerators, air conditioners, etc. with air cooled ones for significant water and energy savings.

General Household

[×] Monitor your water bill for unusually high use. Your bill and water meter are tools that can help you discover leaks.

[×] Listen for dripping faucets and running toilets. Fixing a leak can save 300 gallons a month or more.

[×] Grab a wrench and fix that leaky faucet. It's simple, inexpensive, and you can save up to 140 gallons a week.

[×] Teach your children to turn off faucets tightly after each use.

[×] Know where your master water shut-off valve is located. This could save water and prevent damage to your home.

[×] Use a commercial car wash that recycles water.

[×] Wash pets in the yard where run off can be used to water the lawn.

[×] Avoid recreational water toys that require a constant flow of water.

Yard & Garden

[×] Stay tuned to the weather forecast. Don't water your lawn or garden if it will be raining that same day.

[×] Adjust sprinklers so only your lawn and plants are watered and not the house, sidewalk, or street.

[×] Remember to check your sprinkler system valves, outdoor faucets, sprinklers and hoses periodically for leaks.

[×] Let your lawn go dormant during the summer. Dormant grass only needs to be watered every three weeks or less if it rains.

[×] Spread mulch around outdoor plants in order to conserve more water.

[×] Allow some leaf litter to accumulate on the soil. This keeps the soil cooler and reduces evaporation.

[×] Use a broom instead of a hose to clean your driveway and sidewalk.

[×] To decrease water wasted on sloping lawns, apply water for five minutes and then repeat two to three times.

[×] Reduce the amount of lawn in your yard by planting shrubs and ground covers appropriate to your site and region.

[×] Plant a rain garden with native plants and flowers.

[×] Choose shrubs and groundcovers instead of turf for hard-to-water areas such as steep slopes and isolated strips.

[×] Replace impervious (hard) surfaces with pervious surfaces.

[×] Direct water from rain gutters and HVAC systems toward water-loving plants or gardens for automatic water savings.

[×] Purchase or build a rain barrel or rain catchment device to harvest roof runoff for watering your yard and flower gardens.

[×] Have your plumber re-route your gray water to trees and gardens rather than letting it run into the sewer line. (Check with your city codes and, if it isn't allowed in your area, start a movement to get that changed!)

[×] Install covers on pools and spas and check for leaks around your pumps to avoid evaporation.

[×] Trickling or cascading fountains lose less water to evaporation than those spraying water into the air.

[×] Make sure your swimming pools, fountains, and ponds are equipped with re-circulating pumps.

Plant and Garden Care

[×] Water only when necessary. More plants die from over-watering than from under-watering.

[×] Water your garden in the morning or evening when temperatures are cooler to minimize evaporation.

[×] Check the root zone for moisture before watering and if it's still moist two inches under the soil surface, enough water remains.

[×] Water your plants deeply but less frequently to encourage deep root growth and drought tolerance.

[×] Spreading a layer of organic mulch around plants retains moisture and saves water, time and money.

[×] Plant in the fall when conditions are cooler and rainfall is more plentiful.

[×] When adding or replacing a flower or shrub, choose a low water use plant for year-round color and save up to 550 gallons each year.

[×] Adjust your lawn mower to a higher setting. A taller lawn shades roots and holds soil moisture better than if it is closely clipped.

[×] Install a rain sensor on your irrigation controller so your system won't run when it's raining.

[×] Use drip irrigation for shrubs and trees to apply water directly to the roots where it's needed.

[×] Don't water your lawn on windy days when most of the water blows away or evaporates.

[×] Group plants with the same watering needs together to avoid over watering some while under watering others.

[×] Use the minimum amount of organic or slow release fertilizer to promote a healthy and drought tolerant landscape.

[×] Use a rain gauge, or empty tuna can, to track rainfall. Then reduce your watering accordingly.

[×] Set a kitchen timer when watering your garden to remind you when to stop. A running hose can discharge up to 10 gallons a minute.

Community

[×] Encourage your school system and local government to develop and promote water conservation.

[×] Design and install a rain garden for your school to capture rainwater and reduce stormwater pollution. Ask your local nursery for design help.

[×] Make suggestions to your employer about ways to save water (and money) at work.

[×] Support projects that use reclaimed wastewater for irrigation and industrial uses.

[×] Share water conservation tips with friends and neighbors (like this checklist!).

[×] Report broken pipes, open hydrants and errant sprinklers to your neighbor or water provider.

Check the Do It Green! Minnesota website for more water tips and water-related articles at **WWW.DOITGREEN.ORG**.

Funding for the Rain Drop Project was provided by the Mississippi Watershed Management Organization.
www.mwmo.org

MISSISSIPPI WATERSHED MANAGEMENT ORGANIZATION

LEFT: **Score extra eco-points by biking to pick up your food from the co-op!**
RIGHT: **A little herb garden is a great way to get involved in producing your own food.**

Strengthening our Local Food Systems

By **LIZ MCMANN**
MISSISSIPPI MARKET CO-OP

In a country where rivers of high fructose corn syrup flow through our food system and the food recalls never seem to stop, something really miraculous is happening. In the shadows of genetically modified corn fields and pre-made frozen peanut butter sandwiches, people are starting to see past the industrial food system that we've grown accustomed to these past 50 years. People are starting to take the American food system into their own hands and become personally invested in where and how their food is produced. People are starting to care about their food.

Each time we choose to find out the source of our food, we not only learn about our food supply, but we also have the opportunity to make a choice. Turning over a package of food or checking out those little stickers on our apples can open our eyes to the size and scope of the food supply. And we can choose an alternative. In fact, the alternatives are practically mainstream these days.

Gardening, farmer's markets, food co-ops, and community-supported agriculture (CSA) — all of these food sources are growing stronger with every new gardener, shop-per, member-owner and subscriber! Having a personal involvement and connection to our food is part of what has been missing in our convenience- and price-driven diets. And this connection to our food could be what changes our food system.

Think about it: When a child takes the time to plant a seed, water it, nurture it through its lifecycle and harvest its fruits, that child is more likely to eat that fruit or vegetable. We know that getting children involved in growing and preparing their food encourages them to eat healthy foods. The same holds true for any of us. ❧

Introduction, CONTINUED

One of the most radical and effective actions we can take to change our food system is to get involved in it!

You can start small with buying some locally-grown apples from a co-op, visiting the farmer's market, or growing some herbs on a windowsill. Be careful, though. The freshness and flavor of real, sustainably produced food is addictive. You'll want more! Before long, you'll be digging up your yard to plant kale, joining a food co-op, harvesting onions at your CSA farm, canning peaches, and sharing recipes for home-cooked organic meals with your neighbors. And the outcome of all this? You'll know what you are eating. You'll know the people who worked so hard to grow your food. And you'll strengthen the local food systems that are changing how America eats, one community at a time.

ON THE WEB!

- Food co-ops across the country, strongertogether.coop
- Twin Cities Food Co-ops, themix.coop
- Minnesota Farmers' Market Association, mfma.org
- Land Stewardship Project's CSA Farm Directory, landstewardshipproject.org /csa.html

READ UP!

- *Grace from the Garden: Changing the World One Garden at a Time*, by Debra Landwehr Engle, Rodale, 2003.
- *The Town That Food Saved: How One Community Found Vitality in Local Food*, by Ben Hewitt, Rodale, 2010.

ACT LOCALLY!

- Mississippi Market Co-op St. Paul, MN, msmarket.coop
- EggPlant Urban Farm Supply eggplantsupply.com

What is a Vegan?

By **UNNY NAMBUDIRIPAD, KARA FANCY** *and* **AMI VOELTZ**

A spread of delicious vegan foods. Sharyn Morrow

Veganism is a lifestyle which avoids using animals for food, clothing, or other purposes. Vegans try to minimize suffering and cruelty by not purchasing products that are derived from animals. Vegetarians do not eat meat, fish, or poultry. Vegans, in addition to being vegetarian, do not use other animal products or by-products such as eggs, dairy products, honey, leather, fur, silk, wool, cosmetics, and soaps derived from animal products.

Animals suffer immensely in modern "factory" farms. They are confined in small areas for most of their lives, in a space too small to stretch their wings or turn around. The animals must constantly face filth, disease, and lack of individualized care. Cows also are hurt by the human consumption of dairy products. For factory farmers, the cow producing milk or producing meat is no different. Dairy cows are still slaughtered after 5–6 years of producing milk for human consumption. It is especially hard on the mother cow that often has her calf taken away at birth.

By not consuming the products that come from animal exploitation, each individual is making a statement against inhumane practices. They are undertaking an economic boycott, and supporting the production of vegan products. These decisions, and the message they send to others, help to move society away from industries that use animals as a means to human ends. Although the end goal is generally the same, the path an individual takes towards veganism is a unique one. Some people follow a methodical process of cutting out foods in the order they consider to be the cruelest, or the foods they find the easiest to avoid. Others, initially concerned with health, eventually cut out products such as chicken and fish as they become more aware of the suffering involved in the production of these goods.

Others go "cold-tofu," giving up all animal foods, donating their leather goods to charity, returning products that have been tested on animals, etc. Changing to a vegan diet can at first seem like a daunting task, but with time and a little motivation, new habits become easy to follow.

ON THE WEB!

- Vegan resources, vrg.org
- Vegan advocacy and nutrition, veganoutreach.org
- Replacing animal products when baking, doitgreen.org/article/food/ NonAnimalSubstitutes

READ UP!

- *Eating Animals*, by Jonathan Safran Foer, Back Bay Books, 2010
- *Becoming Vegan: The Complete Guide to Adopting a Healthy Plant-Based Diet*, by Brenda Davis and Vesanto Melina, Book Publishing Company, 2000.

ACT LOCALLY!

- Animal Rights Coalition/Ethique Noveau Minneapolis, MN 612 822-6161 animalrightscoalition.com *and* ethiquenouveau.com
- Compassionate Action for Animals Minneapolis, MN 612-276-2242 exploreveg.org
- Earthsave International 952-930-1205 twincities.earthsave.org
- Fast and Furless Minneapolis, MN 612-FUR-LESS fastandfurless.com

Tips: How to Begin Eating a Vegan Diet

Cook vegan at home. This is a pretty easy task with a wide variety of tasty vegan recipes available over the internet such as vegweb.com and the spread of vegan cookbooks, such as Veganomicon, available at most bookstores.

Start with fast and easy vegan foods. This could include bean burritos, spaghetti, salads, veggie burgers, chili, french fries, tofu lasagna and veggie stir fries.

Learn how to cook vegan. Check with your local co-op at themix.coop for cooking classes on vegan cooking and baking.

VEGAN NUTRITION

Vegan diets can be healthy at all stages of life. When eating a diet based on whole grains, fruits, vegetables, and legumes, a few nutritional needs of vegan diets are often of concern. With a little planning, none of these are hard to reach:

- **Calcium:** Kale, broccoli, calcium-set tofu, fortified orange juice, and almonds are good sources of calcium. Unless you're eating a lot of these and other high-calcium foods regularly, you may want to take a mineral supplent. For healthy bones, be sure to get adequate exercise and vitamin D, and avoid excessive amounts of caffeine, sodium, and protein.

- **Iron:** Many plant foods are high in iron. Beans, tofu, whole wheat and spinach are just a few examples of iron-rich foods.

- **Protein:** Protein requirements are easy to meet on a vegan diet, since protein is readily available in most plant foods. Tofu, lentils, peanut butter, and brown rice are all good sources of protein.

- **Vitamin B12:** Plant sources are not reliable sources of B12, so supplements should be taken. They are available at grocery and natural food stores. You

can also use some nutritional yeast, found at co-ops in the bulk section or prepackaged. It's tasty sprinkled on top of your foods or on popcorn!

The quest for personal purity is practically impossible. All around us are items connected in some way to animal suffering: some brands of white sugar (bone char used in processing), beer and wine (animal blood, egg whites, etc. used in refining), bicycles (animal fat in tires), roads and buildings (animal products used in curing concrete), medicine (tested on animals).

Any steps you can take to remove your support from animal exploitation are valuable. Alleviating the suffering of others is the essence of veganism. Regardless of any other beliefs we hold and however else we choose to lead our lives, we can make a conscious decision to act from kindness and compassion rather than habit and tradition.

Veggie & Green Restaurants

By **ALENA HYAMS** *and* **JEFF BARTLETT**
DO IT GREEN! MINNESOTA

Among the signs of progress we've seen in Minnesota in recent years, one of the bright spots is surely the greening of our vibrant restaurant scene. New choices allow us to eat low on the food chain and support responsible restaurants that walk the talk, applying principles that reduce waste, save energy, and support local producers.

According to veteran Dave Rolsky of Veg-Guide, "it used to be that the word vegan was unheard of, and most restaurants had no idea what that meant," adding that now "many restaurants make a point of explicitly labeling vegetarian and vegan items, or providing a separate menu." Reliance on local producers, better packaging and efficiencies, and vegan spreads from bread to ice cream are now part of the landscape.

All in all, it is a great time to eat out, with restaurants greening in the Twin Cities and

greater Minnesota: From Northfield's Just Food to Duluth grill and Whole Foods Deli, vegetarian selections, and green practices are catching on. We cannot do justice to all those great restaurants out there, but here is a sampling you might want to try:

Willowgate Chinese Restaurant, Roseville
willowgateonline.com
A family-run business around since 1983, Willowgate has a fantastic lunch menu allowing guests to order a main dish, rice, and sides—all for less than seven dollars! An entire section of vegetarian friendly food with a tofu or mock duck option and an atmosphere that is always very fun and welcoming.

Red Stag Supper Club, Minneapolis
redstagsupperclub.com
This new Northeast club is the state's first LEED-certified restaurant, proving that wasteful and energy-intensive restaurant practice need not be the norm. The owners take "local" to a new level, offering Meet the Farmer nights. Locally sourced, organic ingredients include a variety of meats and sandwiches, but vegetarian options are available.

The Black Sea, St. Paul
blacksearestaurant.com
With fewer than ten tables, "Minnesota's first Turkish restaurant" is very cozy—you feel right at home. The Black Sea has cheap, delicious food and a wide selection of vegetarian options. A personal favorite dish is the Meze Platter, which includes ➛

Green Restaurants, CONTINUED

cabbage rolls, pita bread and hummus, olives and feta cheese, and falafel.

Namasté, Uptown
namastechai.com

A relative newcomer already famous for chai drinks and people watching, Namasté offers great Nepalese and Indian dishes with organic ingredients. The vegetarian section includes vegan-friendly dishes and a great outdoor patio to enjoy them.

Ginkgo Coffeehouse, St. Paul
ginkgocoffee.com

With a great selection of vegetarian food, as well as fantastic coffee and desserts, Gingko is a popular place for college students to come and study, or just to hang out and listen to some live music.

Seward Community Café, Minneapolis
sewardcafempls.net

True to its name, this community icon has enhanced the local vibe for decades with a mainly vegetarian/vegan menu, great breakfast, and an alternative casual crowd. Great baked goods include vegan items, and you can get the "Earth" on a plate.

Fasika, St. Paul
fasika.com

An Ethiopian restaurant in the Midway area of St. Paul, Fasika has a menu of vegetarian options including lentils in berbere sauce and curried vegetable stew. Use the traditional injera bread in place of flatware to grab bite-sized portions of food. Fasika is a great place to eat if you are looking to try something truly authentic.

Birchwood Café, Minneapolis
birchwoodcafe.com

Food, setting and atmosphere all reflect the true neighborhood style of this green leader. Wonderful dishes on a dynamic, changing menu and a casual but lively sensibility lend a great feel to the place. Vegetarian and vegan fare from named local sources are amazingly fresh, and luxurious desserts crown the menu.

Mesa Pizza, Minneapolis
mesapizzamn.com

This Dinkytown hotspot is hugely popular among local college students. With a wide variety of pizza by the slice, as well as whole pizzas and salads; Mesa is a great choice for a fast, cheap, delicious meal. With choices like Macaroni and Cheese, and Avocado Delight pizza and extended hours, Mesa has something to please everyone.

Galactic Pizza, Uptown
galacticpizza.com

Uptown's Galactic Pizza is a prime example of what can be done to make the restaurant scene more earth-friendly. Pop on 3D specs and browse the menu for vegan and vegetarian ingredients, local produce and simply outstanding selections, enjoyed under their grassy tiki awnings or delivered by ultra-efficient electric vehicles. Add to that composting initiatives and local ownership, and this place has it all!

ON THE WEB!

- VegGuide, vegguide.org
  A great resource providing extensive lists and reviews of the hundreds of vegetarian and vegan-friendly establishments in Minnesota

- Make Dirt Not Waste, makedirtnotwaste.org
  Eureka Recycling's listing of restaurants leading in composting programs

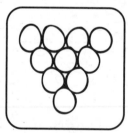

Macrobiotics: Diet for a Healthy and Peaceful World

By **GABRIELE F. KUSHI, BFA, MEA, CHC, AADP**
BOARD CERTIFIED HOLISTIC HEALTH PRACTITIONER, MACROBIOTIC NUTRITIONAL CONSULTANT, COOKING TEACHER, AND DIRECTOR OF KUSHI'S KITCHEN

The goals of macrobiotics are the realization of planetary health and happiness, world peace and human evolution. Macrobiotic, derived from the Greek word macrobios (large life), is associated worldwide with living and eating in harmony with the season. Macrobiotics embraces the 5,000-year-old philosophy of yin and yang, wherein yin represents expanding energy and yang contracting energy. Yin and yang are the building blocks found in all phenomena in varying proportion. Scholars have classified the relationship of yin and yang in many phenomena, including food groups, body types, organs and meridians.

What is a macrobiotic diet?

Macrobiotics supports traditional foods that people ate before the dawn of our modern civilization. Thus, the macrobiotic diet emphasizes natural and whole foods such as grains, land and sea vegetables, legumes, beans and bean products, seasonal fruits, seeds, nuts and vegetable oils. These foods eaten in season provide a healthy body and a peaceful mind. Foods to be avoided are excess animal products (meats, dairy, eggs, honey, fish), refined and processed products (sugar, white flour) and stimulant foods (nicotine, coffee, spices), which seem to contribute to sickness, aggression and disharmony.

A variety of cooking techniques such as steaming, pressure cooking, sautéing, baking, juicing, sprouting, pickling, soaking, fermenting or raw are used to enhance the nutritional value and seasonal energy of food.

The macrobiotic diet provides guidelines (proportional as well as food-wise) that can be modified depending on one's individual health, personal needs, climate, environment and other considerations. Thus it differs from a vegetarian/vegan/raw diet, which does not take such considerations.

In the context of disease treatment, or for more detailed guidance regarding dietary change, it is recommended that individuals seek advice from a qualified macrobiotic health consultant.

Daily macrobiotic dietary guidelines for a temperate climate:

- 30%–60% Whole Grains: Major portion of whole cooked grains like short- and medium-grain brown rice, sweet and wild rice, millet, spelt, barley, oats, kamut, quinoa, wheat or corn. Minor portion of whole grain sourdough bread or other baked whole flour products, pasta and flakes.
- 20%–30% Vegetables: Green leafy vegetables, including collard, kale, broccoli, Nappa cabbage or mustard greens; root vegetables such as daikon, carrots and burdock; and round vegetables, preferably cabbage, onions and squash.
- 5%–10% Legumes and Beans: Chickpeas, azuki beans, lentils, white and black soybeans, and bean products like tofu or tempeh.
- 3%–5% Sea Vegetables: Nori, wakame, dulse and sweet water algae daily. Arame, hijiki and kombu seaweed three times per week.
- Small volume of locally grown fruits. Choose locally grown fruits that are in season to prepare delicious desserts. You can use dried or fresh fruits. Prepare fruits with a pinch of sea salt, or cook them with kudzu, a vine with starchy roots. Minimize or avoid eating fruits that cannot be grown in your area.
- Small amounts of seeds, nuts, and raw foods like vegetable juices and salads.
- Fermented Foods. Complement each meal with a small amount of fermented pickles to enrich your meals with enzymes. Include a pressed or ⤳

➠ *Macrobiotics,* CONTINUED

raw salad and sprouted seeds or beans. Prepare homemade quick pickles from a variety of vegetables. Use long-term traditional pickles like raw sauerkraut, takuan (a white radish) daikon, or ginger pickles

- Very small volume of seasonings and condiments such as sea salt, miso, soy sauce, goma-shio, umeboshi vinegar and plums.

Why do people choose to eat this way?

Millions of people on this planet are actively practicing macrobiotic principles, and its dietary benefits have been published in numerous scientific and medical journals. Because the macrobiotic diet prevents and protects against degenerative disease, it may be the best diet to follow in this time of high cancer rates, heart disease, obesity, allergies, HIV/AIDS and the hazards of environmental pollution. These conditions are considered to be a result of our imbalanced modern way of life.

Macrobiotic benefits for the body

Research about the macrobiotic diet indicates that because of its low-fat and high-fiber content, it benefits people by: reducing high cholesterol, preventing heart disease, reducing cancer risks, assisting with weight management and strengthening the immune system.

Macrobiotic benefits the environment

Macrobiotics supports organic, natural agriculture and natural food processing and production. It raises environmental awareness, while preserving a clean, natural environment and respecting natural and animal life. Macrobiotics promotes natural water conservation as well as natural technologies to purify contaminated water.

Nutritional information about the macrobiotic diet

The American Journal of Clinical Nutrition published a study by Dr. B.L. Specker that points out that some sea vegetables provide sufficient sources of Vitamin B12 within a macrobiotic diet (Specker, 1988). It is, however, important to eat balanced meals with all food groups in order to obtain the nutrients the body needs. If for some reason a person cannot always follow a balanced diet, vitamin and mineral supplementation is recommended. Since very few people can make a radical transition from a diet of primarily meat and sugar to a diet based on grains and vegetables, most people make the transition to macrobiotics step by healthy step.

ON THE WEB!

✿ Kushi's Kitchen, kushiskitchen.com

READ UP!

✿ *Embracing Menopause Naturally,* by Gabrielle Kushi, Square One Publishers, 2006.

✿ "Increased urinary methylmalonic acid excretion in breast-fed infants of vegetarian mothers and identification of an acceptable dietary source of vitamin B-12," by BL Specker, D Miller, EJ Norman, H Greene, and KC Hayes. *American Journal of Clinical Nutrition,* Jan 1988; 47: 89–92.

Living Simple V

By **ELLEN TELANDER**
WINSTED ORGANICS FARM

Rescued horse and goats at Winsted Organics Farm.

There are so many new things on the farm this year, and I can only talk about a few for this article. I call this year "Reduce my workload please!" I am trying to make time for more play in my farm life.

I sold off the dairy herd this year. I was up to 20 heads! They all sold on Craigslist for $150–$200 each to other small farms or people trying to live off the land. Apparently, dairy goats are more popular than ever with the increased interest in the raw foods movement. Everyone wants raw milk for health reasons. I kept my best doe and a buck for our own use: I didn't want to get rid of my only source of good quality organic milk. I also needed a way to start making fresh yogurt! It's so easy! I ended up purchasing a $25 electric yogurt maker. Wow, talk about easy, and it makes a great quality yogurt using goat's milk.

➠

HOW TO MAKE YOUR OWN YOGURT:

What you'll need:

- 3–4 small, pint-sized glass jars. Do not use big quart jars. In this instance, smaller *is* better.
- Clean lids for the glass jars.
- Store-bought organic yogurt (just a small single serving will do or if you plan to make a lot each week, buy the larger bulk size). Make sure it has *live* cultures. Look at the date on the package, and don't buy yogurt nearing its expiration.
- Blender or whisk and bowl.
- 1 C of raw milk or store bought milk.

Cheapo Instructions if you don't own a yogurt maker:
Most people say you need to heat pasteurize your milk, but don't bother.

1. Put the milk in the blender (or bowl with whisk) and blend one cup of yogurt in milk *entirely*. Do not leave clumps of yogurt in the mixture.
2. Pour mixture into glass jars and screw on lids.
3. Put jars in a warm place in your house. I've used the warm window or up high in the kitchen above the stove. It needs to be warm, but *not* too hot to kill the yogurt cultures. Do not use the oven, heating pad or crock pot. All are too hot even on low.
4. Leave alone for 16–24 hours. Yes, that's right! As long as the cultures are alive, then you will have yogurt and not spoiled milk!

TIP: Fresh yogurt will look like the consistency of kefir sometimes. This is due to your jar size (too big), not enough time allowed to sit, not enough heat, or poor yogurt starter.

Tomatoes Galore!

I had a *bumper* tomato crop this year. I planted 30 various heirloom plants, including some I've never heard or seen before. I'm an Italian and our family of course has its own family recipes for spaghetti sauce. I've perfected *fresh* tomato sauce. Use the best tomatoes you can find, ones that taste sweet. I prefer to add large yellow tomatoes: they add a nice tangy acid to the sauce.

HOW TO MAKE YOUR OWN TOMATO SAUCE

Yield: Makes enough for a large gathering or to freeze for later. Sauce is always better the next day.

What you'll need:
- one huge pot or crock pot
- wooden spoon
- 1–2 chopped onions
- 8 cloves garlic, chopped
- 20–25 large tomatoes, cored and skinned. Don't use small tomatoes.
- olive oil
- small can of tomato paste (organic)
- 3 T dried oregano
- 2 T dried basil
- 1 tsp marjoram
- 1–2 T sea salt
- 1 tsp pepper
- a little sugar to taste if you need it
- a splash of red wine, more if you like that taste

Instructions:

1. Sauté onions and garlic in olive oil in pot.
2. Then add meat to pot to sauté: I make meatballs or add a nice sausage and goat chops. Alternative: you can use sliced, sautéed mushrooms—a lot of them. This will offer a meaty flavor to the sauce if you are a vegetarian or trying to reduce your meat intake. You can always use meat alternative crumbles by MorningStar™.
3. Simmer this all day long. You need to allow for at least 8 hours of cooking. You need to simmer this slowly on *low*. Don't try to do this in 3 hours and burn the sauce!

How to remove tomato skins: You can do this by dipping the tomatoes in boiling water for 1 minute and skins remove easily. Or a lazy way is to freeze the tomatoes overnight (cored with skins on) and put the frozen tomatoes on the counter. As they thaw, you can easily remove skins and throw them in the pot.

Green Your Child's School Lunch

By **KATRINA EDENFELD**
Do It Green! Minnesota

Home-packed lunches can be fun, healthy, and green, with very little time or money required. I calculated that my child's lunch, including organic fruit, required less than five minutes on average and $1.00 per day last year—compared to over $2.25 for school lunch. Try these suggestions to green your packed lunches, whether for children, adults, or picnics!

Reduce waste: Avoid disposables and look for high-quality reusable items—for instance, an insulated lunch bag with sturdy zippers and a leakproof, child-friendly stainless steel water bottle. Polypropylene plastic containers (#5) do not contain BPA and are a lightweight option for packing cold foods. A stainless steel food jar makes home-packed hot lunch possible. Finish the lunch setting with a reusable ice pack, a cloth napkin (in a fun fabric, if you're crafty!) and washable spoon or fork.

Choose greener foods: An environmentally friendly lunch will limit packaged and processed foods and focus low on the food chain. Avoid food waste, too: many schools have a very short lunch period, and your child may only be able to eat a small amount of food in that time. Consider thinking of lunch and an after-school snack as two small meals, both consisting of healthy foods, to substitute for a larger lunch.

Add a surprise: A funny note or a short poem tucked into the lunchbox is fun for young ones.

Be prepared: Don't expect to be very inspired in the middle of the morning school rush. Take a few minutes during a quiet time to make a list of the foods your child would like to eat for lunch, and add the ingredients to your grocery list. It doesn't need to be an extensive list: some children are happy eating the same lunch for a surprisingly long string of days.

Leftovers such as this Szechuan noodle salad and fresh fruit make a perfectly easy, green lunch when packed in reusables. Katrina Edenfeld

A few ideas to inspire your own creation:

Cold

- Cheese sandwich
- Cream cheese and vegetable sandwich
- Peanut butter and jelly, if permitted
- Pita bread and hummus, beans, vegetables
- Yogurt (make or buy in bulk) and granola (pack separately)
- Wrap with baked tofu or a bean spread, vegetables
- Hard-boiled egg
- Pasta salad

Hot, in food jar

- Your child's favorite soup or chili
- Pasta with tomato, cheese, or pesto sauce
- Beans, mashed or not, with tortilla and cheese on the side

On the side

- Fruit
- Vegetables, sliced as needed, raw or lightly steamed
- Pickled cucumber or other veggies
- Roasted chickpeas
- Trail mix

ON THE WEB!

- ⚙ Waste Free Lunches, wastefreelunches.org/HowTo.html
- ⚙ Creating Less Trash at School, pca.state.mn.us/index.php/download-document.html?gid=11345
- ⚙ Healthy Kids' Lunches and Tips, eatingwell.com/recipes_menus/collections/healthy_kids_lunch_recipes

READ UP!

- ⚙ *Vegan Lunch Box: 130 Amazing, Animal-Free Lunches Kids and Grown-Ups Will Love!*, by Jennifer McCann, DaCapo Press, 2008.
- ⚙ *Lunch Boxes and Snacks: Over 120 Healthy Recipes from Delicious Sandwiches and Salads to Hot Soups and Sweet Treats*, by Annabel Karmel, Atria, 2007.

ACT LOCALLY!

- ⚙ Wedge Community Co-op Minneapolis, MN 612-871-3993 wedge.coop/recipes/whats-in-lunch-box
- ⚙ Linden Hills Natural Home Minneapolis, MN 612-279-2479 lindenhills.coop/naturalhome
- ⚙ Lands End Not-Quite-Perfect Store, Roseville, MN 651-633-7004 *Lunch boxes, food jars*
- ⚙ Lands End Inlet, Woodbury, MN 651-714-9000 landsend.com

How to Be a Locavore

By **LIZ MCMANN**
MISSISSIPPI MARKET CO-OP

Eating locally isn't just a fad diet or a trend. On the contrary, global, mega-farm sourcing for nearly all of our foods is a relatively new practice. It wasn't long ago that citrus, coffee and avocados were treats to be savored rather than kitchen staples. Those concerned with the environment, survival of small family farms and food freshness are embracing a local diet that supports their values. As we return to the common-sense practice of sourcing food locally whenever possible, it helps to have some tools and tips on hand for navigating the road to locavorism. After all, while our ancestors ate locally because that was the norm, it takes more effort for modern-day Americans to be involved with their food supply and stay committed to local foods.

#1: Know why you want to eat locally.

You will encounter those who disagree, so be prepared to explain why you have decided to eat more local foods. Perhaps it's the pollution associated with "food miles" or simply the superior taste of produce eaten within hours of harvest. Whatever the reason, keep it in mind both for self-motivation and explaining to curious lunch-mates.

#2: Define what you consider local

Local means something different to everyone: 100 miles, MN grown, regionally produced, etc. Choose where you want to source your food and become familiar with what is grown locally. Don't forget the importance of supporting local food processors and restaurants. Our local food system includes more than just farmers!

#3: Find a community

Eating locally by yourself can get lonely. Seek out fellow locavores to share recipes, favorite farms and insight into the art of eating locally. Networks abound online — check out the resource list. And don't be too shy to approach fellow shoppers at your local co-op or farmer's markets!

#4: Choose some simple "busy night meals"

We all have nights when we want to forget our values and order some greasy (non-local) pizza. Plan a couple of meals that are simple to prepare and keep the ingredients on hand at all times. Cook and freeze some Whole Grain Milling Co. black beans for quick tacos or never let your omelet-ready Schultz organic eggs run out.

TOP LEFT: **Brian from Ames Farm shows off his single-source honey from right here in MN.** ABOVE: **Omelets and scrambled eggs are a simple local meal (and not just for breakfast!)** BELOW: **Hoch Orchard's organic apples provide a crunchy local treat throughout the Fall and Winter.**

#5: Don't worry if you're not 100% local

Nobody's perfect and eating an avocado won't undo all the good you've done with your locally grown meals. Choose a goal for how local you want to eat. Find a balance between sourcing local foods and allowing yourself some non-local indulgences.

ON THE WEB!

- Eat Local America, eatlocalamerica.coop
- Simple Good and Tasty, simplegoodandtasty.com
- Real Food Minnesota, realfoodmn.wordpress.com

READ UP!

- *The Minnesota Table: Recipes for savoring local food throughout the year,* by Shelley N.C. Holl and B.J. Carpenter, Voyageur Press, 2010.
- *Coming Home to Eat: The Pleasures and Politics of Local Food,* by Dr. Gary Paul Nabhan, W.W. Norton, 2009.

ACT LOCALLY!

- Find a co-op near you at coopdirectory.org
- Mississippi Market Co-op St. Paul, MN, msmarket.coop
- Golden Fig St. Paul, MN, goldenfig.com

Remaking the Way We Make Things

PRODUCT STEWARDSHIP AND ZERO WASTE

By **DIANNA KENNEDY**
EUREKA RECYCLING

Have you found yourself holding onto a household item or package that you cannot recycle or compost (or get fixed for less than buying two new ones) and yet you just can't stand to "throw it away?" Are you an avid recycler and composter so now your trash can looks like a collection of plastics that are suitable for nothing except maybe a modern art piece? Sometimes it looks like these items really should be recyclable but those pesky recyclers just won't take it. Truth is, your best efforts to recycle and compost (and ours at Eureka Recycling) will not stop our trash cans from filling up. However, there are ways to redesign these products in the first place and *you* have the chance to influence it!

One way people talk about moving beyond reuse, recycling and composting is through legislation called "product stewardship." Product stewardship is an assignment of responsibility for the management of a product *once it has been discarded*. You might recognize product stewardship as a fee collected by government, at point of sale for a product, that is used to subsidize a government-run recycling program or a "take-back" program that is significantly run and/or funded by the government to keep materials out of the trash (such as for electronics).

To date, these programs have not stopped the ocean of discards or stemmed the har-vesting of the last of our natural resources. So where is the progress? Many local governments, and a few of our Minnesota state representatives and senators, recognize that for many products and their packaging there is a lack of stewardship and the burden is placed on the residents through increased pollution, negative health impacts, and growing taxes and other fees. They will create legislation to help. They want to hear from their constituents. So what will we say when we have our chance?

Where product stewardship is falling short is in the answer to the question: Who should hold responsibility? Right now we are still the ones holding the bag… box… or bottle. Consumers and governments are given the responsibility for these items at the end of the pipe—with no say in how they are made or designed.

So, we can say that product stewardship is effective if it includes *extended producer responsibility* where the producers take full responsibility for their products and packaging. Making producers responsible to share in some or all of the cost of assuring authentic reuse, recycling or composting of the products, packaging and the byproducts, provides an incentive for them to use their engineering and design capacity to create items that include all environmental considerations in their product design, packaging and choice of materials. This has been tested with great success in a country just a stone's throw north of here (Canada, of course)!

Product stewardship should be a strategy to *prevent* waste, not just manage it better *once it has been discarded*. There is much debate about the "best" way to manage waste, but there is no disagreement that the least expensive and least environmentally-damaging waste is the waste that is never created. Yes, zero waste is better than recycling or composting. It is the manufacturer who develops designs and chooses the materials for a product or package. The most efficient place to reduce waste and encourage reuse, reduction, recycling and composting is at the product development stage. This is the most economical place to minimize the environmental impact of the product. Any product stewardship in Minnesota that doesn't include *extended producer responsibility* will not be the change we want to see in our world.

ON THE WEB!

- Product Policy Institute (PPI),
  productpolicy.org
- Eureka Recycling,
  eurekarecycling.org
- The Story of Stuff Video,
  storyofstuff.com

A Journal from Old Greeting Cards

By **ALENA HYAMS**
DO IT GREEN! MINNESOTA

When you get a card in the mail, what do you normally do with it? Do you post it on the fridge? Maybe save your cards in a box? Or do you read it and throw it away (or recycle it)? In an effort to cut down on the amount of waste created by greeting cards, we would like to offer some ideas on ways to re-use your old greeting cards!

Some options include cutting the cards into strips to use as bookmarks or folding them into origami holiday ornaments or gift boxes. However, the option that we will illustrate is how to "make your own mini journal."

How to Make Your Own Greeting-Card Journal:

1. Gather old greeting cards of similar sizes.

2. Cut off the front, decorative, parts of the cards from the message half on the back.

3. Fold the cut off card pieces in half.

4. Use a hole puncher to punch two holes in each card (one near the top and one near the bottom of each fold line). Make sure the holes line up with the other holes as best as possible.

5. Cut a piece of string to use as the journal binding. Try to avoid buying anything new. Yarn, twine, or ribbons work best. The length of string will vary depending on the size of the cards selected—but try to cut enough to loop through the book twice before tying.

6. Select which card you would like to use as the "cover" and arrange the rest of the cards from there. There is no right or wrong way to arrange the cards—just do whatever feels right to you!

7. Thread string through the top hole of each page of the book, and then through the bottom hole of each page; repeat, making sure to leave a little string hanging, from both the top and bottom holes, on the outside of the book.

8. Tie the string on the outside of the book. Make sure to double knot. Tie a bow for added charm!

ON THE WEB!

- "Making Your Own Mini Journal," craftydaisies.com/2007/07/05/making-your-own-mini-journal/

Other Ways to Reuse Greeting Cards:

- squidoo.com/recycleholidaycards
- makingfriends.com/readers_cards.htm

ACT LOCALLY!

- ArtScraps
  St. Paul, MN
  651-698-2787
  artstart.org/reusestore.html

Sewing to Transform Old Clothing into Something New

By **NIKOL GIANOPOULOS**
SEWTROPOLIS

Before and after. Nikol Gianopolous

There's an old saying, "Use it up, wear it out, make it do, or do without," which can be traced back to WWII days when people conserved in order to help the war effort. These days the saying is "reduce, reuse, recycle." Everybody knows to recycle their plastic, newspapers and glass, but what about clothing?

Taking a piece of clothing and transforming it into something new in order to extend the life of that item is called up-cycling, recycling or up-scaling. Sewing is a wonderful way to transform old clothing into something new. Up-cycling is not a new concept for quilters; quilts were traditionally made by sewing together bits of fabric from old clothing. The whole process could sometimes take years before the clothing was cut up, as the clothing was often passed down from oldest child to youngest child.

As the owner of Sewtropolis, I frequently see creative up-cycled clothing projects. My favorite was the leather jacket (a thrift store find) made into a tote bag. I loved it so much I made two of my own and have another two leather jackets waiting to be transformed. One young girl took an old eyelet lace curtain, sewed up the sides, added elastic, and walked out with a cute skirt.

Last month my sewing group members challenged one another to up-cycle an item of clothing. We each brought in an item for an exchange and were given one month to transform our clothing item into something creative and new. I was given a kid's pullover rain jacket. Since the rain jacket was waterproof, I decided to make sandwich pouches.

Another member took an old corduroy shirt and made a picnic basket cover.

When you know how to sew, transforming clothing into something new is easy. But you don't necessarily have to transform the item into something new. Consider turning a pair of too-short pants into a pair of shorts or maybe a pair of pedal-pushers. How about changing a long-sleeved shirt with a hole in the elbow into a short-sleeved shirt? The possibilities are endless with a little sewing know-how. The Internet is full of sites where people have creatively up-cycled—I encourage you to take a look and get inspired.

ON THE WEB!

- Do-it-yourself site for recycling just about everything from jewelry to clothing, diyfashion.about.com/
- Threadbanger, the home of DIY fashion how-to, home décor tips and more, threadbanger.com

READ UP!

- *Subversive Seamster: Transform Thrift Store Threads into Street Couture,* by Melissa Alvarado, Hope Meng and Melissa Rannels, Taunton Press, 2007.
- *Generation T, 108 ways to transform a T-shirt,* by Megan Nicolay, Workman Publishing Company, 2006.

ACT LOCALLY!

Visit the many thrift shops in your area to find used goods to make into something new:

- Sewtropolis
  Minneapolis, MN
  612-387-6966
  sewtropolis.com
- Crafty Planet
  Minneapolis, MN
  612-788-1180
  craftyplanet.com

Eco-Friendly Bakeries in the Twin Cities

By **ALENA HYAMS**
Do It Green! Minnesota

When you think "eco-friendly," bakeries might not be the first thing that come to mind; but Minneapolis and St. Paul each have their fair share of eco-friendly bakeries. Do It Green! Minnesota visited a selection of these bakeries in order to taste some of their delectable treats and find out just how delicious baking green can be.

The Wedge Natural Foods Co-Op
wedge.coop
2105 Lyndale Avenue S, Minneapolis

The Wedge is a "Certified Organic" grocery store in the Uptown area of Minneapolis. With a bakery that has fresh baked goods daily, The Wedge is a convenient and scrumptious place to treat yourself. While visiting The Wedge I sampled their "Fruit with Mascarpone Mini Tart" and was delighted by its subtle sweetness. The crust was thick and slightly buttery, and the Mascarpone tasted like whipped cream yet was the consistency of cream cheese. I very much enjoyed how simple this pastry was and appreciated being able to taste and recognize each individual fruit, as opposed to only tasting sugar. How they do it green: The Wedge is a certified organic retailer and buys locally.

Salty Tart
saltytart.com
920 East Lake Street, Minneapolis

The Salty Tart is a small bakery located inside the Midtown Global Market. The staff is friendly and the cupcakes are phenomenal. I purchased a vanilla cupcake with

raspberry filling and red wine butter cream on this visit. The butter cream frosting was unique, but the raspberry filling is what made this cupcake for me. How they do it green: Salty Tart buys local and organic produce in addition to composting. Pastry chef Michelle Gayer says they are "just trying to reduce everyone's carbon footprint."

Madwoman Foods Bakeshop and Foodery
madwomanfoods.com
4747 Nicollet Ave S, Minneapolis

Madwoman is known for an entirely gluten-free menu. While visiting this distinctive bakery I decided to sit down and have what was the best (and, granted, first) gluten-free brownie I'd ever had. The brownie tasted rich and was almost fudge-like—making for a very satisfying treat. What was nice about Madwoman was that the service was as wonderful as the brownie. The staff was very friendly and greeted regular customers by name—even being able to recall what their regular guests usually order. How they do it green: Madwoman uses minimal packaging as well as "supporting local sustainable organic agriculture."

3 Tiers, Inc.
3tierscakes.com
5011 34th Ave S, Minneapolis

3 Tiers had my favorite of the baked goods I sampled; a seemingly simple carrot cake cupcake. From the first bite, I was blown away by how delicious this cupcake was. The frosting was rich and not piled on as heavily as other bakeries sometimes do. The cake was buttery and had a wonder-

ful texture. I was surprised and delighted to find that nuts had been included in the batter and found the overall combination absolutely marvelous. I would not hesitate to make my way back to 3 tiers in order to try even more menu items. How they do it green: 3 Tiers uses real dishware throughout their establishment, composts, and reuses everything!

Sweets Bakeshop
sweetsbakeshop.com
2042 Marshall Ave, St. Paul

Sweets enticed me with a small Tiramisu cupcake. The cupcake consisted of a vanilla cake bottom filled with espresso chocolate ganache, all topped with a mascarpone frosting. The cupcake was delightful, but the location was disappointing in that it did not really encourage people to stay and enjoy their purchases. The store itself was very small and while it did have a few tall tables, there were no chairs. How they do it green: Sweets Bakeshop buys locally and buys organic products.

You Are Where You Eat

Contributions by **EUREKA RECYCLING, THE GREEN INSTITUTE, LAND STEWARDSHIP PROJECT, TRACY SINGLETON,** OWNER OF BIRCHWOOD CAFÉ, *and* **KIM BARTMANN,** OWNER OF RED STAG SUPPER CLUB, BRYANT LAKE BOWL, AND BARBETTE.

When you cook and enjoy a meal at home, it reflects your values and the choices you make every day. You know where the food came from and how it was grown. You can compost your food scraps and store your leftovers in your energy-efficient fridge in reusable containers. But what about when you go out to eat? How can you make sure the restaurants you support are making the right choices for the environment and our community?

Consider asking your favorite restaurants the following questions, and offer them encouragement, suggestions, and resources to help them learn and do more!

1. Do they source local and sustainable food?

Sourcing food from local farms means fewer food miles from farm to table, requiring less fuel, less refrigeration, and fewer carbon emissions. Sustainable agriculture uses less energy than industrial agriculture that relies on energy intensive processes and chemical inputs. Sustainable agriculture builds soil, preserves our rivers and lakes and provides safe habitat for pollinators, birds, wildlife, and people

2. Do they have their sights set on Zero Waste?

Through recycling and composting, restaurants can reduce their waste 90% or more, making our air and water healthier and safer by reducing greenhouse gas emissions and pollutants. Many restaurants are taking additional steps towards zero waste, offering to-go packaging that consumer can recycle or compost at home where available, and purchasing fewer plastic items and less disposable plastic in their kitchens.

3. How are they working to conserve energy?

There are many no-cost or low-cost actions that restaurants can take to save energy. For example, for as little as $30, a low-flow pre-rinse valve for dishwashing can result in approximately 65% savings in energy to heat the water used for rinsing dishes.

4. Do they serve tap water?

Many restaurants in the Twin Cities area serve tap water instead of bottled water out of a commitment to reduce waste and a belief that water is a common resource, not a commodity. Every year, according to Tap Minneapolis, producing bottled water requires enough crude oil to fuel a million American cars for a year, and results in two and a half millions tons of carbon dioxide emissions.

5. What else is important to you?

Does the restaurant offer bicycle parking? Or source fair trade products? Do they pay a living wage and offer health insurance to employees? Do they make efforts to reduce harmful chemicals in their kitchens and cleaning products?

There are many ways for restaurants to make a difference—make sure you let them know you appreciate it when they do!

ON THE WEB!

- Small Business Energy Saving Guide, greeninstitute.org/media/documents /SmallBusinessEnergy ReductionGuide_001.pdf
- Benefits of Sustainable, Local Foods, landstewardshipproject.org /foodfarm-main.html
- Tap Minneapolis, tapmpls.com

ACT LOCALLY!

- List of local restaurants composting with Eureka Recycling, MakeDirtNotWaste.org

Green Product Shopping Tips

By **KATE RIME**
CHINOOK BOOK, THE ORIGINAL BLUE SKY GUIDE

When looking for green products it helps to return to the ol' Three Rs: Reduce, Reuse, and Recycle.

First and foremost is reduce—ask yourself: **do I really need this product?** No need to be a martyr, yet in our society it's helpful to remind ourselves that we can live with less. We're frequently sent messages by clever marketers that can easily fool us into believing we need items.

The second R, reuse, reminds us to **shop for used items**. There are many shops in Minnesota that offer quality used goods such as clothing, kids' toys, sporting goods, etc. Take advantage of used products to save resources and money!

The third R, recycle, guides us to **look for products that are made from recyclable materials and are recyclable**. Businessdictionary.com defines "cradle-to-grave" in the following way: Responsibility to monitor every aspect of a product or program through its entire life cycle; from design or acquisition to disposal, or from proposal to termination. If the product you're purchasing isn't available with recycled content, see if there is an option made from renewable resources. Consider the life cycle of the product you're looking to purchase and let that guide your decisions. Often products are labeled as recyclable but recycling facilities in your area may not accept that type of material (typically plastic). Don't be fooled by a label that indicates you can recycle.

Some products carry **labels that indicate they are environmentally preferable**. Examples of labels include: Fair Trade: transfairusa.org, FSC (Forest Stewardship Council)-certified: fsc.org and Energy Star rated: energystar.org.

READ UP!

- *The Consumer's Guide to Effective Environmental Choices*, by Michael Brower & Warren Leon, Three Rivers Press, 1999.
- *The Better World Handbook: Small Changes That Make A Big Difference*, by Ellis Jones, Ross Haenfler and Brett Johnson, New Society Publishers, 2007.

ACT LOCALLY!

- Use these links to find green and recycled products in Minnesota:
- Chinook Book, chinookbook.net
- Do It Green! Directory, doitgreen. org/directory
- Moss Envy, mossenvy.com
- Recycled Products Guide, recycleminnesota.org/htm /ReProd.htm

Demystifying Recycling in Minnesota

By **SARA GROCHOWSKI**
DO IT GREEN! MINNESOTA

The average Minnesotan generates more than seven pounds of waste per day and more than one ton annually! In fact, in the Twin Cities area alone, we generate enough waste to fill the Metrodome 11 times every year. Although Minnesota has one of the highest recycling rates in the country, we could be recycling more. Often the problem is not what you know that can be recycled, but what you don't know. Those items usually end up in the trash. For complete details on disposal for specific items, refer to your county website and consider the following items which can also be recycled outside of your residential pick-up program:

1. **#5 plastics, including Brita filters:** Whole Foods started a program called Gimme 5 for recycling #5 plastics by partnering with Preserve (best known for their recycled plastic toothbrushes), Organic Valley and Stonyfield Organic. Bring in your yogurt tubs, cottage cheese containers, medicine bottles and even Brita water filters—just look for the #5 on the bottom. If you do not live by a Whole Foods, the Gimme 5 program also has a mail option. (preserveproducts.com/recycling/**gimme5**.html)

2. **Old holiday lights:** The Recycling Association of Minnesota (RAM) sponsors the Holiday Light Recycling Program with partners WCCO, Snyders Drugs, CERTS and Xcel Energy. RAM will accept old holiday lights and electrical cords. Refer to the link for a detailed listing of drop off sites in your specific area. (recycleminnesota.org)

3. **Building materials:** Remodeling part of your home? Call the ReUse Center of Minneapolis to see what old items you can donate. (thereusecenter.com)

4. **Compact fluorescent lights:** Recycle them at some county household hazardous waste collection sites or bring them to the service center at all Home Depot and Menards locations in Minnesota. (RethinkRecycling.com)

5. **E-Waste:** This includes old computers, printers, fax machines, televisions, radios, audio equipment, and cell phones. These items can be harmful to the environment if not properly recycled. Refer to the Minnesota Pollution Control Agency for drop off sites. (RethinkRecycling.com or pca.state.mn.us)

6. **Plastic garden pots:** Plastic garden containers can now be returned to specific garden centers throughout Minnesota. Go to Garden Minnesota for a complete list of dates and locations. (gardenminnesota.com)

7. **Bathroom tissue rolls and paper towel rolls:** Toss them in with your paper or cardboard recycling.

8. **Excess art supplies:** By donating your discards or scrap to ArtScraps, a creative materials reuse store, your material donation reaches literally hundreds of individuals, families, and organizations, including Head Start programs, child care associations, daycare providers, social service organizations, schools, neighborhoods and many arts organizations, who shop the store. (artstart.org)

9. **Phone books:** Place them at the curb with the rest of your recycling.

10. **Hair:** Send your cut hair to Locks of Love (minimum length of longest layer is 10 inches) to be made into hairpieces for financially disadvantaged children under age 21 suffering from long-term medical hair loss from any diagnosis. Refer to specifics at their website. (locksoflove.org)

11. **Empty aerosol cans:** Most cans are made out of steel or aluminum and can be recycled if empty. Check out earth911.com for your local options.

12. **Aluminum:** This includes anything: tin foil, house siding, lawn furniture, pie tins, etc.

13. **Asphalt shingles:** Check out shinglerecycling.org (this site really is more targeted to industry) and consider this when interviewing roofers. You may want to refer to **dem-con.com**, they seem to be the only option in town right now.

14. **Crayons:** The **crazycrayons.com** community service program has made it possible to stop more than 53,000 pounds of unwanted crayons from going into landfills.

15. **Eyeglasses:** New Eyes For The Needy is just one of many programs that have a global reach and make the 'gift of sight' available to deserving individuals around the world. Other reliable programs include those operated by LensCrafters, Lions Club, and Unite For Sight. (neweyesfortheneedy.org)

16. **Metal clothes hangers:** Ask your local dry cleaner as most of them will re-use what you bring back.

Use the resources below for even more on recycling ideas and options.

ON THE WEB!

- Recycling Association of Minnesota, recycleminnesota.org
- Rethink Recycling, RethinkRecycling.com
- Recycle More Minnesota, recyclemoreminnesota.com
- 1-800 Recycling database, 1800recycling.com

A Sampling of Minnesota's Sustainable Building History

By **THE WEIDT GROUP** ON BEHALF OF THE USGBC-MISSISSIPPI HEADWATERS CHAPTER

1945
Andersen introduced the Pressure Seal double hung window, which uses a removable sash and pressure-seal weather-stripping to keep out wind and precipitation.

1966
The Perm-Shield System, by Andersen, made its debut. The patented, tough vinyl exterior for wood windows was low maintenance and energy efficient with insulating glass.

1972
The University of Minnesota's School of Architecture designed and constructed the Ouroboros House, a self-sufficient house with passive solar systems, integrated composting waste systems and a green roof, in Rosemount.

1974
The Minnesota Energy Agency was created.

1976
The first State Energy Code went into effect with design requirements and criteria for new buildings, additions and remodels.

Williamson Hall Bookstore opened at the U of M as one of the first commercial earth-sheltered buildings featuring deep daylighting, green roofs and active solar collectors.

1977
The U.S. Department of Energy and partners commissioned The Weidt Group to perform research on the performance of wall and ceiling insulation materials. Findings lead to restrictions on the use of urea formaldehyde foams and stricter federal and state code requirements for the thermal and fire retarding values for all insulation materials.

1978
The Department of Energy and partners commissioned The Weidt Group to perform air infiltration studies. Publication of results created broad code changes reducing the acceptable air-leakage limits of installed windows.

The 4,000 SF, earth-sheltered Taft Residence was built in Edina in response to the energy crisis of the 1970s, utilizing passive solar features that reduced energy costs and consumption.

1979
The Underground Space Center was established in Civil Engineering at U of M. The Center researched and published seminal works on earth-sheltered, passive solar buildings and other energy efficient technologies.

The State of Minnesota opened a new alternative energy initiative using waste wood to heat a 22,000 sq.ft. building.

The Regional Headquarters for the Minnesota DNR opened in Grand Rapids, designed for maximum solar orientation and winter solar gain, including a wood burning heating system.

1980
The Minnesota Legislature established requirements for electric and gas utilities to perform pilot conservation programs.

The City of Minneapolis took its first efforts to address energy challenges by establishing the Energy Futures Committee and the Minneapolis Energy Plan and Energy Action Program.

The Center for Energy & Environment (CEE) established the House Doctor program, performing diagnostic tests, conducting homeowner education workshops, and providing materials and assistance for residential energy efficiency improvements.

1982
The Civil/Mineral Engineering Building opened at the U of M, featuring the world's first Passive Solar Optic and Active Solar Optic Systems, hybrid Trombe wall technologies, and ground source heat pumps.

Minnesota began the monitoring of wind speeds around the State for wind energy development potential at 30-meter heights.

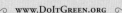

1983

Andersen introduced low-emissivity (Low-E) High-Performance glass with a specialized metallic coating that retards the loss of radiant heat from the inside in the winter and the gain of radiant heat in the summer.

CEE initiated a multi-year program of field tests of energy efficiency strategies for multifamily building mechanical systems, which later became the basis for multifamily efficiency programs throughout the country.

1986

The Regional Daylighting Center was established by the U of M's School of Architecture, in collaboration with The Weidt Group, as a resource to the design and construction community.

The City of St. Paul installed its district water heating system.

1987

The Minnesota Building Research Center (MNBRC) was established at the University of Minnesota to coordinate building research, including indoor air quality and models of professional practice for design team integration.

Three 25 kilowatt grid-connected wind turbines was installed in Crookston—the first small, commercial scale wind turbines in the state.

1990

AIA Minnesota established its Committee on the Environment (COTE) following the formation of the national COTE in 1989.

1993

Xcel Energy launched its Energy Design Assistance Program, then known as Energy Assets℠. By 2003, the program had addressed over 230 projects and reduced air pollution by over 209,000 tons per year while saving building owners more than 20 million dollars annually.

Johnstech International created the Healthy Office with low VOC materials and IAQ HVAC performance specifications.

The OEA held a Buy Recycled Workshop and Product Show, attended by 150 business and government professionals, featuring a session with nationally recognized experts.

1994

The American Lung Association of Minnesota completed the design of its first Health House, one of the nation's first single-family healthy demonstration homes.

Xcel Energy installed an interactive photovoltaic system exhibit at the old Science Museum to educate visitors on energy from the sun and to collect data.

1995

The State of Minnesota's Office of Environmental Assistance (OEA) published the Resource Efficient Building Guide.

Hennepin County made its Public Works facility a sustainable design pilot project which led to the development of the County's sustainable design guidelines, incorporating on-site wastewater treatment, graywater recycling and recycled materials.

Several northeastern Minnesota counties developed a mock house (trailer) that displayed recycled content building products.

1996

The Material Reuse Center, a retail store that handles salvaged building materials, was opened by the Green Institute in Minneapolis.

Xcel Energy completed eighteen 2 kW photovoltaic systems for the Solar Advantage green-leasing program.

1997

The Green Institute Phillips Eco-Enterprise Center (PEEC) was constructed with award winning green building features including operable windows, a demonstration green roof, geothermal heating and cooling, 100% on site storm water management, and many salvaged materials including structural joists.

Northland College developed the Environmental Living & Learning Center, a student housing live-in learning center that demonstrated energy efficiency, composting toilets, wind power and 3 types of photovoltaic power monitored by the students.

Beautiful Savior Lutheran Church in Plymouth completed construction of a 32,000 SF project incorporating a 100-ton loop field geothermal heating system.

1998

OEA held a green building workshop at the U of M for local government officials.

Great River Energy installed three 660 kW wind turbines in Chandler for the State's first green pricing program.

1999

The Millennium Star Energy House was built in Duluth, demonstrating advanced energy techniques with an interactive educational website.

The West Metro Education Program (WMEP) completed its Interdistrict Downtown School, a "green living school" achieving energy efficiency 40% above MN code with Daylighting, recycled content materials, superior indoor air quality and incorporating the SolarWall product.

Six state agencies collaborated to form the "Smart Buildings Partnership" and produce "High Performance Building Goals."

Minnesota Solar Resource Assessment Project began to collect data on solar potential in Minnesota.

2000

The National Council of Architectural Registration Boards (NCARB) published an educational monograph on Sustainable Design.

Minnesota installed more wind energy capacity from 1995-2000 than any other state.

2001

The Center for Sustainable Building Research (CSBR) was established at the U of M.

The OEA funds LHB Inc. to develop a predesign manual titled, "Sustainable Schools Minnesota."

The State of Minnesota passed legislation requiring sustainable guidelines be applied to all projects receiving funds from state bonds.

Carleton College in Northfield adopted the MN Sustainable Design Guide for all new and renovated projects on its campus.

Offering green pricing as an option to customers was made mandatory for all Minnesota electric utilities. ❧➡

2002

The Metropolitan Council built a new Demonstration Administration Building for its Eagle's Point wastewater treatment plant that was 70% more energy efficient than code, using strategies including Daylighting and the effluent tank as a source for geothermal energy.

Minnesota Planning published "Return on Investment—High Performance Buildings" which called for the State to improve standards of its buildings through high-performance measures.

OEA's Green Building Website was launched (pca.state.mn.us), search 'green building'.

The Minnesota Solar Electric Rebate Program began, reducing the cost of grid-connected photovoltaics by 20–25%.

The first Living Green Expo drew 5,000 attendees to the State Capitol to learn about sustainable lifestyle choices.

2003

The Science Museum of Minnesota opened the Science House, a Zero Emissions Building.

Minnesota's U.S. Green Building Council (USGBC) members formed a committee to establish a Minnesota Chapter of the USGBC.

The American Lung Association of Minnesota built a new national demonstration Health House, using geothermal energy and Masterfit, a waste-free wood structural framing system.

The City of St. Paul added new efficient burners and biomass to its downtown district heating system.

MN Power and the Duluth Zoo built three renewable demonstration projects, including photovoltaic recharges for vehicles, solar water heating for the farm animal barn, and geothermal cooling for the polar bear pond.

OEA awarded a grant to U of M to develop a database of green affordable housing technologies.

Lebanon Hills Trail Head & Visitor Center was completed using Dakota County Sustainable Design & Construction Standards.

MN Health House townhouses at Jackson Street Village opened, featuring geothermal, waterproof exterior technologies and resource efficient materials.

The Living Green Expo moved to the State Fairgrounds and more than doubled attendance to 11,000 attendees.

Clean Energy Resource Teams in seven regions of Minnesota were formed to promote grassroots education and project development.

The Weidt Group received the 2003 Firm Award from AIA Minnesota for having "led the local, national and international architectural profession in one of architecture's most significant changes in the last 26 years: the formal incorporation of sustainability into the design process."

2004

The Minnesota Building Materials Database was completed.

Sustainable Building Guidelines (B3) Version 1.0 were developed and in effect for all projects using funds bonded by the State of Minnesota.

Phillips Eco Enterprise Center installed a 34-kilowatt photovoltaic system, the largest solar array in the 5-state area.

EnvironDesign8, Affordable Comfort, and Energy Smart America national conferences came to Minnesota.

The U of M Graduate School approved the College of Architecture and Landscape Architecture's proposal for a new MS program with an option for an emphasis in Sustainable Design.

2005

The "Green Remodeling Group" was created by members of the remodeling, design, trade association, and building supply communities to develop sustainable, green remodeling standards. The group evolved to become Minnesota GreenStar, a voluntary, third-party green certification program for new and renovated homes.

Minnesota Green Communities was created to foster the development of affordable, healthy, energy-efficient, environmentally friendly housing in Minnesota.

2006

The first Eco Experience displays were set up at the Minnesota State Fair held in the Progress Center.

Minneapolis City Council voted to use LEED standards for all new or significantly renovated municipal facilities 5,000 square feet or greater.

2007

Legislature passed the Next Generation Energy Act, **mnclimatechange.us**

2008

Great River Energy opened its new headquarters in Maple Grove. The building was the first in Minnesota to receive LEED Platinum certification from USGBC.

Minnesota Sustainable Building 2030 (www.mn2030.umn.edu/download/ SB2030_OnePager.pdf), a MN legislative initiative patterned after Architecture 2030, was launched.

2009

St. Paul City Council adopted a Sustainable Building Policy governing all new private development projects that received more than $200,000 in city funds.

The new TCF Bank stadium at the U of M received LEED Silver certification.

Excelsior & Grand development project in St. Louis Park, a pilot project of the USGBC's LEED for Neighborhood Development was officially certified.

2010

Target Field, home of the MN Twins and the recipient of a LEED Silver certification from the USGBC, opened in the spring.

LEED for Neighborhood Development was officially launched nationally after a 2½ year pilot phase, usgbc.org.

Shades of Green: Healthy Basement Renovations

By **ERIN BARNES-DRISCOLL**
GREEN BUILDINGS TEAM — MINNESOTA POLLUTION CONTROL AGENCY

Basements are notorious for being damp, dark, inhospitable places—the antithesis of what we like to associate with green and healthy living. As a rule, the basements in older homes were not designed to be functional living spaces. Yet for many of us, the basement represents potential bedroom, recreational or home office space at an affordable cost.

While some basements are unsuitable as living space, others *can* be transformed as long as some "green building science" principles are followed. The following is a partial list of things to consider:

- Test for radon, lead, mold, asbestos, and moisture at the outset and at the end of the renovation to help identify and subsequently rectify pollutants and problems that could impact your health or that of your family.
- Make certain that gutters and downspouts are cleared of debris and diverting water away from the foundation, and that there is proper grading or slope next to the house. Seal cracks in foundation walls and consider installing exterior water-management controls. Interior waterproofing as a primary or sole means of long-term water management is unreliable. Combined with other measures discussed here, however, it can be useful.

- Building scientists frequently recommend that basement walls be insulated, where possible, on the outside using rigid foam or a similar material, and that they dry towards the interior; the use of a dehumidifier is important. Avoid products like vinyl wallpaper, which can trap moisture inside the wall, leading to mold and structural damage.
- Have a thorough energy analysis done of your home to determine where air leakage is occurring. Air seal as needed.
- Install materials and products that are mold and moisture-resistant, such as paperless (a.k.a. mold resistant) drywall, hard-surface flooring, and insulation that is non-water sensitive.
- Ensure that proper drainage techniques, such as flashing, are installed for all windows and doors.
- Sufficiently ventilate and dehumidify, especially in the summer. Leave basement windows closed during the summer when humidity is high. Consider adding mechanical ventilation to improve air quality. Use an ENERGY STAR rated dehumidifier.
- Add energy-efficient lighting, such as CFLs and/or LEDs. Use occupancy-sensors and timers to reduce unnecessary energy use.

- Improve indoor air quality by using products that are free of formaldehyde and any VOC (volatile organic compound). This includes paint, particleboard, MDF, insulation, flooring, furniture, cabinetry, and wood finishes, among others.
- Consider upgrading to a closed-combustion, high-efficiency water heater, furnace, and air conditioner. If replacing the furnace with a high efficiency version, take care not to "orphan" the water heater—it may have a hard time venting up the chimney by itself, potentially backdrafting CO_2 into the home, along with moisture. You're better off simultaneously replacing both mechanical systems with closed combustion versions.

Select a contractor who is trained and experienced in green-remodeling. Look for companies whose personnel are trained on the MN GreenStar standards and in building performance and building science. Registering and certifying your project through MN GreenStar is a particularly good way to ensure that healthy, green remodeling practices are followed.

ON THE WEB!

- Minnesota GreenStar Certified Green Homes and Remodeling, mngreenstar.org
- Minnesota Office of Energy Security, state.mn.us/portal/mn/jsp /home.do?agency=Energy
- *Read This Before You Design, Build, or Renovate,* buildingscience.com /documents/guides-and-manuals
- *University of Minnesota Extension, Moisture in Basements: Causes and Solutions,* by John Carmody and Brent Anderson; Revised by Richard Stone, extension.umn.edu /distribution/housingandclothing /DK7051.html

Top: Before renovation; project is registered with MN GreenStar). Bottom: Carpet has been replaced with engineered hardwood floor. Paneling has been removed. New walls are painted with low VOC paint. Wood burning fireplace now has a gas insert. Recycled glass tile surrounds the fireplace.

Native Plantings

A BEAUTIFUL SOLUTION FOR MINNESOTA SHORELINES

By **ANGIE HONG**

EAST METRO WATER RESOURCE EDUCATION PROGRAM

Left: Chuck and Joan Taylor of Lake Elmo completed a shoreline planting project on Lake Jane in 2003 with assistance from the Washington Conservation District. Courtesy of Washington Conservation District

Right: Rice Creek Watershed District shoreline planting on Lake Josephine in Arden Hills. Courtesy of Blue Thumb: Planting for Clean Water

Here in Minnesota, shoreline living is not limited to the rich and famous. According to the MN DNR, Minnesota has 11,842 lakes and 69,200 miles of natural rivers and streams. We have over 13 million acres of lakes, streams, and wetlands, which is equivalent to one quarter of the area of the entire state. Correspondingly, 200,000–225,000 lucky Minnesota families own lakeshore homes, and countless others live along rivers, streams and wetlands.

Living close to the water provides many benefits, including a beautiful view, easy access for water recreation and higher property values. The advantages of waterfront living, however, also come with the responsibility to maintain the health of the lakes, rivers, streams and wetlands so that those of us not so lucky to own shoreline property can still enjoy clean water for fishing, boating, and other forms of recreation.

The water quality data for developed lakeshores can be quite alarming. On average, the development of a lakeshore lot reduces aquatic vegetation along that lot by 66%. There is a direct correspondence between the amount of aquatic vegetation and the number of fish able to live in a lake, and studies have shown that even small changes, paving over or building on 8% of the land on a lot, for example, can impact water quality and fish survival rates.

Shoreline property owners have perhaps more to benefit than anyone from maintaining healthy water bodies, and the most important thing they can do to protect their property investment is to minimize impervious surfaces and maximize native vegetation.

Often, there is pressure from neighbors to maintain a tidy yard by mowing the grass down to the water's edge or removing tall vegetation from the shoreline. Many people are afraid that their property values will decrease if they plant native vegetation; however, recent planting projects in the local area have shown that a natural shoreline can actually be quite beautiful. Deep-rooted plants and trees also help to control erosion, a major problem for many shoreline properties. In most cases, a buffer of native plants is actually more effective at limiting erosion than a retaining wall, and has the added benefit of discouraging geese from visiting and dropping "presents."

At first, some people are resistant to planting native vegetation along their shoreline because they are afraid it will limit their access to the water. It is fairly easy, however, to design a yard plan that allows for a dock and a trail to the water while still keeping a healthy buffer along the shoreline. For sample shoreline planting plans and step-by-step instructions for doing a shoreline project, as well as local partners that may be able to provide technical or financial assistance for shoreline planting projects, visit **BlueThumb.org**.

ON THE WEB!

- Blue Thumb: Shoreline Planting for Clean Water, bluethumb.org/shorelines
- Minnesota DNR on Lakescaping, www.dnr.state.mn.us/lakescaping
- U of M Extension on Shoreland Education, extension.umn.edu/shoreland

READ UP!

- *Lakescaping for Wildlife and Water Quality*, by Carrol Henderson, Carolyn Dindorf and Fred Rozumalski, Minnesota Department of Natural Resources, 1999.
- *Restore Your Shore* (CD-ROM), Minnesota Department of Natural Resources, 2002.

ACT LOCALLY!

- Landscaping professionals that specialize in Shoreline Plantings, BlueThumb.org/partners
- Mary Blickenderfer, Shoreland Education, Extension Regional Center, Grand Rapids, MN 218-244-7966 extension.umn.edu/shoreland /programteam.html

Greener Design and Remodeling

By **MICHAEL ANSCHEL**
OTOGAWA-ANSCHEL DESIGN + BUILD

Cabinets made from salvaged wood out of Lake Superior and salvaged granite countertops; proving green can be beautiful.

If you are reading this article, you may already know the importance of considering our planet's resources when designing our homes. Determining the most sustainable solutions is a real challenge. Should you invest in solar panels? Should you buy the carpet with the Green label? Which design solutions have the highest impact?

In order to help you make these important decisions for your home, designers Greg Kraus, Chie Morioka, and Scott Barsness of Otogawa-Anschel Design-Build provide some helpful tips.

1. "**Remodel rather than build new**," says designer Kraus. "It is always the first place

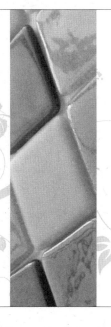

Greener Design, CONTINUED

to start when considering your home." An existing home already has the embodied energy built in: the stone was quarried long ago, the lumber represents trapped carbon, and the millwork and cabinets may have been made from local wood by local craftspeople. Additionally, older wall studs are able to handle up to 30 times as much moisture compared to today's young pine. Greg suggests you find a designer who is well versed in "transforming existing spaces rather than just building new ones."

2. Kitchens offer lots of opportunity when remodeling. Kraus suggests you "minimize, or better yet, eliminate upper cabinets in a kitchen. This saves building materials and costs," while also allowing more natural light to enter the room. If no pantry option exists and upper cabinets are needed, placing them on interior walls allows light to flow into kitchen space without disruption.

3. "Don't design your kitchen for 10 people if the majority of the time there are only three of you," advises Barsness. "Layout and function are the same to me. I don't want to design things larger than they need to be."

4. "Water conservation is easy! Start by swapping out old shower heads for 1.5 gpm models," adds Kraus. "The technology has vastly improved so that you can hardly tell the difference between the old and new efficient models." Delta has a series of attractive and excellent performing models to choose from. "Look for the Water Sense label," suggests Kraus, when shopping for a new water saving device. Toto and Sterling make affordable, attractive, and incredible performing toilets. Dual flush units like the Aquio or the Rockton are obvious choices at around $300. The new 1.28 gallon per flush units from Toto and Kohler are quieter and can also save thousands of gallons of water per year.

5. Improving the efficiency of your windows might help you save some energy, but controlling solar gain and maintaining privacy are sometimes overlooked issues. Designer Chie suggests using "honeycomb blinds for the added insulating benefit. If you have west facing windows, then darkening the rooms with honeycomb blinds may help keep the rooms from over heating in the summer months." If considering window replacement, calculate payback and energy savings before making a decision. Matching the material and detail of older windows is an expensive proposition. You

Super insulated and super comfortable space adds real livability to this old home.

might get similar energy savings by simply adding a good storm window and filling the weight pockets with a low density spray foam.

My own tip

Be cautious of products that sound too good to be true. Beware of exaggerated, unsubstantiated, or irrelevant claims, and don't get fooled by a "self awarded" green label. Look for actual data on projects, such as R-values for insulating materials or window coverings, and check local codes before buying and installing a product.

ON THE WEB!

- U.S. Green Building Council, usgbc.org
- All things green building, greenbuildingadvisor.com
- Materials database, pharosproject.org

READ UP!

- *Cats' Paws and Catapults:Mechanical Worlds of Nature and People*, by Steven Vogel, Norton, 2000.
- *A Pattern Language: Towns, Buildings, Construction,* by Christopher Alexander, Oxford University Press, 1977.
- *Not So Big Remodeling: Tailoring Your Home for the Way You Really Live,* by Sarah Susanka, Taunton, 2009.

ACT LOCALLY!

- Otogawa-Anschel Design-Build Minneapolis, MN
  612-789-7070
  otogawa-anschel.com

Funding A$$istance for Green Building Projects

Established in 1995, the Database of State Incentives for Renewables & Efficiency (DSIRE) is an ongoing project funded by the U.S. Department of Energy's Office of Energy Efficiency and Renewable Energy (EERE).

Here are some examples of financing programs, tax incentives, loan programs and rebates:

FINANCING
- Local Option: Energy Improvement Financing Programs

PERFORMANCE-BASED INCENTIVE
- Austin Utilities: Solar Choice Program
- Minnesota: Renewable Energy Production Incentive

PROPERTY TAX INCENTIVE
- Wind and Solar-Electric (PV) Systems Exemption

SALES TAX INCENTIVE
- Solar Energy Sales Tax Exemption
- Wind Energy Sales Tax Exemption

STATE GRANT PROGRAM
- Renewable Energy Equipment Grant
- Solar Energy Legacy Grants for Local Governments

STATE LOAN PROGRAM
- Agricultural Improvement Loan Program
- Home Energy Loan Program
- Methane Digester Loan Program
- MHFA Rental Rehabilitation Loan Program
- NEC Minnesota Energy Loan Program
- Rental Energy Loan Fund
- Sustainable Agriculture Loan Program

STATE REBATE PROGRAM
- Residential Small Wind Rebate Program
- Solar Hot Water Rebate Program
- Solar Space Heating Rebate Program
- Solar-Electric (PV) Rebate Program

Visit the following link for up to date information on these financing options and scroll down to Minnesota listings: **dsireusa.org/incentives**

Getting Started with Green Building and Remodeling

By **MICHAEL ANSCHEL**
OTOGAWA-ANSCHEL DESIGN + BUILD

Getting creative with high recycled content commercial tile is an inexpensive solution.

The key to successful green building lies in two things: planning and communication. One of the big challenges in green construction and design is sorting through the vast ocean of information including all of the facts, fictions, and applications. Location, climate and building type all can change the assembly of materials and methods of installation. Consider also the composition of the actual building materials, and concerns such as sustainability, safety, and durability.

Here are some helpful solutions:

1. Start by hiring a design professional who has experience in green design and construction. Make sure you can communicate easily with this person. Common questions include: Have you designed a certified green project? Do you have a green accreditation such as MN GreenStar AP, NARI CGP, or LEED AP? If you find a designer whom you really like, and there just isn't enough time for them to learn everything, consider hiring a green consultant who can guide everyone through the process. Get everyone involved *before* you draw a single line.

2. Before starting your new project, **test your home for air leaks and possible moisture problems** as well as "combustion spillage." This will help you better understand how your house is currently performing, areas that could be improved in addition to your new project, and possible problems that exist before you make your plans.

3. As you are designing your project, **utilize a reference guide** such as MN GreenStar, MN Green Communities, or LEED for Homes. This will allow you to keep your project in balance among the numerous green concerns: energy efficiency, water conservation, resource efficiency, indoor environmental quality, site impact, and community impact. Certification has become less costly and planning for it from the start is a simple and invaluable step.

4. If you are planning an addition to your home or considering replacing your heating and cooling equipment, **require that your designer obtain Manual J load calculations** from an HVAC contractor or energy efficiency expert. These will help you determine the proper size for your new mechanical system, and may also help identify elements in the design that could be changed to reduce the size and the cost of the mechanical system.

5. Selecting your contractor at the same time you select your designer is ideal. Some companies have both design and contractor in house, which helps to integrate the process. Having your contractor involved during the design phase will help to manage cost expectations and provide better communication of the goals and importance of details in the green design.

6. During the designing phase, your designer should **involve the various trade contractors who will be working on the project** so they can familiarize themselves with the space and help identify solutions that will improve efficiency and reduce cost. This is called a multidisciplinary approach, and is proven to be very successful in reducing cost and avoiding mistakes.

7. Select all of your materials during the design phase. Never start construction or sign a contract without knowing all the details of the project, whether it is the color, size and performance of the windows or the knobs on the cabinets. It all impacts the overall cost and the execution of the project. In green building, every step of

ABOVE LEFT: **No upper cabinets allows sunlight to fill the kitchen.** RIGHT: **Small spaces require creativity and flexibility. Light, line, color, and texture make it come alive.** BELOW: **90% reduction in Nat Gas usage, 40% reduction in electrical usage, 90% storm water retention, ultra-low VOC finishes and no carpet are some of the highlights of this certified MN GreenStar Gold Remodel.**

ON THE WEB!

- Green Building Advisor: building science, forums & experts, greenbuildingadvisor.com
- U.S. Green Building Council, usgbc.org

READ UP!

- *The Integrative Design Guide to Green Building:Redefining the Practice of Sustainability*, by 7group, Bill Reed, and S. Rick Fedrizzi, Wiley, 2009.
- *Building Green in a Black and White World*, by David R. Johnston, Home Builder Press, 2000.
- *Builders Guide to Cold Climates: Details for Design & Construction*, by Joseph Lstiburek, Taunton Press, 2000.

ACT LOCALLY!

- Minnesota GreenStar
  Roseville, MN
  651-493-0294
  mngreenstar.org
- Verified Green
  Minneapolis, MN
  612-789-7070
  verifiedgreen.org

≫ *Green Building*, CONTINUED

the process is documented to ensure that things are done as specified.

8. **Test your project at the beginning,** at the end, and during construction. Blower door tests and infrared thermometers are two means of measuring air infiltration. Insulation of all types is difficult to properly install. Take the opportunity to catch errors before they turn into an expensive and highly disruptive problem.

9. **Finally, make sure the work is done as you and your team determined it should be.** The easiest way to do this is to have your project certified by a third party reviewer. Even if you choose not to certify the project, take an active role in the process and require that everything be documented and collected as if the project were to be certified. After all, if you paid for something built green, you should get it green.

As you can see, getting your team together to start the process is truly the key to successfully remodeling or building green. Following these three steps will help ensure your project is a success: include the people who will build it from the beginning; test the project thoroughly; utilize third-party reviewers.

Live simply, ride efficiently.

Metro Transit can help you Go Greener with options to fit your lifestyle: taking the bus or train, biking, carpooling or walking. Leaving your car behind and sharing the ride—even one day a week—can make a difference.

metrotransit.org/gogreener

a service of the Metropolitan Council

The North Star commuter rail, picking up passengers.
Transit for Livable Communities

Becoming Multi-Modal in the Twin Cities in the Last Ten Years

By DAVE VAN HATTUM
TRANSIT FOR LIVABLE COMMUNITIES

The Twin Cities metro area has greatly expanded non-auto options over the past decade. Cities across the metro are actively seeking a new transitway for LRT, BRT or commuter rail, new bike lanes and more walkable public spaces. Since 1990, the Twin Cities:

- Opened in 2004 its first light rail transit (LRT) line—the Hiawatha line, which runs every 15 minutes for 22 hours a day and carries approximately 30,000 riders per day
- Secured funding for, and ensured all communities are served on, the Central Corridor LRT—set to open in 2014.
- Opened its first commuter rail line—the Northstar, which runs 12 times each weekday between Big Lake and downtown Minneapolis, carrying 3,500 passengers daily.
- Opened its second bus rapid transit (BRT) line—on I-35W South.
- Installed bike racks on all buses and trains (note: New York City does not have bike racks on buses!).
- Opened dual-lane bus routes on two key thoroughfares in downtown Minneapolis—greatly speeding travel for tens of thousands of commuters.
- Greatly expanded bike lanes in Minneapolis and St. Paul including the 5.5-mile midtown Greenway and artistic Sabo

bridge over Hiawatha Ave.
- Secured federal funding (i.e. Bike Walk Twin Cities program) for bike/walk expansions in Minneapolis and neighboring communities.
- Opened two car-sharing organizations: the non-profit HOURCAR with a fleet of 20 cars, and the for-profit ZIPCAR with a fleet of 5 cars.
- Opened a state-of-the-art bicycle sharing option, Nice Ride, with 65 kiosks and 1000 bikes in Minneapolis.
- Effectively created and marketed transit tax breaks for employers and employees.
- Created the first dedicated funding sources for transit—motor vehicle sales

tax revenues in 2006, and sales tax in five metro counties in 2008.

- Located the new Twins ballpark at the crossroads of Minneapolis transit routes and good bicycle access, leading to hordes of fans—20% or more—leaving their cars at home.
- Experienced dramatic increases in transit and non-motorized trip-making. In 2008, 10.4% of daily commutes in Minneapolis were by bicycling or walking, up 26.8% from 2005, while in St. Paul the 2008 figure was 6.1%, an increase of 45.2% over 2005.
- Passed Complete Streets legislation to ensure that new roads and bridges are built to serve all users regardless of age or ability.

Twin Cities residents overwhelmingly support further expansions of alternatives to driving alone. Where good transit service and safe bike routes are available, people of all ages flock to these healthy and economical choices.

Given our starting point—we have one

of the nation's largest metro highway systems, we are among the most sprawling cities our size, and we were behind other cities in adding rail service—we have made progress, but still have a long way to go. Our transit fares are higher, and transit availability lower, than in peer regions. Tragically, 13 people lost their lives in the 35W bridge collapse—highlighting the importance of a "fix-it-first" approach (i.e. fix before expan-

sion) to road and bridge infrastructure.

The good news is that most residents experience, and all benefit from, the myriad of new transportation choices described above. Young and old, city and suburban dweller, as well as business and union leaders are increasingly vocal in demanding that elected officials and public agencies build a 21st century transportation system that serves all communities equitably, and provides safe, energy-efficient, healthy options to get people where they need to go.

ON THE WEB!

- Finding your way on bus or rail, metrotransit.org
- Regional planning agency serving the Twin Cities, metrocouncil.org/transit
- Hourcar car sharing, hourcar.org
- Zipcar car sharing, zipcar.com
- Nice Ride Minnesota bikeshare, niceridemn.org
- Resources for biking and walking, bikewalktwincities.org

ACT LOCALLY!

- **Minnesota Complete Streets Coalition**
  mncompletestreets.org
  651-294-7141
  Get involved to influence street design in your community
- **Transit for Livable Communities**
  St. Paul, MN 55104
  651-767-0298
  tlcminnesota.org
  Working to expand transportation choices for all Minnesotans

Walking as Transportation

By **AMBER COLLETT**
Transit for Livable Communities

We walk to raise money and awareness for causes, to get exercise, and to grab a cup of coffee at the nearby coffee shop, but is walking considered transportation? Despite the fact that walking is all about getting your body from point A to point B, it is often left out of the definition of transportation.

However, according to the U.S. Census, in 2008, 6.1% of people in Minneapolis choose to walk to work every day. Since there were 382,605 people living in Minneapolis in 2008, that means more than 6,200 people were walking to work every day! That is far above the national average of 2.8%. And folks aren't just walking to work: 2009 data

from the National Household Transportation Survey showed that walking accounts for 10.9% of all trips made in the U.S.

The trick is integrating walking into your daily schedule. Twenty-five percent of all "trips" are less than one mile in length—and therefore perfect for walking. Walk with your child to school in the mornings or form a walking group with other children in the neighborhood. Walk to the nearest grocery store or to the post office.

Small trips taken by foot add up and come with benefits galore. You're powering your own engine—regular exercise not only keeps you healthy, it also gives you extra energy to enjoy your favorite activities. By being out and about in your neighborhood, you connect with neighbors, the natural environment, and you might even discover a new shop or café. ❧

Walking, CONTINUED

TOP: **Stone Arch Bridge, Minneapolis.**
BOTTOM: **Nicollet Mall, Minneapolis.**

This year, the Minnesota legislature took a step in the right direction by passing a Complete Streets bill that makes sure the needs of all road-users are considered when designing or reconstructing roads in Minnesota. Implementation of the Complete Streets bill could mean wider sidewalks and safer intersections for pedestrians, making walking the easy choice for residents.

And in case you needed another reason to step off your doorstep, just remember —you never have to bail your shoes out of an impound lot!

ON THE WEB!

❖ National Center for Bicycling & Walking, bikewalk.org

❖ Walk Score, walkscore.com

❖ Mn/DOT Safe Routes to School, dot.state.mn.us/saferoutes/

ACT LOCALLY!

❖ Bike Walk Twin Cities
St. Paul, MN
651-767-0298
bikewalktwincities.org

❖ Minnesota Complete Streets Coalition
St. Paul, MN
651-294-7141
mncompletestreets.org

Bus-Only Shoulders Move Transit Commuters Past Congestion

By **METRO TRANSIT**

Nearly 20 years ago, Metro Transit pioneered a simple way to get buses out of congestion by traveling on the shoulder instead of sitting in rush-hour congestion.

In 1992, it experimented on a few miles of freeway and liked the results: bus drivers could stay on schedule, commuters got to work or home faster and ridership increased.

After that initial success, Metro Transit teamed up with the state Department of Transportation and others to create Team Transit, a group dedicated to enhancing infrastructure to create transit advantages.

When roadways are being built or reconstructed, Team Transit makes sure that shoulders are wide enough to safely accommodate buses and the roadway is strong enough to withstand the weight of full buses. Since shoulder use is built into the project, the transit advantage is a cost-effective alternative to building new lanes.

For a time, bus-only shoulders were being added at a rate of 20 miles per year. While expansion has slowed, in 2010 there are 290 miles of bus-only shoulders across the region, ensuring fast, reliable travel times for commuters on thousands of buses each day. Transit customers save between five and 15 minutes thanks to shoulder use.

Metro Transit ensures that speed is secondary to safety. While bus drivers are authorized to use designated shoulders, they follow strict guidelines. Buses can merge onto the shoulder only when general traffic speeds are lower than 35 mph. Maximum bus speed on the shoulder is 15 mph faster than traffic.

Thanks to these measures, bus-only shoulders have been extremely effective and very safe. In 18 years of use, there has been just one crash involving injuries.

Those in other metropolitan areas have modeled the shoulder concept to make bus service more efficient. Transit providers in 10 states now use bus-only shoulders.

ON THE WEB!

❖ metrotransit.org *or* transit-advantages.org

New Transitways:

HIAWATHA, CENTRAL, SOUTHWEST AND MORE!

By **DAVE VAN HATTUM**
POLICY AND PROGRAM MANAGER,
TRANSIT FOR LIVABLE COMMUNITIES

This map of transitways depicts a system that is bold but achievable by 2020.

NOT TO SCALE
Many of the lines and stations depicted on this map are in various stages of planning and are subject to change.

The opening of exciting new transitways in the Twin Cities is on the horizon over the next 10 years. At the same time, funding and integration challenges remain.

The Twin Cities region is poised to add two new light rail (LRT) lines — Central Corridor in 2014, and Southwest in 2017. Construction has begun on the Central Corridor project, which will connect downtown Minneapolis and downtown St. Paul, traveling most the distance on University Avenue. The Southwest LRT — traveling from downtown Minneapolis to Eden Prairie (with stops in St. Louis Park, Hopkins and Minnetonka as well) — Is expected to begin preliminary engineering this fall. Both promise huge ridership: approximately 30,000 riders per day.

The Bottineau Corridor, traveling northwest from downtown Minneapolis to Maple Grove or Brooklyn Park, and the Gateway Corridor, traveling east from downtown St. Paul potentially as far as the St. Croix River, are also being studied for LRT. Current uncertainty regarding state and federal funding makes these projects a long shot for completion by 2020.

Watch for enhanced bus rapid transit (BRT) service on I-35W South and Cedar Avenue. When the Crosstown (Highway 62) reconstruction is complete, bus riders will enjoy free-flow conditions in the MN/Pass lane from Lakeville to downtown Minneapolis and a few stops in between, including the new 46th street on-line station. The Gateway corridor may operate as BRT if ridership estimates don't support investment in LRT.

A pleasing transit system relies on downtown transit stations to efficiently move people from corridor to corridor and from train or bus to their office or other destination. St. Paul's Union Depot and the Minneapolis Transportation Interchange will provide this function while also providing exquisite public spaces.

The Counties Transit Improvement Board (CTIB), a collaboration of Anoka, Dakota, Hennepin, Ramsey, and Washington Counties, deserves most of the credit for accelerating transitways in the region. Thanks to County Board votes in 2008 and bold legislative action, a small increase in the sales tax in these counties is leveraging large matching funding from the Federal Transit Administration.

Twin Cities residents shouldn't be content with current plans for the transit system. The Metropolitan Council, Mn/DOT, and county and local government all have a critical opportunity to set a new course for a safer and more sustainable transportation system. Getting there means prioritizing transit projects over road expansion. It also requires crafting local land use and housing plans that allow for new development (housing and commercial) that follows the increased access provided by better transit service.

ON THE WEB!

- MN Rides — the web site of the Counties Transit Improvement Board, mnrides.org
- City of St. Paul web page for Central Corridor, stpaul.gov/index.aspx?NID=85
- University of Minnesota web page for Central Corridor, lightrail.umn.edu

READ UP!

- *Region: Planning the Future of the Twin Cities*, by Myron Orfield and Thomas Luce, University of Minnesota Press, 2010.

ACT LOCALLY!

- Transit for Livable Communities St. Paul, MN 651-767-0298 tlcminnesota.org

Why Consider Electric Cars?

By **JUKKA KUKKONEN**
PLUGINCONNECT

Jukka in a Tesla Roadster after a fun test drive.

For the last century we have relied heavily on oil to provide energy for our transportation needs. Gasoline- and diesel-powered internal combustion engines (ICE) have monopolized as the propulsion provider for cars and trucks. They have worked fairly well for us, but we are also paying a heavy price in environmental effects. Fortunately, we are starting to explore new alternatives, and electric vehicles (EVs) are emerging as the most viable new alternative for most of our driving. Here are some reasons to consider the switch:

Freedom
With EVs we aren't tied to one energy source, so we have the flexibility to choose how we produce the energy for our transportation. We can drastically reduce our dependency on oil and move toward more renewable energy sources. Owning an EV even allows you the option of producing your own transportation energy directly from the sun by adding solar panels to the roof of your home.

Efficiency
Even the best ICEs do a poor job in turning the energy from the gasoline into propulsion power. On average, 20% goes to propulsion and about 80% is thrown away as waste heat. Electric motors are just the opposite. They turn 80% of the battery's energy to propulsion power, while only 20% goes to waste heat. So EVs consume much less energy than traditional ICE-powered cars.

Simplicity
ICEs are very complex machines, and in most cases they are coupled with automatic transmissions that are even more complicated. Together, they consist of hundreds of moving parts. A modern AC electric motor has just one moving part, a rotor, and is coupled with a simple reduction gear. This simplicity means cheaper production costs in mass manufacturing, and the whole power train is practically maintenance free.

EVs work for most people's daily driving needs
The capability of batteries to carry energy is still limited, but the technology is developing fast. Present technologies limit the range of sensibly-priced family sedans to less than 100 miles/charge. This means that EVs are not yet ready to take you on interstate trips, but they are still well-suited for the daily driving needs of most people, since according to a U.S. Bureau of Transportation study, 78% of people drive fewer than 40 miles per day on average. For longer trips, people could rent a car, use public transportation or, in two-car households, they could use their second car, a traditional ICE powered vehicle.

Low emissions
Even though electric cars don't emit any exhaust gas, electricity production does cause emissions. The amount of these emissions depends on how big a portion is produced by coal-fired power plants. Still, even if the electricity were exclusively produced by coal, the exhaust emissions per mile driven would be less with EVs than with ICE vehicles. The more electricity produced by renewable sources such as solar and wind, the smaller the amount of emissions. For ICE vehicles, when we add the emissions for finding and drilling the crude oil, transporting it to refineries, refining it, transporting it to gas stations, pumping it to the storage tanks and even using electric pumps to pump it into cars, we start to get a better picture of the total emissions of oil-based energy sources. And how do you measure the costs of catastrophic oil spills like on the Gulf Coast?

ON THE WEB!

- ⚙ Plug In America, pluginamerica.org
- ⚙ Electric Auto Association, eaaev.org
- ⚙ Electrification Coalition, electrificationcoalition.org
- ⚙ The Plug-In Hybrid Consortium, hybridconsortium.org

ACT LOCALLY!

- ⚙ PlugInConnect, Jukka Kukkonen St Paul, MN PlugInConnect.com
- ⚙ ReGo Electric Conversions Minneapolis, MN 612-822-1626 regoelectric.com
- ⚙ Minnesota Electric Auto Association MNEAA.com

Cheaper to own and use

The high efficiency of the EV drive train means electricity costs for driving your EV are about half of what you would pay for gas for even the most efficient ICE car. The simplicity of the EV drive train means maintenance costs are also reduced drastically. Even the brake system sees very little wear, because most of the energy needed to slow down is collected to batteries by using the motor as a generator when the brake pedal is pressed. The new lithium-ion battery packs found in most of the mass-manufactured EVs coming to market are expected to last eight to ten years. Even though these packs are fairly expensive now, the rapid development of battery technologies will make these packs much cheaper by the time they need to be replaced.

Why pure EVs might not work for you

If no one in your family commutes fewer than 40 miles per day, I would advise you to consider plug-in hybrid (PHEV) models like the Chevrolet Volt, the Toyota Prius Plug-in, or the Fisker Karma. Those will give you some pure EV driving range (12–40 miles), and then the ICE engine will provide the extended range you need. There aren't yet many bigger truck and van options available as EVs, but keep your eyes open for new models coming to the market in the future.

Some EV and PHEV Options

The following EVs and PHEVs are already driven on U.S. roads or are expected to be available in the next couple of years. Check out the links to find out more about the models.

- **Aptera.** Designed from ground up to be an efficient EV or PHEV. *aptera.com*
- **BMW Mini-E.** Test fleet of 500 Mini-Es are driven around the east and west coast every day. *miniusa.com/minie-usa*
- **BYD e6.** Chinese battery manufacturer BYD is planning to enter to U.S. market with this crossover EV. *byd.com/showroom.php?car=e6*
- **Coda.** After extensive development and testing, the Coda sedan is expected to arrive in the U.S. market at the end of 2010. *codaautomotive.com*
- **Fisker Karma.** This luxury PHEV sports car is coming to the U.S. at the beginning of 2011. *karma.fiskerautomotive.com*
- **Chevrolet Volt.** Chevrolet's answer to the market demands is the PHEV Volt, which will be launched in November, 2010. *chevrolet.com/pages/open/default/future/volt.do*

- **Ford Focus BEV.** Ford will bring the new Focus model to the U.S. market at the end of 2010 and the electric version should arrive in 2011. *en.wikipedia.org/wiki/Ford_Focus_BEV*
- **Ford Transit Connect BEV.** Ford and Azure Dynamics are starting to sell this small commercial EV van in the U.S. at the end of 2010. *azuredynamics.com/products/transit-connect-electric.htm*
- **Mitsubishi i-MiEV.** Mitsubishi has been selling this 4 seater EV in Japan for some time. *mitsubishi-motors.com/special/ev*
- **Nissan Leaf.** Nissan is investing heavily in EV development and is launching the Leaf in the U.S. in December, 2010. *nissan-zeroemission.com/EN/LEAF*
- **Smart ED.** Daimler is bringing a test fleet of 250 Smart ED EVs to the U.S. at the end of this year and will be starting mass production in 2012. *smartusa.com/smart-fortwo-electric-drive.aspx*

- **Tesla model S.** Tesla is starting the mass production of its luxury sedan EV, Model S, in 2012. *teslamotors.com/models*
- **Tesla Roadster.** Tesla's luxury sports EV, the Roadster, has been sold in the U.S. since 2008. *teslamotors.com/roadster*
- **Think City.** The Think City EV has been sold in Europe for years and it is coming to the U.S. in 2011. *thinkev.com*
- **Toyota Plug-in Prius.** Toyota is presently testing the PHEV Prius and planning to start selling it in 2012. *en.wikipedia.org/wiki/Plug_in_Prius*
- **Toyota RAV4 EV.** Toyota is working with Tesla Motors to develop a second generation RAV4 EV that should come to the market in 2012. *en.wikipedia.org/wiki/Toyota_RAV4_EV*
- **Wheego Whip.** Wheego is bringing its two seater Whip to the U.S. market during 2010. **wheego.net**

Nice Ride Minnesota is Here

By **JAKE QUARSTAD**
NICE RIDE MINNESOTA

Nice Ride Minnesota launched the largest public bike sharing system in America on June 10, with 65 stations spread across the city, housing 700 bikes.

Sign up for a 24-hour to year-long subscription with your credit card online or at a station. 1-year and 30-day subscribers receive a Nice Ride key that makes using the system even easier to use. One-year subscribers also receive a coupon booklet within their User Manual worth roughly $500. If you like deals like free dinner at Common Roots Café, free lunch at Lucia's, free brunch at Butter Bakery or 50% off almost every theater in town, you'll dig the rest of the coupons.

Subscription rates are:
$60 = 1-year (online)
$50 = Student 1-year (online)
$30 = 30-day (online)
$5 = 24-hour (at the station)

So the time has come, and you want to hop on a gorgeous green bike to grab something different to eat on your lunch hour, soak up some rays and get a little exercise while you're at it. Walk to a station, swipe your credit card at the pay station to pay for your 24-hour subscription, print out your access code and find the bike that seems to scream your name. Adjust the seat to the proper level for you, and remember your seat number for future Nice Ride excursions.

Punch the access code into the number pad to the left of the bike. Skip the pay station altogether if you have a 1-year subscription, and simply insert your Nice Ride key in the slot to the left of the bike.

Once the light above the keypad has turned green, yank the bike out and get pedaling. There's no need to roll up your pant legs, or wear spandex; the bike is fully self-contained so that riders can even wear dresses! Did we mention there are ⮞

Minneapolis Bikeways Expansion

COMING YOUR WAY!

By **HILARY REEVES**
COMMUNICATIONS MANAGER, TRANSIT FOR LIVABLE COMMUNITIES

The Twin Cities are has long been known for its extensive system of off-road bike paths, from the Grand Rounds to the Cedar Lake trail, Luce Line trail, and others. Minnesota also has several great "rails to trails" bike paths around the state. All of these trails have given Minneapolis a well-deserved reputation for being a great place for recreational bicycling.

In 2010, the gears shifted a bit as Minneapolis was recognized by *Bicycling Magazine* as the nation's #1 bike-friendly city. What finally put Minneapolis on top, bumping Portland from its 14-year perch, was not only our great bike trails—including the Hiawatha LRT Trail, the Sabo Bridge, and the amazing Midtown Greenway—but also the Cities' growing network of on-street bicycling options and an embrace by more and more residents of bicycling as a viable and fun means of transportation—of getting around.

Minneapolis is one of four locations around the country participating in a federal non-motorized pilot program dedicated to expanding the options for bicycling and walking. Bike Walk Twin Cities, a program of Transit for Livable Communities, runs the Minneapolis area pilot—and is investing upwards of $25 million in new facilities for biking and walking. As a result of this funding and of allocations by local cities and counties, there are several new on-street routes coming in 2010 and 2011. The new routes make it easier for cyclists and walkers to reach important destinations. They connect with off-road bike trails. They provide new ways to move between Minneapolis, St. Paul, Richfield, Edina, Roseville, Golden Valley, and other cities in the metro area.

Here are some highlights from a new network of bikeways that cyclists will be able to consider for getting around by the fall of 2012:

North-South bikeways in South Minneapolis
- The Bryant Avenue bikeway from Loring Park to 50th Street.
- A bikeway from the Longfellow neighborhood near Lake Street to the University of Minnesota and Augsburg. This route will connect to the Hiawatha LRT Trail and Midtown Greenway.
- The "Southern Connector" from Minneapolis to Richfield, with bikeways on 17th, 18th and Bloomington Avenue.
- 1st and Blaisdell Avenues—two one-way streets in South Minneapolis.

North-South routes in North and Northeast Minneapolis
- A new route connecting to the Stone Arch Bridge, along Fillmore and 6th Avenues in Northeast.
- In North Minneapolis, a bikeway will extend down two one-way streets, Emerson Avenue and Fremont Avenue.
- A new bikeway will connect Falcon Heights, Lauderdale, and Roseville to both the St. Paul and Minneapolis campuses of the University of Minnesota, along Fairview Avenue North, Larpenteur Avenue, and Gortner Avenue.

East-West routes
- Bikeways along Como Avenue in St. Paul and Minneapolis. ⮞

Subscriber Key

Pay Station

Price = Subscription + Trip Fees
✔ All subscriptions give you an unlimited number of trips.
✔ A trip starts when you take a bike and ends when you return it to any station in the system.
✔ There are no Trip Fees for the first 30 minutes of every trip.
✔ Take as many trips as you want during a subscription.

Subscriptions:
1yr (365 days) ....$60 ($55 students)
30 days $30
24hrs $5

Trip Fees: (per trip)
0-30 min...................................no fee
up to 60 min $1.50
up to 90 min $4.50
Each additional 1/2 hr ....+$6.00

trip fees below will apply.

But wait, 95% of Minneapolis riders have avoided these trip fees.

How'd they do it?

Every time you dock the bicycle into place and the light turns green, your trip has ended. So if you want to keep riding around the city all day, just dock the bicycle within 30 minutes and take the same bike out again, either with your Nice Ride key, or by swiping your credit card again for a brand new access code at no additional charge.

The trip fees keep folks from keeping the bikes in their offices, garages or cars. Trip fees are incentives to keep the bikes in circulation and available to you when someone else isn't using it.

Have a Nice Ride!

built-in lights and a rack on the front so that you can bring your leftovers back to the office for your coworkers to drool over?

Once you've removed the bike from the dock, the first 30 minutes of every trip is paid for. If you don't stop at a station the

ON THE WEB!

⚙ For additional details visit Nice Ride Minnesota, niceridemn.org.

- A bikeway will extend along Jefferson Avenue in St. Paul, connecting to Mississippi River Road bike paths at both ends.
- In South Minneapolis, the new Riverlake Greenway will extend from I-35 to the Mississippi River.

The last American Community Survey, a part of the census, showed Minneapolis at #2 in bicycle commuting, behind Portland. To be number 1 by all measures, Minneapolis and the whole Twin Cities region still has room to crank it up.

ON THE WEB!

⚙ Minneaplis Bicycles Page, ci.minneapolis.mn.us/bicycles
⚙ #1 Biking City article, bicycling.com/news/featured-stories/1-bike-city-minneapolis
⚙ Nice Ride bike share program, niceridemn.org
⚙ Bike Walk Ambassador program, bikewalktwincities.org/ambassadors
⚙ Bike Walk Twin Cities, bikewalktwincities.org

ACT LOCALLY!

⚙ Bike Trails in the Twin Cities

Minneapolis Named Best Biking City

Excerpts reprinted from **ci.minneapolis.mn.us/bicycles**

Our more than 120 miles of bikeways, many bike amenities and strong, vibrant bicycling community has prompted *Bicycling* magazine to name Minneapolis as America's best bike city in its May, 2010 issue, stating that "The unforgiving and frigid city of Minneapolis is the country's top spot to be an urban cyclist." In the article, Minneapolis is noted for having a large and supportive biking community and extensive infrastructure in place for cyclists.

DID YOU KNOW?

- Minneapolis has 43 miles of streets with dedicated bicycle lanes and 84 miles of off-street bicycle paths.
- There is more bike parking per capita in Minneapolis than any other city in the country.
- The city has hired bike ambassadors to help educate and promote biking.
- Minneapolis has the second

highest percentage of bicycle commuters in the nation, according to a U.S. Census comparison of the nation's 50 biggest cities.

- Minneapolis has been ranked the #2 bicycling city in the nation by the U.S. Census Bureau.
- The city has also been awarded the League of American Bicyclists' Bicycle Friendly Community Award.
- Minneapolis is home to Nice Ride Minnesota, the Bike Walk Ambassadors, and the Midtown Bike Center.

By choosing to bike instead of drive, residents decrease traffic congestion, cut the production of greenhouse gases and reduce our dependence on oil. Plus, biking is a healthy way to get around. The Minneapolis Bicycle Program helps those who live and work in the city to use bicycles as a low polluting, cost-effective, and healthy way to travel. Join us on the trails!

Pass Along Your Cycling Passion to Your Kids

Excerpts reprinted from **REI.COM**

"How do I get my child started in cycling?" It's one of the first questions bike-riding parents ask. Happily, kids and bikes seem to be drawn together by a natural kind of magnetism. By following the tips we outline here, you can quickly strengthen that attraction.

A Child's Bike Progression

To get children started early, don't wait until they can pedal. Connect a child carrier to your bike, strap in your child and go for rides regularly. When you do, be sure to show enthusiasm for the activity on every ride to set an example and to get your kids fired up about cycling.

As they become more comfortable and their bodies become better equipped to handle physical activity, progessively move children to bikes that offer greater degrees of independence. Few motivators will generate greater enthusiasm for cycling within a child than a growing sense of self-sufficiency.

Step 1: Child Bike Seat

Toddlers must be able to easily sit up and fully support their head before they can join you for a ride. Many areas have laws requiring children to be at least 1 year old and to wear a helmet while riding in a bike seat. Most carriers attach to the back of the bicycle and are suitable for children weighing up to 40 pounds. They have high backs to support a child's shoulders and head. The seats themselves are lightweight, though you may find your bike is a bit harder to manuever. Remember, should you fall, your child falls, too.

Tip: The bike seat is directly over your rear axle, so your child will feel bumps more than you do. To provide some cush-

Lukas Grochowski riding up the tree on his pedaless balance bike with Dad.

ioning, inflate your tires to slighly below their maximum setting. Less-inflated tires allow a softer ride.

Step 2: Bike Trailer

This is a popular option for toddlers and children up to 6 years old. You get to cycle; the kids get to sit and see the sights. Trailers are stable and easy to steer. Even if you fall, your child won't. Tip: Give your toddlers a pillow so their head doesn't bounce around too much.

Trailers have a few downsides. Kids sit low to the ground, so they're less visible to others and they are a bit more exposed to the exhaust of cars. Also, keep in mind that older children can get bored with such passive transport.

Step 3: Push Bike

This is a bike in its simplest form—no pedals or chain, just wheels and a frame. As the child walks or coasts along on their push bike, their feet act as their brakes. A push bike helps teach 2- to 5-year-olds how to coordinate steering and balance. The better they get, the easier their transition to pedaling will be.

Step 4: Trailer Bike

A trailer bike (sometimes referred to by the brand name Trail-a-bike) attaches to your bicycle so your child can pedal and feel independent, though he or she is still relying on you for balance and control. This single-wheel bike attaches either to your seatpost or on a rear rack so it can pivot for turning. A trailer bike is good for 4- to 7-year-olds who may have some trepidation about cycling. It also allows you to cycle farther than your child's stamina might otherwise allow.

Step 5: Training Wheel Bike

Bikes with training wheels can give children the confidence boost needed so they can start riding on their own. Once the confidence is there, the training wheels can be removed. These are single-speed bicycles with coaster brakes, though some models have an additional linear-pull rear brake to ready them for future hand brakes.

Step 6: Kids' Bike

Once they are ready for their own 2-wheeler, make sure you avoid the common mistake of buying a bike that they'll "grow into." Doing so can set your child back a couple of years. When shopping, be aware that children's bikes are measured by their wheel size (not frame size). The most common sizes are 16", 20" and 24". The right size is one where your child can comfortably get on the bike and stand with his or her feet on the ground.

Fore more outdoor adventure articles bike options visit **rei.com**.

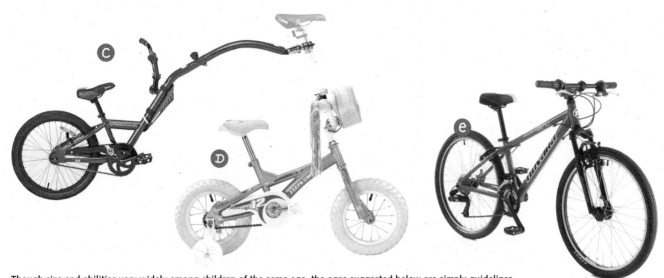

Though size and abilities vary widely among children of the same age, the ages suggested below are simply guidelines…
A Ages 1-5: Give them the feel of the road in a bike trailer or a bicycle-mounted seat. **B** Ages 2-5: Help them discover their center of gravity on a balance bike. **C** Ages 4-7: Take them on their first family ride on a trailer bike where they can pedal too. **D** Ages 4-6: Let them earn their independence on a two-wheeler. **e** Ages 8–10: 24″ bikes are made for those tweens who are ready to ride.

How to Take Your Kids Biking

LEFT: **Get your child used to wearing a helmet at a young age to help them form the habit.** RIGHT: Madix Schakel enjoying a ride in the bike trailer with his Dad along Lake Nokomis.

Children make good cycling companions because they're adaptable, energetic and want to have fun. However, cycling with kids is not as easy as hopping on your bike and taking off. Here are some saddle-savvy tips.

BEFORE THE RIDE

Do your homework: Make certain you are familiar with the bike route so that you do not get lost or find the route is longer than expected.

Start early: Children tend to tire quickly in the afternoon. Take advantage of their energy in the morning.

Invite playmates: Cycling is more fun when shared. If your child has a friend who is at the same level of competency on a bike, bring them along.

Slow down: Realize that a 4-mile ride may take 2 hours. Don't expect to ride as fast as you would on your own.

Be aware of traffic: What might seem like light traffic to you could be a more dangerous situation for your child, whether biking separately or in a trailer.

Be prepared: Carry a tool kit and know how to use it. Also, carry a first-aid kit.

Dress right: Bring a daypack to hold extra jackets in case the weather changes.

ON THE RIDE

Take breaks: Plan on taking a lot of short breaks. Allow time to stop, get off the bike and explore.

Drink water: Always bring water on your trip and have everyone drink it regularly throughout the ride.

Eat snacks: A well-timed snack can defuse a squabble or bad mood and keep energy going.

Make it fun: Choose an interesting route that goes by gardens, streams, views, farms or a favorite shop.

Express enthusiasm: If you convey a genuinely upbeat attitude, children most often will be inclined to mimic it.

Rain Barrel & Compost Bin SALES!

Compost Bin
Sale $55
Reg. $105

Rain Barrel
Sale $65
Reg. $115

• Additional Styles Available

For more info & to order visit:
www.recycleminnesota.org

RECYCLING
ASSOCIATION
of Minnesota

Hosting several sale events this spring!

The daily harvest, whether from an urban yard or a dedicated vegetable garden, varies, but is rewarding throughout the season.

Home Grown

By **THERESA ROONEY**
HENNEPIN COUNTY MASTER GARDENER

Why grow your own food? For many people, it is one simple and rewarding thing they can do to make a difference in their own lives and help the environment at the same time. Some may wish to reduce their use of natural resources such as oil, or to provide some food security to their families in the wake of a major event such as a terrorist attack or a massive food recall. As a Master Gardener, I have observed an increase in questions regarding all types of food gardening over the past several years. Vegetable growing classes are often filled, and not always with just young, first-time gardeners. Our gardening students are from all age groups, income levels and nationalities, making each class a melting pot.

Farmers' markets are experiencing a strengthening of support in their communities as their customer base expands. Many visitors first learn here that produce is a seasonal commodity, which may spark interest in eating in harmony with the seasons. These market visitors soon realize that the vegetables are fresh and flavorful in comparison to supermarket vegetables, and they become interested in growing their own. And so the journey to learn about growing food starts.

For some, popular books such as *The Omnivore's Dilemma* by Michael Pollan, movies such as *Food, Inc,* or thumbing through a classic gardening book may spark an interest in knowing how and where their food is grown. Others begin with a desire for safe, fresh food, grown locally, and discover that they can produce some of the food needed by their family and save money at the same time. Community gardens are a popular option for people who lack their own growing space. These gardens bring a wonderful sense of connection to their community.

Some may view this interest as a return to the old way of doing things, but I think it reaches beyond that. Many of us see how interdependent we all are, and that our actions influence others. People are seeing that some resources may be finite, and that we need to look at our lifestyles in a new way. Growing vegetables in your garden or landscaping your yard can have a positive impact on your health and your financial bottom line, your community and even the world. The money you save with creative landscaping is money that you then have available for other purposes. The food you grow and eat helps you to be a healthier, more productive member of society, which benefits the entire community. ❧➤

❧ → *Home Grown,* CONTINUED

So, pull out that trowel and take action! Exchange some lawn for a vegetable or flower plot; spend time in the front yard and meet the neighbors while weeding; bring a bounty of fresh vegetables to the potluck at the office or the next block party. Cut a bouquet of flowers from your yard for the elderly neighbor who can no longer garden. Take a community class on gardening, chickens, rain gardens or native plant landscaping. Plant your boulevard for the enjoyment of all who pass. Recycle everything you can. Whatever you use, use it wisely and with knowledge of where it came from, how it got to your hands, and where it will go once it leaves your hands.

As for me, I have a few 'weeds' to pick and feed to the chickens, some beans to harvest and share with my neighbor, and then I will enjoy a cup of mint tea, fresh from my garden, while I decide where I can plant some more blueberry bushes.

ON THE WEB!

- University of Minnesota extension, extension.umn.edu/Garden
- Presentation about edible landscapes, www.slideshare.net/UMNfruit/edible-landscapes-3186210
- Edible Landscaping, rosalindcreasy.com

ACT LOCALLY

- Hennepin County Master Gardeners
  Eden Prairie, MN
  612-596-2110
  hcmg.umn.edu

READ UP!

- *Fresh Food from Small Spaces: The Square-Inch Gardener's Guide to Year-Round Growing, Fermenting, and Sprouting*, by R.J. Ruppenthal, Chelsea Green, 2008.
- *The Backyard Homestead: Produce all the food you need on just a quarter acre!*, by Carleen Madigan, Storey Publishing, 2009.
- *All New Square Foot Gardening: Grow More in Less Space!*, by Mel Bartholomew, Cool Springs Press, 2006.

- *Landscaping with Fruit*, by Lee Reich, Storey Publishing, 2009.
- *Gaia's Garden, Second Edition: A Guide To Home-Scale Permaculture*, by Toby Hemenway, Clelsea Green, 2009.
- *Landscaping with Native Plants of Minnesota*, by Lynn M Steiner, Voyageur Press, 2005.

MAGAZINES:
- *Northern Gardener*
- *Mother Earth News*
- *Backyard Poultry*
- *Organic Gardening*

Raingarden Maintenance

By **LAURA DOMYANCICH**
ENERGYSCAPES, INC.

Choosing to go green by installing a rain garden is a choice for clean water, reduced resource use, and healthy habitat. Rain gardens reduce run-off and create a beautiful landscape feature. These benefits, however, rely on seasonal maintenance. Simple, proactive steps ensure that a rain garden functions properly and benefits the landscape.

Erosion is a consideration as rainwater or snowmelt moves through the rain garden inflow. Deep-rooting native plants and the inclusion of shredded, hardwood mulch prevent erosion by physically slowing water flow, stabilizing soil, assisting with water infiltration and moisture retention, and limiting weed growth. Thoughtful placement of 6- to 12-inch boulders can also absorb the force of water and add a distinctive feature to a rain garden.

Consideration should be given to **new plants versus mature plants**. Young plants

Implementing small boulders and shredded hardwood mulch to absorb the force of water, stabilize plantings, and suppress weed growth.
Laura Domyancich

are more susceptible to failure from both dry and wet conditions. Large, established plants tolerate drought and saturation. New plants should receive 1 inch of water **❧ →**

per week, easily measured by placing an empty tuna can in the rain garden while watering. During subsequent growing seasons, plants have established root systems and only need supplemental watering during excessively dry periods or if species prefer consistent moisture. If an extended rainy period follows a rain garden installation, cut a temporary notch in the outlet berm.

The removal of **debris and sediment** that is carried into the rain garden with inflow will prevent ponding. This issue is likely if the rain garden is adjacent to a road or driveway and receives meltwater in the spring.

As with any garden, **weeding** is necessary to maintain aesthetics and limit competition. Desirable plants that become dominant can be split or their seed collected and sown in other areas of the landscape. Timely pruning and the removal of last year's growth from grasses and perennials will also provide a maintained appearance.

ON THE WEB!

- Metro Watershed Partners, cleanwatermn.org
- Metro Blooms, metroblooms.org
- Wisconsin Department of Natural Resources (Rain Garden Manual), dnr.wi.gov/org/water/wm/dsfm /shore/documents/rgmanual.pdf
- Blue Thumb: Planting for Clean Water, bluethumb.org

READ UP!

- *The Blue Thumb Guide to Rain Gardens,* by Rusty Schmidt, David Dods, and Dan Shaw, Marion County, IN Soil and Water Conservation District, 2007.
- *Rain Gardens: Managing Water Sustainably in the Garden and Designed Landscape,* by Nigel Dunnet and Andy Clayden, Timber Press, 2007.

ACT LOCALLY!

- EnergyScapes, Inc. Minneapolis, MN (612) 821-9797 energyscapes.com

Creating a Bird & Butterfly Haven Garden

By **CRAIG STARK**
Ecoscapes Sustainable Landscaping

Many of us look at gardens as a way to create something, enjoy the outdoors, and restore our spirit. As a landscape designer and contractor I am often asked, "How do I draw more birds and butterflies to my gardens?" I have always looked at attracting them from the point of view of what plants they eat. However, I think I have been missing several vital parts of the puzzle. What if we looked at everything they need and not just the pretty flower filled with nectar? Just like humans, birds and butterflies need food, shelter, and water. Here, I'll explore each of these needs individually, although they are often interconnected.

FOOD: What do birds eat? Well, a lot of things: nectar, worms, insects, berries, and other fruits. When trying to create an ecosystem that is hospitable to birds, we should create places that are also hospitable to worms and invertebrates, as well as adding plants that provide nectar and berries. The diet of butterflies is simpler: generally nectar from flowers.

SHELTER: What do birds need for shelter? This varies widely between species. Often a nest in a tree works, but some like shrubs, and yet others nest on the ground. Some birds like the protection of evergreens, and some like our small native trees and shrubs with thinner branches that keep ground predators away. Many birds need standing dead trees, which we often clear from urban areas. Consider leaving the trunk of a tree on your lot next time a tree dies.

Butterflies need structure as well to keep them out of potentially fatal rains and to provide a place to roost at night. They also need places to safely lay eggs and a place for their larvae to feed and eventually pupate and complete the life cycle.

WATER: Finally, both birds and butterflies need a clean and safe water source. For example: Cup Plant (*Silphium perfoliatum*)

TOP: **Monarch (***Danaus plexippus***) feeds on Showy Goldenrod (***Solidago speciosa***).** BOTTOM: **White-lined Spinx (***Hyles lineata***) feeds on nectar of Blue Lobelia (***Lobelia siphilitica***).**

holds water in its leaves after rain events and often dries up before mosquitoes' eggs can hatch, therefore making a great source of water for birds and butterflies without breeding pesky mosquitoes. Birdbaths and butterfly water dishes will also work. Be sure to keep these filled with fresh water.

Creating an Ecosystem:

Looking at all these needs makes this task seem very complex, especially when you consider all of the species. Essentially, you just have to supply the basic needs of the species you would like to attract. Following is a list of many plants that are good for butterflies and birds as well as some cultural practices that can help create a healthy ecosystem for them, even if on a small ❧

Butterfly Haven, CONTINUED

scale. Again we need to create an ecosystem, even if it is on a small scale, providing all the necessities for their existence.

I always start any landscape design with trees or at least one tree. Trees are vital for most songbirds of the upper Midwest, as well as being good shelter for butterflies. Then I look at small understory trees and shrubs. They provide the layer that is often completely missing in our urban environments, because we have been trained to like park-like landscapes. In much of the Twin Cities, this layer has been replaced by invasive buckthorn, which has very little, if any, habitat value for our native feathered friends. Finally, I try to integrate native grasses, sedges and flowers. For most gardeners this is the part we focus on already, but we can do better by sticking to native plants.

When selecting plant species, locally native species are the best for creating habitat for our native fauna. It seems obvious that our native fauna has evolved with our native flora, but we have overlooked this and opted for pretty exotic cultivars instead. The nursery industry has pushed for bigger, brighter, and showier in our cultivated plants and this has resulted in a large-scale replacement of native plants, especially in urban and suburban environments. The result is habitat loss for our beloved native fauna because many of these non-natives cultivated plants do not provide them quality habitat.

The following list contains species that have significant habitat value for our native birds and butterflies. Some species of birds and butterflies need specific plants, called host plants. Many of the plants below are host plants for specific species, while others will attract a wide range of insects to feed our bird populations or supply nectar to many species. When selecting plants for your bird and butterfly garden, the more diversity of native plants you use, the more animal diversity you will be privileged to experience.

ON THE WEB!

- EcoScapes, www.ecoscapes1.com
- bluethumb.org
- metroblooms.org

READ UP!

- *Trees and Shrubs of Minnesota,* by Welby R. Smith, University of Minnesota Press, 2008.
- *Bringing Nature Home, How You Can Sustain Wildlife with Native Plants,* by Douglas W. Tallamy, Timber Press, 2009.

ACT LOCALLY!

- Ecoscapes Sustainable Landscaping, ecoscapes1.com

Landscape Plants for Birds and Butterflies

TREES & SHRUBS:

- Bur Oak – *Quercus macrocarpa*
- White Oak – *Quercus alba*
- Red Oak – *Quercus rubra*
- Northern Pin Oak – *Quercus ellipsoidalis*
- Swamp White Oak – *Quercus bicolor*
- Bebb's Willow – *Salix rostrata*
- Pussy Willow – *Salix discolor*
- Prairie Willow – *Salix humilis*
- Black Willow – *Salix nigra*
- Black Cherry – *Prunus serotina*
- Pin Cherry – *Prunus pensylvanica*
- America Wild Plum – *Prunus americana*
- Chokecherry – *Prunus virginiana*
- River Birch – *Betula nigra*
- Paper Birch – *Betula papyrifera*
- Yellow Birch – *Betula alleghaniensis*
- Bigtooth Aspen – *Populus grandidentata*
- Quaking Aspen – *Populus tremuloides*
- Prairie Crabapple – *Malus ioensis*
- Sugar Maple – *Acer saccharum*
- Red Maple – *Acer rubrum*
- American Elm – *Ulmus americana* (Dutch Elm Disease Resistant Selections)
- Hackberry – *Celtis occidentalis*
- Downy Serviceberry – *Amelanchier arborea*
- Saskatoon Serviceberry – *Amelanchier alnifolia*
- Black Chokeberry – *Aronia melanocarpa*
- Pagoda Dogwood – *Cornus alternifolia*
- Red-osier Dogwood – *Cornus sericea*
- American Hazel – *Corylus americana*
- Downy Hawthorn – *Crataegus mollis*
- Showy Mountain Ash – *Sorbus decora*
- Bush Honeysuckle – *Diervilla lonicera*
- Ninebark – *Physocarpus opulifolius*

GRASSES & SEDGES:

- Little Bluestem – *Schizachyrium scoparium*
- Big Bluestem – *Andropogon gerardii*
- Indian Grass – *Sorghastrum nutans*
- Side Oats Grama – *Bouteloua curtipendula*
- Bebb's Sedge – *Carex bebbii*
- Fox Sedge – *Carex vulpinoidea*
- Bottlebrush Sedge – *Carex hystericina*
- Longhair Sedge – *Carex comosa*

FLOWERS/FORBS:

- Anise Hyssop – *Agastache foeniculum*
- Giant Hyssop – *Agastache scrophulariifolia*
- Pearly Everlasting – *Anaphalis margaritacea*
- Wild Columbine – *Aquilegia canadensis*
- Swamp Milkweed – *Asclepias incarnata*
- Butterfly Weed – *Asclepias tuberosa*
- Whorled Milkweed – *Asclepias verticillata*
- Smooth Aster – *Aster laevis*
- New England Aster – *Aster novae angliae*
- Lance Leaf Coreopsis – *Coreopsis lanceolata*
- Prairie Coreopsis – *Coreopsis palmata*
- White Prairie Clover – *Dalea candida*
- Purple Prairie Clover – *Dalea purpurea*
- Pale Purple Coneflower – *Echinacea pallida*
- Fireweed – *Epilobium angustifolium*
- Purple Joe Pye Weed – *Eupatorium purpureum*
- Sneezeweed – *Helenium autumnale*
- Sawtooth Sunflower – *Helianthus grosseserratus*
- Maximilian Sunflower – *Helianthus maximiliani*
- Rough Blazing Star – *Liatris aspera*
- Northern Plains Blazing Star – *Liatris ligulistylis*
- Thick Spike Blazing Star – *Liatris pycnostachya*
- Marsh Blazing Star – *Liatris spicata*
- Scaly Blazing Star – *Liatris squarrosa*
- Cardinal Flower – *Lobelia cardinalis*
- Great Blue Lobelia – *Lobelia siphilitica*
- Wild Blue Lupine – *Lupinus perennis*
- Bergamot – *Monarda fistulosa*
- Smooth Penstemon – *Penstemon digitalis*
- Yellow Coneflower – *Ratibida pinnata*
- Orange Coneflower – *Rudbeckia fulgida*
- Compass Plant – *Silphium laciniatum*
- Cup Plant – *Silphium perfoliatum*
- Ohio Goldenrod – *Solidago ohiensis*
- Showy Goldenrod – *Solidago speciosa*
- Blue Vervain – *Verbena hastata*
- Hoary Vervain – *Verbena stricta*
- Ironweed – *Vernonia fasciculata*
- Culver's Root – *Veronicastrum virginicum*

Emerald Ash Borer

By **TESSIA MELVIN**
CITY OF SHOREVIEW

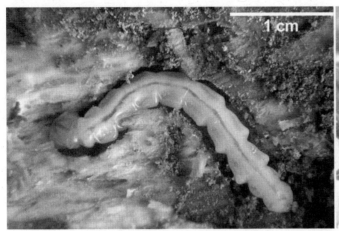 

LEFT: **The larval form of the emerald ash borer is lethal to trees.** D. Cappaert, MSU RIGHT: **Many other insects resemble the adult emerald ash borer, but online photo resources can help you identify it.** Michigan State University

The emerald ash borer (EAB) is an exotic beetle native to Asia which attacks and kills ash trees. The adult EAB measures 0.5 inch and can be recognized by its sparkly green coat and purplish red abdomen. However, it's the larvae that have been damaging and killing ash trees across the eastern and midwestern parts of the United States. Measuring up to an inch in length, these cream-colored pests burrow through ash in S-shaped patterns, feeding on the living tissue in the phloem layer of the ash trees, between the bark and the wood. This interrupts the transport of nutrients and water in the tree, causing it to die.

First found in Michigan in 2001, EAB has spread all over the region, including 13 states and two Canadian provinces. Seven years after it was first discovered, millions of ash trees have already died as a result of EAB. In spring 2009, EAB was identified in St Paul, Minnesota. This poses a threat to all of Minnesota's estimated 867 million ash trees, our local economies, plant communities, dependent wildlife, and the quality of our water.

Signs and Symptoms of EAB:
- Decline in growth at the top of the canopy
- Roots sprouting from the trunk
- Vertical fissures in the bark revealing the S-shaped galleries of the larvae
- Increased woodpecker activity on the bark of the tree
- D-shaped exit holes on the outside of the tree, 3 to 4 mm in diameter

Prevention and Treatment
Experts suggest considering preventive treatment if you have ash trees and live within 10–15 miles of a known infestation. In Minnesota, this includes a large portion of the metro Twin Cities area, as infestations have been found in St. Paul and Falcon Heights. Research into the most effective treatment is ongoing at several large universities.

Treatment options are available for EAB via local arborists, and some treatments can be applied by the homeowner. Methods include either soil drench or direct injection, using chemicals such as Imidacloprid, but can become costly because they must be repeated annually. These insecticides are relatively new for EAB and are not perfected, meaning that success rates are less than 100 percent. For further details on treatment options, visit the web resources below.

If You Suspect Your Ash is Infected:
Contact the Minnesota Department of Agriculture's Arrest the Pest Hotline at 651-201-6684 to speak with an EAB First Detector, a trained volunteer who will help you determine if this is, in fact, EAB, and if so, guide you through reporting the infestation.

Prevention
To prevent the spread of emerald ash borer, observe the Hennepin and Ramsey County quarantines which prohibit the following transport of Ash:
- Entire ash trees (mature or nursery)
- Ash limbs or branches
- Ash logs
- Untreated ash lumber with bark attached or ash bark chips
- Any firewood of non-evergreen species

ON THE WEB!
- emeraldashborer.info (Minnesota-specific information: emeraldashborer.info/minnesotainfo.cfm)
- USDA: Invasive Species invasivespeciesinfo.gov/animals/eab.shtml
- Emerald Ash Borer Prevention, Early Detection & Rapid Response" www.mda.state.mn.us/plants/pestmanagement/eab.aspx

ACT LOCALLY!
- Find a certified arborist at the Minnesota Society of Arboriculture msa-live.org/certified-arborists.html

Choosing a Rain Catchment System

By **KURT MILLER**
DO IT GREEN! MINNESOTA

The remodeled Roseville Library, which is seeking LEED certification, features a Children's Reading Garden that is irrigated with rainwater collected in this cistern. Katrina Edenfeld

Anything you can do to make your environmental footprint a little smaller on this earth is always exciting. Looking at Earth from space, you see all greens and blues; however, only three percent of all the blue water we see from space on Earth is usable by humans. Many countries lack a consistent source of water or have a reliable source of water that is too expensive to utilize. Thus far in Minnesota, many of us have been fortunate enough to have a consistently clean, dependable, and safe source of potable water coming right from the tap. This type of system is by no means the standard in many countries, developed or undeveloped.

One of the many things you can do to decrease your water consumption is to install a rain catchment system. Rain catchment systems allow you to capture rain water from your roof and store it for later use. You do not want to use this water for drinking, cooking, or washing dishes; however, you can use it for almost anything else. The goal is to use the captured water for anything that does not require potable water—also known as that clean, dependable, and safe water that comes from your tap. One use can include watering your flower garden; it is **not** recommended for use on vegetable gardens. You can use it to wash your car, driveway, sidewalk, or deck. One indoor use that may sound crazy is using your captured water to flush your toilet!

There are several things to consider when determining the type of rain catchment system to purchase. First, consider what you can do around your home. Do you own your property? Do you need to obtain permission from your landlord, local government, or neighbors? The next question you must ask yourself is whether you have the infrastructure to get going. While there are numerous low-cost and affordable options, few of them are free of cost. In addition to the vessel to hold the water, you need to get it there first — do you have gutters and downspouts?

Next you must consider the size of the system needed for your project. Some important questions to consider are: How much space do you have to physically accommodate the vessel? How much 'roof-real estate' is there? What uses are there for the captured water? If you have a lot of room next to your house, a huge roof, and ten cars to wash, why not get a three-thousand gallon tank? If that is not you, perhaps a 55-gallon plastic tank— or two— might be a better option for you. You don't want to install something that is so big it will kill half the grass in your yard, nor do you want three thousand gallons of water just sitting for months on end.

Four things are mandatory for any water catchment system: it has to have a screen to prevent mosquitoes from entering and laying eggs; it must be placed and secured in such a manner to keep children, pets, and other wildlife out of it; and it must have overflow relief, which is usually a long, flexible tube directed away from the house. It is important to direct the overflow ❧➤

ON THE WEB!

❀ Ramsey-Washington Metro Watershed District (many informative articles. Search for keywords such as "rainbarrel" or "cistern"), rwmwd.org

❀ Rainwater Cisterns, resources.cas.psu.edu/WaterResources/pdfs/RainCistern.pdf

READ UP!

❀ *Design for Water: Rainwater Harvesting, Stormwater Catchment, and Alternate Water Reuse*, by Heather Kinkade-Levario, New Society Publishers, 2007.

❀ *Water Storage: Tanks, Cisterns, Aquifers, and Ponds for Domestic Supply, Fire and Emergency*, by Art Ludwig, Oasis Design, 2005.

ACT LOCALLY!

❀ The ReUse Center
Minneapolis, MN, 612-724-2608
Maplewood, MN, 651-379-1280
thereusecenter.com

❀ Barrel Depot — Rain barrels and other supplies
Minneapolis, MN
612-290-7427
barreldepot.com

Rainbarrels can be connected in series to harvest additional rain water. Tim Pratt

in a controlled manner rather than allow it to go where you don't want excess water (for instance, next to the foundation of your house). An excellent place for this overflow is a rain garden. A rain garden not only prevents rainwater from entering the storm sewer system, but it lets the ground absorb the water to recharge the aquifer.

The fourth thing you cannot forget is maintenance. All rain barrels **must** be drained and disconnected from downspouts before winter. Recall that water expands on freezing; a rain barrel left in place will turn into a solid block of ice, and that expanding water can damage it permanently. It may be easiest to store it inside a shed or garage if possible, especially if your system is made wood, as snow sitting on top of the barrel will cause it to rot quite quickly. Rain barrels can also be turned upside down and left outside for the winter.

During the "rain catchment season" you should periodically check the gutters, downspouts, spigot, and overflow assembly to ensure there is nothing blocking the flow of water into or out of the vessel. When you check those things, verify that the vessel is still sturdy and not susceptible to tipping over. Check for mosquitoes and small animals that may have found their way into the vessel at the same time.

Visit the Do It Green! Minnesota website for a brochure on a wide selection of available catchment systems.

Planting a Medicinal Garden

By **KAREN OLSON**
WRITER, EDITOR, INVETERATE PLANT LOVER

As a new gardener, I chose plants for my garden because of the shape of their leaves, the color of their flowers or maybe their plant name—like boneset, angelica, lemon balm or feverfew. I later researched the plants I had purchased and was surprised to discover I'd selected many with healing properties.

For hundreds of years, all around the globe, communities have recognized the plants growing around them as healing allies. In fact, the world's first botanic gardens—medieval Italian "physic gardens"—were created so scientists could study the medicinal power of plants. London still has a physic garden: The Chelsea Physic Garden was founded in 1673 as the Apothecaries' Garden and currently researches over 5000 plants. On our side of the Atlantic, Pennsylvania Hospital planted its physic garden in 1976.

Locally, more than 2,000 native plants grow in Minnesota and Wisconsin. A large number of them were, and are, used as medicine by indigenous peoples. Now many medicinal plants imported from elsewhere are available for us to grow in Minnesota.

After decades of a pharmaceuticals-only approach to medicine, people are renewing their interest in natural solutions to common health concerns like colds, scrapes, and headaches. Simultaneously, gardening is becoming more popular again. So, it seems only natural to combine these interests.

It took a few years of getting familiar with the plants I'd brought home before I actually used them. I started with simple infusions, which involve steeping plants in hot water as teas. Some plants are better prepared boiled as decoctions, soaked in alcohol as tinctures, or crushed and placed directly on the skin as poultices. These techniques are not always as straightforward as they seem. **Different plants require different preparations—and some are better for some people than others. Do your research before self-administering.**

Whether you want to grow one special medicinal plant in a pot, incorporate a few into your garden, or plan a special medicinal garden—perhaps in a labyrinth shape, or an English square garden, or in a more naturalistic, woodsy-feeling setting—here are a few basic plants to consider.

Minnesota Natives

Bee Balm is good for fevers and congestion due to colds. Crushed leaves can help alleviate sting of insect bites.

Boneset tea is a laxative and can help alleviate symptoms of cold and flu. Make tea with equal parts mint to help prevent common cold.

Catnip tea can alleviate fevers, insomnia, intestinal problems, headaches and menstrual cramps. ❧

LEFT: **Purple coneflower (***Echinacea purpurea***) is known for its immune-enhancing properties.**
RIGHT: **Lungwort is among the many interesting plants at the Florence Bakken Medicinal Garden.**
Alena Hyams

❦ *Medicinal Garden,* CONTINUED

Mullein's dried leaves can be made into an infusion and used as an astringent or a tea for nonproductive coughs.

Wild Geranium's crushed fresh roots can be applied directly onto sore tooth or gums for temporary relief.

Yarrow is a powerful antiseptic whose tea can be used to treat headaches, fevers, minor cuts and swelling.

Other Medicinal Plants

Comfrey's leaves can be soaked in hot water then used as a gargle for sore throats.

Echinacea tea helps support the immune system. Drink it during cold season.

Lemon Balm makes a delicious tea. It calms and soothes women going through menopause or suffering from PMS.

St Johns Wort is nature's anti-depressant.

Valerian, a very mild sedative, is the leading over-the-counter sleep aid in Europe.

Use With Caution!

Plants can offer wonderful medicines, but people with certain conditions or allergies should avoid some plants. Make sure to consult with a knowledgeable herbalist before you ingest them or put them on your skin. **Pregnant women should be especially careful.**

Here's to your health, and to happy planting!

Karen Olson is a Minneapolis-based writer and editor. Say hey at karen-olson.com.

ON THE WEB!

❖ **American Botanical Council**, visit its "virtual gardens," abc.herbalgram.org

❖ **Steven Foster**, herbalist, author and photographer, stevenfoster.com

READ UP!

❖ *A Field Guide to Medicinal Plants and Herbs: Eastern and Central North America (Peterson Field Guide),* by Steven Foster and James A. Duke, Houghton Mifflin Harcourt, 2000.

❖ *Edible & Medicinal Wild Plants of Minnesota & Wisconsin,* by Matthew Alfs, Old Theology Book House, 2001.

ACT LOCALLY!

❖ Florence Bakken Medicinal Gardens The Bakken Museum Minneapolis, MN 612-926-3878 thebakken.org/ florencebakkenmedicinalgardens.html

Veg Out: Tips for Growing Edible Container Gardens

By **MELEAH MAYNARD**
FREELANCE WRITER AND MASTER GARDENER IN MINNEAPOLIS

If you're short on space but still want to grow veggies, you're in luck. By following a few easy steps, growing vegetables in containers can be easy and fun. The first and most important step is choosing a container big enough to grow the plant you have. This can be a pain because big pots take a lot of soil and are heavy and difficult to move. But small pots dry out quickly in the hot sun and favorites like tomatoes, beets, sweet potatoes, peas, cucumbers, broccoli, carrots and squash mostly need large containers (at least 20 inches wide and 16 inches deep) that offer room for roots to spread out.

Peppers, eggplant and some compact and determinate tomatoes can be grown in pots that are about 15 inches wide and 10 to 12 inches deep. And you can grow lettuce, herbs, arugula, cress and compact peppers like Habañero in 10-inch wide containers that are 10 to 12 inches deep. Always choose containers with good drainage holes at the bottom, or plants could get water-logged and literally drown in the water you lovingly give them.

I like to move my containers around on the patio to follow the sun since I don't get a lot of it in my backyard. So, several years ago, I bought a few four-wheeled stands at IKEA. A handier person could ❦

probably make such a thing, though. If you don't use stands with wheels, you'll want to fill your big pots where you plan to keep them because they'll be back-breakers once they are full.

Choose good potting soil

If you're only doing a few containers, it will be easiest to buy commercial potting mix in bags. (Don't buy garden soil, it's too heavy for pots and won't drain well.) But that gets expensive if you have a lot of pots to do. In that case, you may want to make your own mix by combining equal parts of garden soil, compost and decomposed leaves or some sharp plasterer's sand. Peat moss used to be the organic matter of choice for container plants but conservationists are working hard to make people aware that peat bogs, which take hundreds to thousands of years to develop, are being destroyed to meet demand for this product. While peat hasn't been taken off the market, there is a boycott underway and it's up to gardeners to decide what they want to do.

Water well

The number one reason container-grown crops fail is usually a lack of water. In the heat of the summer, containers may need to be watered twice a day to keep from drying out. When watering, do your best to keep the hose down near the soil so you don't splash dirt on the leaves or get leaves too wet. These things can make plants more susceptible to diseases. If you're not around for long periods of time and can't water in the morning and evening, there are simple, tube-based irrigation systems that loop from pot to pot. Garden centers often sell these and though I've never used them, I have friends who say they work well.

Fertilize regularly

Plants in containers need more nutrients than plants in the garden because all that water washes away nutrients fast. Granulated slow-release fertilizers are your best choice for containers. They feed plants over a long period of time unlike the quick-release kinds that mix with water and offer more instantaneous food. Organic brands will likely require repeated applications where synthetic ones will last the whole season. Fish emulsion can also be used twice a month for added nutrients, if you like.

ACT LOCALLY

- Interior Gardens
  Minneapolis, MN
  612-870-9077
  interiorgardens.com/organic
  -gardening.html

- Minnehaha Falls Nursery and
  Landscaping
  Minneapolis, MN
  612-724-5453
  minnehahafallslandscape.com

- University of Minnesota Extension
  Service Master Gardeners
  *Ask a Master Gardener a question via
  email:* extension.umn.edu
  /gardeninfo/components/questions
  _askmg.html

- Ask a Master Gardener in Hennepin
  County a question by phone:
  612-596-2118

- Ask a Master Gardener in Ramsey
  County a question by phone:
  651-704-2071

ON THE WEB!

- Mother Earth News, "How to Make
  Your Own Potting Soil," December
  2008, motherearthnews.com/
  Organic-Gardening/How-To-Make-
  Your-Own-Potting-Soil.aspx

- Michigan State University Extension
  Service, "Kinds of Fertilizer,"
  web1.msue.msu.edu/monroe/
  soilweb2/kinds%20of%20fertilizers
  .htm

- Better Homes and Gardens,
  "Growing Vegetables in Containers,"
  bhg.com/gardening/vegetable/
  vegetables/growing-vegetables-in
  -containers

READ UP!

- *Grow Your Own, Eat Your Own,* by
  Bob Flowerdew, Kyle Books, 2009.

- *Kitchen Harvest: Growing Organic
  Fruit, Vegetables & Herbs in
  Containers,* by Susan Berry, Frances
  Lincoln, 2007

- *The Garden Primer,* by Barbara
  Damrosch, Rodale Books, 2008.

Vegetables and Fruits for the Lazy Gardener *By* Katrina Edenfeld

A vegetable garden can be a labor of love or a necessary chore, but either way, it is time-consuming. One way to reduce some of the ongoing work and still reap harvests from your yard is to grow perennial food-producing plants. Here are a few that grow well in Minnesota:

VEGETABLES

Homegrown **Asparagus** is one of the most delectable vegetables you will ever eat. Once established, an asparagus bed can produce for years, with shoots jumping out of the ground on warm spring days. *For further information, see extension. umn.edu/distribution/horticulture /M1251.html.*

That **Dandelions** are perennial will not be news to anyone who has tried removing them from a lawn. In fact, dandelions are here in North America because early settlers brought them as a food crop! *For a discussion of ways to serve dandelion leaves, see backwoodshome.com /articles2/kallas82.html.*

Rhubarb is very vigorous and easily obtained from a friend who needs to divide plants. *See extension.umn.edu/dis-tribution/horticulture/m1260.html*

The **Sunchoke** or Jerusalem Artichoke, a relative of the sunflower, is native to much of North America, and is cultivated for its tubers. To grow as a perennial, leave some tubers in the ground for the next year's crop. *Information is available at hort .purdue.edu/newcrop/afcm/jerusart.html*

Sorrel's leaves are among the first spring greens and can be used in soups and salads. *For a discussion of varieties, see the book* Perennial Vegetables, *by Eric Toensmeier (Chelsea Green, 2007).*

FRUITS

In Minnesota, the following fruits grow well: apples, plums, tart cherries, currants, red and black raspberries, and strawberries. Blueberries and lingonberries can be grown in amended, acidic soil. Adventurous gardeners may want to try hardy kiwi, a large vine that requires support and produces small fruits. *For further information, see extension.umn.edu/gardeninfo /components/info_fruit.html.*

Permaculture 101

By **KAREN OLSON**
WRITER, EDITOR, PROUD PERMACULTURE DESIGN COURSE GRADUATE

A backyard slope in this Inver Grove Heights garden, designed by Ecological Gardens, was terraced and planted with fruit trees, berries, and plants to attract beneficial insects and pollinators. Evelyn Hadden

The word *permaculture* is more commonplace now than a few years ago. If you've heard of permaculture—but aren't yet quite sure what it is—chances are you might associate it with a way of living sustainably or a method of growing perennial fruits and vegetables. But permaculture, developed by Australians Bill Mollison and David Holmgren in the early 1970s, goes deeper than that, to the very heart of healthy, natural growing systems.

Because it is a way of seeing, understanding and designing, permaculture, short for "permanent culture," is notoriously difficult to define. Scott Pittman, president of Permaculture Institute U.S.A., defines it this way: "Permaculture is an ecological design system for sustainability in all aspects of human endeavor. It teaches us how to build natural homes, grow our own food, restore diminished landscapes and ecosystems, catch rainwater, build communities and much more." Recently, people have begun applying permaculture design to the way we run our businesses, how we relate to each other, and even how we understand ourselves.

Unlike any other design system, permaculture is based on a set of ethics: care of the earth, care of people, and the contribution of surplus time, money and energy to support care of people and the earth. Drawing on nature's patterns, permaculture's design principles—modeled on cooperation, not competition—include things like bringing food-growing back into cities and towns, restoring fertility of the soil, recycling all wastes, putting your energy to work where you'll make most difference, and, my personal favorite, seeing solutions instead of problems.

Paula Westmoreland, Executive Director of Permaculture Research Institute Cold Climate and owner of the Minneapolis-based landscape design company Ecological Gardens, has noticed a dramatic increase in interest about the design system over the last few years. "Because of changing economic times, people are looking for new ways of doing things," she says. "There's an upsurge right now of people who see that the future is going to be different than the past—and they want to be part of shaping it."

In Minnesota, she says, homeowners and landscape designers are using permaculture principles to rebuild healthy ecosystems on properties and in backyards. They're putting in perennial sources of food, keeping chickens, and slowly turning grassy lawns into places teeming with life. And there's more.

The sustainable agriculture community here is integrating permaculture into business operations. The Minneapolis College of Art and Design offers design courses based on permaculture. In the burgeoning "Transition Town" movement, community members discuss applying the design system at the community level to address peak oil and climate change issues. Permaculture is even making its way into city-level policy discussions, and several Twin Cities neighborhoods—like Seward and St. Anthony Park—are looking toward permaculture for community design ideas.

When we have so many environmental issues to address, it's easy to feel weighted down. But permaculture offers solutions. "It gives people a positive way to interact with the rest of the natural world," Westmoreland says, "and I think that's really liberating."

Karen Olson is a Minneapolis-based writer and editor. Find her at www.karen-olson.com.

ON THE WEB!

- Permaculture Institute U.S.A., permaculture.org
- Permaculture Credit Union, pcuonline.org

READ UP!

MAGAZINES

- *Permaculture Activist*, permacultureactivist.net
- *Permaculture Magazine*, an international magazine from England, permaculture-magazine.co.uk

BOOKS

- *Gaia's Garden: A Guide to Home-Scale Permaculture*, by Toby Hemenway, Chelsea Green, 2000.
- *Introduction to Permaculture*, by Bill Mollison with Reny Mia Slay, Tagari Publications, 1991.

ACT LOCALLY!

- Permaculture Research Institute Cold Climate Minneapolis, MN 612-481-5229 pricoldclimate.org
  PRI Cold Climate offers classes, lectures, a movie series, work and learn opportunities, and the Backyard Harvest program, which pairs gardeners with homeowners to help turn lawns into nourishing landscapes.

Oak Hill Montessori Community Garden

By **ANNE WUSSLER**

LOWER ELEMENTARY TEACHER, OAK HILL MONTESSORI, SHOREVIEW, MN

Maria Montessori, the creator of Montessori education, believed in giving children a powerful connection to the Earth. At Oak Hill Montessori, we strive to give children that connection in many different ways. We have materials and curricula that emphasize learning about plants and animals. These include botany and zoology, as well as geography and history, impressionistic charts and timelines. To bring to life the bounty of the Earth and the cycle of life, we have started a community garden.

Our garden, now in its second year, is a row-style plot, approximately 20 feet square, with straight pathways through the garden to allow movement and tending of the plants by numerous children and adults. Learning from our experiences of last year, we have changed a few things and added some new components. This year we have a variety of easy-to-grow vegetables and flowers. These include carrots, potatoes, beans, pumpkins, squash, kale, tomatoes, oregano, basil, and sunflowers. We harvest throughout the summer and fall. We also have marigolds, cosmos and zinnias to make beautiful bouquets of flowers. Last year we did try corn; although it looked cool, it was more challenging to deal with during the summer and at harvest time. We find that the children particularly enjoy the dramatic, giant blooms of the sunflowers, and the immense pumpkins that are produced from a tiny seed.

The children, like many other gardeners, prefer planting and harvesting to weeding. We have found that keeping the garden

Top: Children love the drama of giant sunflowers. Bottom: Tomatoes ripen at Oak Hill's garden. Katrina Edenfeld

weeded and tended during the summer is a challenge. This year we are engaging our summer campers and staff to help with weeding and tending of the garden. In addition we have a few families who enjoy coming weekly to help tend the garden. We also scheduled some playdates to help keep the school community involved through the summer.

Weeding and tending our garden allow us to sweat, visit and get dirty together. Most importantly, the garden keeps us connected to the source of our food. What better lesson for children than planting a seed in the ground, watching it flourish as a plant, and then harvesting it for a soup or salad? In the fall, our elementary community celebrates with a "Harvest Festival." The students are all involved in harvesting, planning and preparing a meal for our community. This is a wonderful collaboration and celebration of our garden work. Many of the children have tried vegetables that are new to them, and perhaps they will be inspired to help their families begin their own gardens.

ON THE WEB!

- School Garden Wizard, schoolgardenwizard.org
- School Garden and Food Projects, sustainabletable.org/schools/projects
- Starting a School Garden, kitchengardeners.org/group/4-steps-starting-school-garden

READ UP!

- *How to Grow a School Garden: A Complete Guide for Parents and Teachers*, by Arden Bucklin-Sporer and Rachel Pringle, Timber Press, 2010.
- *Schoolyard-Enhanced Learning: Using the Outdoors as an Instructional Tool*, K-8, by Herbert W. Broda, Stenhouse Publishers, 2007.

ACT LOCALLY!

- Oak Hill Montessori
  Shoreview, MN
  651-484-8242
  oakhillmontessori.org

Shade Gardening:

HOW TO LET GO OF SUN-LOVING FLOWERS AND EMBRACE THE BEAUTY OF WHAT GROWS IN THE SHADE

By **MELEAH MAYNARD**
FREELANCE WRITER AND MASTER GARDENER IN MINNEAPOLIS, MN

There's no other way to say it: my heart still aches a little every time I walk by a garden in full sun. There are all the flowers and the veggies I used to grow before I moved to a house with a yard shaded by three enormous oak trees.

It has taken awhile, but I've made peace with the cool, blue-green understated beauty of a garden that grows in the shade. The biggest hurdle, by far, was letting go of the belief that a garden isn't a garden without flowers in bloom at all times.

Of course, without all the blooms, it is the varied hues, textures and shapes of plants that keep a garden interesting. This, I admit, is not an easy task to design; anyone who has seen my yard, which is in a constant state of flux as plants are moved and removed, will agree. The truth is, a shade garden done well is breathtakingly beautiful with its peaceful, almost painterly, beauty. (See for yourself by visiting the Eloise Butler Wildflower Garden in Minneapolis.)

Believe it or not, there are a lot of shade plants with good-looking foliage. Some of my favorites are: lungwort (*Pulmonaria*), Siberian bugloss, Japanese painted fern, snakeroot (*Cimicifuga*), lady fern, epimedium, coral bells (*Heuchera*) and variegated Solomon's seal (*Polygonatum odoratum 'Variegatum'*).

When combining plants, you can create a more dramatic look by using a variety of plants with big, bold leaves and fine, feathery foliage. If you don't have dense shade, you can also plant grasses, including ribbon grass, light blue fescues (they're beautiful), silver spike grass and Japanese forest grass. (A great place to shop for grasses, and all plants, really, is High Country Gardens.

Shade gardening: Trillium Grandiflorum is native to Minnesota and provides bright spring flowers for the shade garden.

They even have no-mow grass mixes that requires very little water.)

Groundcovers play a key role in shade gardens by helping to create the natural, layered look you see when you walk through a woodland and look down rather than up to take in all the amazing plants that make up the understory. Sweet woodruff (*Galium odoratum*) and wild ginger are among my favorite groundcovers for shade. Both spread rapidly, creating a carpet that keeps weeds from taking over.

When you use groundcovers, I recommend going light on mulch, or not using mulch in the area at all, because it tends to inhibit the spread of plants. (Don't skimp on mulch in other areas though, because it helps hold in moisture and breaks down over time into organic matter that helps promote good soil structure.)

Now that I've dashed your hopes about flowers, let me offer some thoughts on bloomers that do well in shade—if only for a few weeks. Virginia bluebells are a sight to behold in the short time they're out and about. If you want something long lasting, you really can't beat astilbe, which you can find in a variety of colors. Foam flowers offer beautiful foliage and flowers ('Mint Chocolate', for example, has mint-green leaves with chocolate-colored veins and white flowers.). White snakeroot is a late-season bloomer

that I recommend highly. Big-root geranium is also a winner, particularly if you are dealing with dry shade.

One last thought about water: you might think that shade plants need less water than those in the sun, and to some extent, that's true. The exceptions are the plants beneath the canopy of trees. Growing in dry shade where rain doesn't reach them, competing with tree roots for water and nutrients, things really couldn't get much tougher—so be sure to provide regular water to shade plants trying to make it in those conditions.

ON THE WEB!

- High Country Gardens: highcountrygardens.com
- University of Minnesota Extension Service "Dry Soil: Shade or Under Trees," extension.umn.edu/distribution/horticulture/dg8464.html
- Department of Natural Resources "Native Shade Garden Landscape Design," www.dnr.state.mn.us /gardens/nativeplants/nativeshade.html

READ UP!

- *Making the Most of Shade: How to Plan, Plant, and Grow a Fabulous Garden that Lightens up the Shadows*, by Larry Hodgson, Rodale Books, 2005.
- *The Natural Shade Garden*, by Ken Druse, Clarkson Potter, 1992.
- *Taylor's Guide to Shade Gardening: More than 350 Trees, Shrubs, and Flowers that Thrive Under Difficult Conditions*, Frances Tenenbaum, editor, Houghton Mifflin Harcourt, 1994.

ACT LOCALLY

- Eloise Butler Wildflower Garden Minneapolis, MN 612-370-4903 friendsofeloisebutler.org.
- Mother Earth Garden Minneapolis, MN 612-724-2296 motherearthgarden.com
- UMORE Park Rosemount, MN 651-423-2455 umorepark.umn.edu

Penny Pinching Tips for Gardeners

By **THERESA ROONEY**
Hennepin County Master Gardener

Everyone has limited resources and must decide how to spend his or her resources of money, time or energy. Gardening does not have to be expensive; in fact, time spent researching may reduce required expenditures.

To maximize your efforts in the garden, know your conditions: have a soil test performed, understand how the sun covers your yard, and then choose plants accordingly. In the correct place and with the proper nutrients, plants will be healthier and perform better.

A hanging basket decorates the rain barrel and recycles water at the same time.

Improving Your Soil

- Whenever possible, build your garden soil with organic amendments such as leaves, compost and manure. The better the soil, the better the plants will do.
- Invest in a worm (vermiculture) or a compost bin and create your own compost. With either choice, use materials already on hand to construct your own bin.
- Save bags of leaves to use as mulch in your vegetable garden, containers, around newly planted annuals, perennials, shrubs and trees. The leaves can also be added as a free "brown" additive to a compost pile or worked into the soil at the end of the season to compost over winter and improve the soil. A layer of leaves over bare soil will protect it from winter compaction. Leaves can also be used as winter mulch around tender plants or as a barrier between plants and salt/sand from winter plowing.

Garden Ergonomically

- Use hand pruners for deadheading plants and pruning shrubs.
- For planting, you will need a trowel.
- A spade is necessary for digging larger holes. Choose one that has a 'lip' or rolled edge for the bottom of your foot to press against. Make sure the handle is the right height for you.
- A kneeling pad will cushion your knees.
- Use a hat, sunscreen and sunglasses for protection from the sun.
- Stay hydrated.
- Keep your tetanus shot up to date.
- Stretch before starting any gardening activity.

Other Ideas

- Sticks and branches can be used for staking your flowers and vegetables. They can also be woven into fences as accents. Tie or nail them together and you have a trellis or tomato cage.
- Rain barrels will collect and save water for you to use for later. This is free water.
- Use anything that will hold soil and has drainage. You do not need to purchase fancy pots. When planting in containers, use potting soil, not top soil.

- Seeds can be saved from year to year. Many (not all) seeds remain viable for many years with proper storage in a cool, dry, dark place.
- Limit your plant selections. Learn to propagate plants, and share plants with neighbors and friends.
- Recycle and repurpose everything you can. Borrow or rent items you don't use often.
- Water your garden properly (at the soil). Take a daily walk through the garden. Doing these two things alone will keep your plants healthier and allow you to spot any problems early before much damage is done.
- Learn about IPM — Integrated Pest Management.
- Decide how much time/energy you have to maintain your garden. It is better to have a small garden that you love than a big garden you hate to take care of.

ON THE WEB!

- "Can a Vegetable Garden Save You Money?" extension.iastate.edu/news/2009/mar/060201.htm
- "Gardening Tips that Save Money," oregonwomensreport.com/2010/03/gardening-tips-that-save-money
- "What's a Home Garden Worth?" kitchengardeners.org/blogs/roger-doiron/home-garden-worth
- "The Best Plants for 30 Tough Sites," extension.umn.edu/distribution/horticulture/dg8464.html

READ UP!

- *Landscaping with Native Plants of Minnesota*, by Lynn M Steiner, Voyageur Press, 2005.
- *Northern Gardener* magazine, northerngardener.org

ACT LOCALLY!

- University of Minnesota Soil Testing Laboratory
  St Paul, MN
  612-625-3101
  soiltest.cfans.umn.edu
- Egg|Plant Urban Farm Supply
  St Paul, MN
  651-645-0818
  eggplantsupply.com

Wind power: one of Minnesota's most valuable homegrown energy resources.

Energy in Minnesota: a history of progress, a future of possibility

By **MICHAEL NOBLE** *and* **KATE ELLIS**, FRESH ENERGY

Over the last two decades, Minnesota has experienced a dramatic change in energy use and energy policies. We are closer than ever to achieving a new energy economy using homegrown resources that create jobs, protect our air and water, and strengthen our state's economy and communities. However, there is still much that needs to be accomplished to reach our state, regional and national clean energy and global warming pollution reduction goals. Looking back, what are some of the biggest energy changes and successes for Minnesota over the past 25 years, and more importantly, what steps need to be taken to continue to improve our energy use and energy policies?

Twenty-five years ago, the energy landscape of Minnesota and the United States looked much different than it does today. Despite tangible examples of the results of our nation's fossil fuel addiction, such as the oil crises of 1973 and 1979, the country seemed to be stalled — or even moving backwards — on the path to a new energy economy. As a significant sign of the times, Ronald Reagan famously removed President Carter's solar panels from the White House. And while the first commercial-scale wind farms were built about 25 years ago, the technology was written off as unreliable and expensive. Massive investments in coal

plants to meet electricity needs were the norm, and utilities were far more concerned about finding customers for a glut of coal-fired power than developing energy efficiency measures or renewable energy. Our country was at an energy crossroads. With rising oil, natural gas and electrical prices, it was clear that the American economy was going to feel the energy squeeze if real leadership wasn't shown. Minnesota's brutal winters meant that our state would be among those that bore the brunt of these increasing costs.

Over the next 25 years, Minnesota gradually turned its attention to new energy and conservation. Landmark change ➥

came in 2007 when the legislature and Governor Pawlenty agreed on sweeping clean energy, energy efficiency and global warming policies. Approved overwhelmingly by a bipartisan Minnesota legislature, this legislation guarantees that 25% of our state's electricity will be generated from renewable energy by 2020. At the same time, all electric and gas utilities will invest in energy-efficiency measures to achieve a 1.5% annual energy savings. The new laws in 2007 also established global warming pollution reduction goals for 2015 and 2025, culminating with an 80% reduction in 2050. This legislation also instituted a statewide moratorium on new coal-fired electricity for Minnesota consumers, preventing new construction of coal-fired power plants to serve Minnesota or new coal power contracts from existing plants.

Today, Minnesota is among the nation's leaders in renewable energy and energy efficiency, and as a state we have many victories to celebrate. Minnesota has over 1,800 megawatts of installed wind power—currently generating nearly 10% of our electricity. We also import wind energy from North Dakota, South Dakota and Iowa, each of which receives 10-20% of its state's electricity generation from wind. Additionally, as the energy landscape rapidly changed, investors in 2009 withdrew support from a $1.6 billion coal-fired power plant after protracted delays and organized opposition, and the Upper Midwest's largest solar farm was recently built near St. Cloud at St. John's University.

As Minnesota aggressively pursues our statewide energy efficiency and clean energy goals, the cleantech industries have become the one bright spot in a troubling economic landscape. Clean energy developers, installers, component manufactures and agricultural landowners with renewable generation on their land are all growing Minnesota's economy and creating sustainable, local jobs. Two Minnesota construction companies—Blattner and Mortenson—are top players in a multibillion-dollar wind farm industry, a competitive edge they gained building wind farms in Minnesota in the 1990s.

Minnesota has also seen many advances in how we use energy in transportation and transit. Just this year, the legislature and governor agreed on a new policy called Minnesota Complete Streets. Under this law, when the Minnesota Department of Transportation builds or rebuilds roads, it must make them safe and accessible for all users, including those traveling on foot,

Minnesota's new Complete Streets policy will make getting around—by foot, bike, wheelchair, and more—safer and easier for all Minnesotans while saving energy. AC Johnson

bike, bus or wheelchair. Minnesotans can expect more focus on providing sidewalks, crosswalks, safe wheelchair ramps, bike lanes and paths, safe bus stops and other road designs that improve safety and use less energy.

While Minnesota has many successes to celebrate, there is still much to be accomplished. Today, as 25 years ago, our country is at another crossroads on energy. Sixty percent of Minnesota's electricity still comes from coal-fired power plants that deposit mercury and global warming pollution into Minnesota's water and air. Worldwide, and right here in Minnesota, we are already starting to see and feel the effects of climate change. Our addiction to oil has only grown, despite record gas prices, and we are now forced to drill the most inaccessible oil in some of the world's most fragile areas. The Midwest is growing its dependence on the oil from Alberta's tar sands, some of the most polluting oil left on earth.

During the summer of 2010, with shocking signs of weather havoc all around the world and with oil spewing from a broken deepwater drilling rig in the Gulf of Mexico, our U.S. Senate was unable to take action on energy—even choosing to skip the debate. Without a clearly defined and stable path set forth by federal legislation, clean energy development on the state level is put in jeopardy. Without federal action, states and industries cannot have the clarity that clean energy is the foundation of our nation's future economic health. With such uncertainty and additional barriers imposed by fossil fuel interests, Minnesota cannot reach its full clean energy and efficiency potential.

If we are to meet our clean energy and carbon reduction goals, Minnesota needs to continue to lead on smart energy policy and build on our previous success. Making con-

tinued progress toward our already-established state goals, pursuing increased and better forms of transit and transportation, developing advanced biofuels and support for electric cars, leading on Midwest-wide and federal carbon reduction legislation and supporting a federal Renewable Energy Standard and Energy Efficiency Standard are just some of the ways that Minnesota can continue to lead the region and nation.

The level of energy innovation and energy policy progress that has been made in the past 25 years is monumental. But now we need to build on and accelerate our past progress to ensure that in the next 25 years we'll be nearing the finish line and realizing a modern energy system, powered by renewables and efficiency.

ON THE WEB!

- Midwest Energy News, midwestenergynews.com
- Union of Concerned Scientists, ucsusa.org

READ UP!

- *Coal: A Human History*, by Barbara Freese, Penguin, 2004.
- *The Green Collar Economy*, by Van Jones, HarperOne, 2009.

ACT LOCALLY!

- Fresh Energy
  St. Paul, MN
  651-225-0878
  fresh-energy.org

Minnesota Wind Energy: One Size Does Not Fit All

Report by **WINDUSTRY**

A commercial-scale wind turbine is just one more piece of equipment on this farm in southwestern Minnesota. Courtesy of Windustry.

Like rich farmland and beautiful lakes, wind is a natural resource in Minnesota and is harvested as a renewable energy source in many areas of the state. Over the past ten years, the wind industry has grown throughout Minnesota, boosting rural economic development and diversifying energy fuel resources.

Minnesota's very early adoption of wind was spurred, in part, by a legislative effort to find an alternative to nuclear power. Financial incentives have made it viable and, now, push is coming from the strong Renewable Energy Standard that requires 25% of power to come from renewable sources by 2025.

Minnesota is currently ranked ninth in the country as a wind resource. The strongest source is along the "Buffalo Ridge," a 60-mile expanse of rolling hills that includes the southwestern corner of the state. Fenton Wind Project, the state's largest wind farm, is located there. Seven miles long and seven miles wide, Fenton has 137 turbines and provides Xcel Energy with energy for more than 66,600 homes.

The Buffalo Ridge is also home to Min-Wind, a community wind project involving a group of nine farmer-owned wind projects. Community wind is commercial-scale development with strong local involvement by way of both ownership and decision making. The economic benefits of community wind projects, where local owners and investors receive revenue from electricity production and sales, can be five times greater than those from wind projects owned by outside investors, where revenue is solely from lease payments, taxes or payments in lieu of taxes. Minnesota is leading the nation with the amount of community wind installed. Not only that, but the participants are diverse: community groups with projects include local small business owners, farmers, schools and universities, Native American tribes, rural electric cooperatives, municipal utilities and religious institutions.

Speeds greater than 14 mph are necessary to power commercial-scale wind turbines economically, but smaller wind turbines will produce energy using lower speeds. These smaller wind turbines are utilized by homeowners, small businesses and farms to produce energy for on-site use. Some also store excess energy in batteries or sell it to their electric utility.

The nation's installed wind capacity is currently at 35,000 megawatts—more than tenfold what it was in 1999. Still, wind provided only 1.8% of U.S. power in 2009. Clearly, more wind energy is needed, from turbines of every size. For that to happen, stronger supportive public policy—including increased net metering and transmission capacity, and support for feed-in tariffs for community renewable energy projects—is also needed.

Windustry promotes progressive renewable energy solutions and empowers communities to develop and own wind energy as an environmentally sustainable asset. Through member-supported outreach, education and advocacy we work to remove the barriers to broad community ownership of wind energy.

ON THE WEB

- U.S. Department of Energy: Windpowering America, windpoweringamerica.gov
- American Wind Energy Association, awea.org
- Renewable Energy Works, renewableenergyworks.org
- Power of Wind, powerofwind.com
- Database of State Incentive for Renewables and Efficiency, dsireusa.org

READ UP

- *Wind Energy Basics, Second Edition: A Guide to Home- and Community-Scale Wind-Energy Systems,* by Paul Gipe, Chelsea Green, 2009.
- *The Citizen-Powered Energy Handbook: Community Solutions to a Global Crisis,* by Greg Pahl, Chelsea Green, 2007.

ACT LOCALLY

- Windustry
  Minneapolis, MN
  612-870-3461
  windustry.org

Reduce the Energy Costs of Home Appliances

By **MARY MORSE**
NEIGHBORHOOD ENERGY CONNECTION

Rein in the cost and environmental impact of common household appliances with the following tips:

Identify your biggest energy wasters

Households spend more money on heating and cooling than any other energy expenditure. Before investing in a new furnace or air conditioner, tame these costs by installing insulation in your attic and walls and sealing air leaks. Caulk baseboards and window and door trim. Install weather-stripping around exterior doors. Wrap your water heater with an insulating blanket and save up to about $25 per year. Adjust thermostat settings in your home by 10 degrees to conserve energy during the hours you are asleep or at work (a programmable thermostat can help you regulate temperatures automatically). When it is time to replace your furnace or air conditioner, install the most efficient units you can afford, and be sure to investigate utility rebates, tax incentives or other conservation programs that might be available.

Tame the cords and cut the power

Cell phone chargers, music players, computers, TVs, gaming systems, microwaves and other electronics pull a surprising amount of power from the plug even when they are turned off. This is pure waste, and you are paying for it. In fact, unused appliances in standby mode account for about 10% of a typical household's energy bill. Pull the plug on chargers when you disconnect your phone. Connect computers, TVs, and their peripherals to a power strip and turn them off when you are done using them with one easy switch, and be sure to enable the power down or sleep modes. Tell family or

Caulk windows in your house to tame energy bill costs.

roommates that they have a choice between following these rules or paying for a larger part of the utility bill.

Read the label and shop around

Do your homework when replacing appliances to learn just how much they cost to run. Find appliance wattage stamped on the bottom or back of the unit, or on its nameplate. Calculate the unit's cost with this handy formula from the U.S. Department of Energy:

$$\text{Wattage x Hours used per day} \div 1000 = \text{Daily kilowatt-hour (kWh) consumption}$$

Multiply daily kWh consumption by the number of days you use the appliance during the year to determine annual kWh consumption. Then multiply annual kWh consumption by your utility's cost rate per kWh consumed. That's the cost per year of operating the appliance.

With the knowledge of how much it will actually cost to use various models, you can choose the most efficient appliances and save both money and energy. Doing a similar assessment of appliances throughout your home may help you decide how to prioritize replacements before you start shopping. Or, take the easy route when comparing new appliances and simply choose an ENERGY STAR labeled model. The additional price you'll pay for a more energy-efficient model will be recovered in about two years. After that, you'll have net savings every year of operation. For the biggest savings, start by replacing the biggest energy hogs: old refrigerators, clothes washers and driers.

Check it off your list by calling the Home Energy Squad

Xcel Energy and CenterPoint Energy offer a terrific service that installs key efficiency measures in your home for a significantly reduced price—cheaper than do-it-yourself! Home Energy Squad appointments are available in the metro area and result in average savings of nearly $200 per year.

ON THE WEB!

- Neighborhood Energy Connection, TheNEC.org
- Minnesota Center for Energy and the Environment, mncee.org
- ENERGY STAR, energystar.gov
- Energy Savers, energysavers.gov

ACT LOCALLY!

- Home Energy Squad assessment and installation service 866-222-4595 homeenergysquad.net

Solar Works for Minnesota

By **DAWN ERLANDSON**

COMMUNICATIONS CONSULTANT, SOLAR AMERICA
CITIES — MINNEAPOLIS AND ST. PAUL

TOP: Pat Mulroy with the new 174-panel solar PV array at his Minneapolis business, Mulroy's Body Shop. BOTTOM: The solar hot water system at the Young-Krueger residence in St. Paul. Gil Young

S olar energy can provide electricity, hot water or space heating depending upon the technology used. According to the Minnesota Office of Energy Security, Minnesota is home to approximately 400 solar photovoltaic (PV) systems as of July 2010. It is estimated that there are also hundreds of solar thermal systems throughout the state. The solar capacity in Minnesota is expected to double in 2010 from two megawatts to four megawatts, with a steady rise in thermal projects, too.

Gil Young and Janet Krueger installed a solar water heating system at their St. Paul home in 2009. They've since reported great results, saying, "We are very pleased with our solar hot water system. It's nice to know we can use the sun to heat our water, even in the wintertime! Over the last two summers, (since we installed our system), we've cut our use of natural gas [used for heating water] by over 75%!" The Krueger-Young residence features two 4x8 collectors that were manufactured by Solar Skies, a Minnesota-based company. A two-collector system is typical in Minnesota's climate and can reasonably supply about 75% of the energy needed for water heating annually.

Businesses are investing in solar too. Mulroy's Body Shop in Minneapolis recently leased a photovoltaic system from Solarflow Energy to supply electricity. The 174 panels atop Mulroy's will provide about 30% of the shop's electricity annually. Pat Mulroy said he made the choice for business reasons and for his grandchildren, adding, "People come in for an estimate for their car and leave more knowledgeable about solar."

In 2008, the federal Department of Energy awarded Minneapolis and St. Paul a grant to expand solar capacity as part of the Solar America Cities program. The goal of the Solar America Cities effort is to increase solar capacity five-fold in the Twin Cities in two years' time. The increased use of solar energy has a number of benefits including power from a secure, endless supply of energy; reduction in air pollution and greenhouse gases; and jobs in manufacturing and installation.

To meet the challenge, the Twin Cities partnered with key organizations and businesses to jumpstart widespread deployment of solar technologies. Both Minneapolis and St. Paul are expected to break ground on large-scale solar projects in 2010: a 600 kilowatt solar electric system on the Minneapolis Convention Center and a large solar thermal system at District Energy in downtown St. Paul.

With an increasing number of people in the Twin Cities enjoying the benefits of solar energy, the Minneapolis St. Paul Solar America Cities initiative recently launched a new statewide awareness campaign to demonstrate that solar is already working in Minnesota and is rapidly growing as a reliable, renewable energy source that is increasingly accessible to those who want it. These efforts are being unified under the banner "Solar Works."

The Solar Works campaign is designed both to increase awareness of existing solar energy systems already in place throughout Minnesota and to inspire more property owners across the state to install their own solar systems. The tagline will be used by solar advocates, the solar installation industry, property owners who already have solar systems and local governments who want to promote solar electric and thermal energy. To find out how solar can work for you, contact the Minnesota Office of Energy Security and the Minnesota Renewable Energy Society.

ON THE WEB!

⚙ Database of State Incentives for Renewables & Efficiency, dsireusa.org

⚙ Up-to-date solar capacity and PV data from the National Renewable Energy Laboratory, openpv.nrel.gov

ACT LOCALLY!

⚙ Department of Commerce Minnesota Office of Energy Security St. Paul, MN 651-296-5175 energy.mn.gov

⚙ Minnesota Renewable Energy Society Minneapolis, MN 612-308-4757 mnrenewables.org

Diversifying Minnesota's Clean Energy Future with Biogas

By **AMANDA BILEK**
GREAT PLAINS INSTITUTE

Minnesota is blessed with an abundance of renewable energy resources to provide a clean energy future for our state. An often overlooked renewable energy resource is biogas. Biogas holds tremendous potential to help meet our future energy needs. As a versatile and constant energy resource, biogas can be produced from organic feedstocks such as manure, crop residues, and a variety of wastes from food (particularly milk) processing, wastewater treatment, biomass processing byproducts (such as ethanol stillage or biodiesel glycerol), fats, oils and greases. Once biogas is produced, it can be converted into usable forms of energy on a constant basis. It can be utilized for electricity, combined heat and power, natural gas replacement, vehicle fuel and chemical production. Conservative calculations estimate that biogas energy could replace up to 5% of Minnesota's electricity or natural gas use.

The dominant technology used to produce biogas is anaerobic digestion. An anaerobic digester vessel is heated to accelerate the biological breakdown of organic feedstocks using bacteria, and gas released from the feedstock decomposition is collected and utilized for energy. On-farm projects in Minnesota have begun to utilize anaerobic digestion technology to produce biogas for electricity production. A 250-cow dairy operation in Stearns County is collecting manure from 130 milk cows and adding cheese whey, a by-product of milk processing, from a local processing plant to successfully produce and sell electricity to a local electric utility. There are an additional four on-farm anaerobic digestion projects in Minnesota today. These projects are not only supplying a source of clean, renewable power but the agricultural producers are able to offset their energy use, sell the excess to a local utility and reduce methane emissions (a greenhouse gas with 25 times more heat trapping potential than carbon dioxide).

City sewers carrying household sewage and wastewater to treatment facilities hold another powerful source of biogas production that could be converted into useable forms of energy. A wastewater treatment facility in Fergus Falls is adding thick corn stillage syrup from a local ethanol plant to wastewater sludge to produce six million cubic feet of biogas a year. The biogas is used to offset conventional natural gas used by the plant, saving thousands of dollars every month for the municipal plant.

Landfills provide an additional source of biogas production. Because landfills are the second largest source of human-related methane emissions, landfill gas recovery projects are a critical greenhouse gas reduction strategy. As trash decomposes and methane is released, landfill gas recovery projects can capture that methane and use it to produce electricity and/or heat. Currently Minnesota has six operational landfill gas recovery projects and an additional eight are planned for future development.

TOP: **Large-scale biogas plant using multiple organic materials to produce biogas.** BOTTOM LEFT: **Small-scale digester in Stearns County, Minnesota.** RIGHT: **Food waste is an untapped potential source of biogas production.**

Biogas is a unique renewable resource because it can provide energy on a constant basis and destruct or avoid heat-trapping methane emissions. The time is ripe for biogas development to increase in Minnesota. Technology advancements in recent years have diversified ways to produce and use biogas. It is time for biogas to step into the spotlight and become a significant part of our clean energy future.

ON THE WEB!

✿ **Great Plains Institute, gpisd.net**
✿ **U.S. EPA AgStar, epa.gov/agstar**
✿ **Association of State Energy Research & Technology Transfer Institutions (ASERTTI), asertti.org**

ACT LOCALLY!

✿ **Great Plains Institute**
Minneapolis, MN
612-278-7118
gpisd.net

✿ **American Biogas Council**
Washington, D.C.
202-457-0868
americanbiogascouncil.org

Minnesota GreenStep Cities

TAKING ACTION WITH PROVEN BEST PRACTICES

By **PHILIPP MUESSIG,** MINNESOTA POLLUTION CONTROL AGENCY
and **DAN FRANK,** GREATER PINE RIVER AREA HEALTHY GREEN COMMUNITIES PARTNERSHIP

Members of the Healthy Green Communities Partnership, excited to be helping Pine River take on the new Minnesota GreenStep Cities program.

Cities all over the state are considering ways to protect the environment and reduce costs, and many of them are looking to a new program called Minnesota GreenStep Cities. GreenStep Cities is an action-oriented voluntary program offering a cost-effective, simple pathway to implementation of sustainable development best practices. The actions that make up each best practice are tailored specifically for Minnesota cities, focus on cost savings and energy use reduction and encourage innovation.

Energy is at the center of the GreenStep Cities program. Best practices include energy efficiency for public and private buildings, constructing green buildings and developing land and roads efficiently. GreenStep Cities helps city government and community members reduce the use of transportation fuels, too, with more efficient vehicles and by supporting active living and alternatives to single-occupancy car travel. GreenStep Cities can also spur job growth, help green businesses thrive, and assist with renewable energy projects.

GreenStep Cities launched in June 2010, and over 20 cities are already involved. One of the first was Pine River, Minnesota, three

hours north of the Twin Cities and with a population of about 900. In 2009 Pine River citizens and organizations approached the Initiative Foundation and together they formed the Greater Pine River Area Healthy Green Communities Partnership (HGCP) to work in large part on GreenStep Cities best practices.

The goals of HGCP are to develop citizens' capacity to create a shared green vision and plan, and to mobilize local, regional and other assets to implement that plan. In early 2010, HGCP recruited and trained a core local team, hosted a GreenStep Cities program representative, held a community visioning session and selected key goals aligned with GreenStep Cities best practices. HGCP is now in the process of working in small task forces to implement these plans for a resilient and sustainable Pine River.

HGCP has already achieved a number of accomplishments: convincing the Pine River City Council to pass a resolution to officially become a GreenStep City, securing a GreenCorps member to staff HGCP, co-hosting a series of neighborhood energy efficiency workshops for residents and businesses and starting a community garden, among others. HGCP is also excited to be

completing the first phase of a feasibility study to add renewable hydroelectric energy production to an existing local dam.

In the coming year the collaborative group in Pine River will move forward with current initiatives, while also taking a close look at energy use in the city's facilities. The greatest challenge will be to retain momentum and to continue to engage local citizens—but HGCP members know that their efforts are creating a leaner, greener Pine River.

Your city can be a part of the action! To learn more about the program and how GreenStep Cities can help you achieve your sustainability goals, visit **MnGreenStep.org**.

ON THE WEB!

- Minnesota GreenStep Cities, MnGreenStep.org
- Pine River Green Steps, PineRiverGreenSteps.org

READ UP!

- *Sustainable Urbanism: Urban Design with Nature,* by Douglas Farr, John Wiley & Sons, Inc., 2008.
- *How Green Is Your City? The SustainLane US City Rankings,* by Warren Karlenzig et. al, New Society Publishers, 2007.

ACT LOCALLY!

- Minnesota Pollution Control Agency St. Paul, MN 651-757-2594 MnGreenStep.org
- Clean Energy Resource Teams (CERTs) St. Paul, MN 612-624-2293 CleanEnergyResourceTeams.org

Park Rapids Wind Energy Project Provides Clean Energy and Education

By **MAO LEE** *and* **KATHLEEN MCCARTHY**
CLEAN ENERGY RESOURCE TEAMS (CERTs)

The Park Rapids Area Century School in Minnesota knows the importance of saving energy, producing clean, renewable energy, educating the community and raising the next generation of young leaders—grades K–8, specifically. In 2007, the school received funding from CERTS and other organizations and individuals to install and monitor the production of a 20kW Jacobs wind turbine.

The turbine is tied directly to the ball field irrigation system and the vending stand for the school; excess energy production goes out to the grid. The project director, Del Holz, states that "While the small turbine is not expected to significantly reduce electricity costs for the school district, its constant presence on the grounds and its use in the classroom will help guide today's students into becoming tomorrow's energy conscious citizens."

Teachers at Park Rapids Century School have been able to incorporate lessons about energy sources in general and wind energy in particular into their course curriculums on a regular basis, engaging students with this vital technology. "In addition to anticipated energy savings, the project helps teachers incorporate information about renewable energy into their curricula, touching on subjects from physics, engineering and chemistry to biology, ecology and meteorology," said former Minnesota Power Conservation Improvement Program (CIP) Specialist Dean Talbott. "The project also helps prompt classroom discussion on generation sources—from wind, coal and hydro to natural gas, biofuels and nuclear."

"The most rewarding experience with the project was going into the classrooms and teaching the kids about wind energy and about the tower. Teaching the next generation about how to care for our environment

20kW Jacobs wind turbine installed at Park Rapids Area Century School.

better than we did … that's why we put in the long hours on this project," said lead teacher Shawn Anderson.

To make the wind turbine an even more accessible educational opportunity, the Park Rapids Wind Energy Committee decided to share the energy production data in real time on the Park Rapids Century School website at **www.prwind.org**. "This service allows students and the community at large to study the output of the wind turbine, as well as research the wind resources in the Park Rapids area," said Anderson.

To complete this project, the Wind Energy Committee had to look for funding in many different areas. One obstacle they came across was that many organizations providing grants had very specific guidelines. Shawn Anderson explained how they overcame this: "This barrier challenged us to reach out to the community and be creative about how we put this project together. We gathered volunteer excavators, surveyors, electricians, as well as people who were able to contribute financially to

the project. This is truly a community project." A seed grant from the Clean Energy Resource Teams was used to pay for the installation and monitoring of the real-time, web-based clean energy monitoring service.

Anderson closed by saying, "Our greatest success and asset in this project is our team. Local citizens had the interest, but not the knowledge about wind energy. By tapping into the expertise and generosity of CERTS and community volunteers we were able to create a hands-on tool for generations of students to experience." The small, educational wind energy project at Park Rapids Century School is a model that many other schools in Minnesota can follow.

For more information, please contact Shawn Anderson at ***esa@unitelc.com*** *or 218-255-0655.*

ON THE WEB!

- CERTs Small Wind Resources, smallwind.mncerts.org
- Minnesota Wind Energy Directory, REDIresources.org

READ UP!

- *Home Power Magazine,* homepower.com

ACT LOCALLY!

- Clean Energy Resource Teams, mncerts.org
- Minnesota Schools Cutting Carbon, SchoolsCuttingCarbon.org

A Quick Guide to Lighting Options for Your Home

By **NEELY CRANE-SMITH**
CENTER FOR ENERGY AND ENVIRONMENT

Incandescent Light Bulbs: These old-school bulbs work through the principal of incandescence—or producing light through heat. The electricity heats a filament (that little wire in the middle of the bulb) to such a temperature that it produces visible light. Incandescent bulbs are very inefficient: 90% of the electricity used is wasted as heat. While incandescents are impractical for most lighting situations, they can be a good solution for closets, unheated garages and outdoor lights during the winter.

Compact Fluorescent Light Bulbs: There are two parts to a compact fluorescent light, or CFL: the bulb, which contains about 3 milligrams of mercury vapor, and the ballast. The ballast contains electronic components that produce an electric current, causing the vapor to emit ultraviolet light. The UV light excites a coating on the inside of the bulb, which produces visible light. CFLs come in a range of applications and colors, and they use 75% less electricity and last 7–20 times longer than incandescents. Once they finally burn out they do need to be recycled, which you can do for free at Menards, Home Depot, IKEA and most local hardware stores!

Light Emitting Diodes: Unlike CFLs, LEDs are a "solid state" lighting technology, meaning they don't use mercury gas. They produce electroluminescence using a diode, which is a type of semiconductor. Basically, LEDs are to incandescents what microwave ovens are to open fires: same result, different level of sophistication. LED lights use almost 10 times less energy than incandescents and half the electricity of CFLs. LEDs are ➤

Community Energy Services

By **KYLE BOEHM**
CENTER FOR ENERGY AND ENVIRONMENT

Learn how to reduce your energy use and save money! The City of Minneapolis has partnered with the Center for Energy and Environment, CenterPoint Energy and Xcel Energy to offer more Minneapolis homeowners Community Energy Services, a full service residential energy program.

Community Energy Services (CES) Provides:

- Free educational workshops to teach homeowners how to lower their energy use and save money;
- Materials which may include: low flow showerheads, setback thermostat, compact fluorescent light bulbs, gasket seals, faucet aerators, pipe insulation and more to help participants save now;
- Customized home energy visits from qualified professionals who will identify additional ways for residents to save in their homes. Up to $400 in services and materials for a co-pay of only $30 (some neighborhoods choose to buy down the co-pay);
- Personalized energy use inventory for the last 12 months and feedback for the next 12 months to show the homeowner how these low- or no-cost measures resulted in decreased energy use, also allowing participants to compare their energy use to that of their neighbors also participating in the program; and
- Access to financing, incentives, and rebates for those wishing to complete larger projects such as insulation or a furnace replacement.

Funding for this project was provided by the City of Minneapolis' Energy Efficiency Conservation Block Grant Funding and the Minnesota Environment and Natural Resources Trust Fund as recommended by the Legislative-Citizen Commission on Minnesota Resources. ➤

great to use as holiday lights, flashlights, night-lights and under-counter lighting, but there are still some drawbacks. Most notably, the price: you can currently pay up to 10 times more for an LED than a CFL that produces the same light. In the next three years, however, we can expect this mercury-free option to rise in quality and come down in price, making it an even more practical way to light your home efficiently.

ON THE WEB!

- U.S. Department of Energy: Energy Saver's Blog, eereblogs. energy.gov /energysavers *Search for "Changing How You Choose Light Bulbs" to learn about new federal labels for lights.*

- Focus on Energy Interactive Light Guide, focusonenergy.com *If you're wondering what kind of CFLs to put in various areas of your house, access a fun and easy interactive guide when you search "light guide."*

- Mercury Fact Sheet from ENERGY STAR, energystar.gov *Search for "mercury" to learn more about mercury, CFLs, and tips for their safe disposal.*

ON THE WEB!

- Minnesota Center for Energy and the Environment, mncee.org
- Community Energy Services, mnenergychallenge.org/Community-Energy-Services/About-CES.aspx

ACT LOCALLY!

- Participate in the Community Energy Service program Center for Energy and Environment Minneapolis, MN 612-219-7334 kboehm@mncee.org

Reckmeyer vs. Rivers: A Family Energy Challenge

By **NEELY CRANE-SMITH**
CENTER FOR ENERGY AND ENVIRONMENT

Looking for inspiration to save energy in your home? Two Minnesota families have taken it to the next level with a three-year competition happening amidst new jobs, new babies and new challenges.

It all started in 2007, when Tim Reckmeyer mentioned to coworker John Rivers that his family had been tracking their electricity use. During one of the hottest years on record, the Reckmeyers had a new baby and a new 42″ plasma TV, and Tim had started working from home 2–3 days a week. By taking steps to conserve energy in their home, the Reckmeyers actually consumed over 7% less electricity despite these factors! When John heard about this a light went off in his head: "Being competitive by nature, we decided to challenge each other and our families to defeat the other by using less electricity and the game was on."

Both families began with simple low-cost, no-cost actions. The Rivers borrowed an electricity meter from the Reckmeyers to see how many watts of power the electronics and appliances in their home were using. "This made creating a priority list fairly simple," says John. Both families installed compact fluorescent light bulbs, fought phantom load with power strips and implemented smart computer power management.

John says that "the easiest and likely most important thing from a long-term savings perspective" was to make this contest fun and engaging for their two kids. "It has become a habit for them to do these things that are common sense." The Reckmeyer's 7-year-old daughter Madeline has also become involved and "knows that it's important to not waste electricity. She accomplishes this by turning off the lights when she leaves the room and turning off the power strip when she's done watching television."

Along with encouraging good energy habits, both families have retired older appliances for newer, more energy efficient versions. The Rivers retired an old fridge and whole-house HEPA filtration system; the Reckmeyers replaced a dead water heater with an instantaneous unit and their old clothes washer with a used front-loading ENERGY STAR model.

In 2008 the Reckmeyers claimed victory, while Tim admits "in 2009 we ceded the electrical energy conservation trophy to Team Rivers. Congrats to them. However, we have a plan to get it back this year." Both families are now using less than 10 kilowatt-hours per day, or about 300 kWh per month—less than half the average for a Minnesota family! With the challenge far from over, Tim believes that Team Reckmeyer will consume less than 8 kWh per day, shaving another $262 off their 2010 electricity bill. We can't wait to see the results!

ON THE WEB!

- Energy Challenge blog, mnenergychallenger.wordpress.com

READ UP!

- *The Low Carbon Diet*, by David Gershon, Empowerment Institute, 2006.

ACT LOCALLY!

- Minnesota Energy Challenge mnenergychallenge.org Minneapolis, MN 612-335-5858 *Join the Minnesota Energy Challenge!*

Tar Sands Oil: Where Minnesota Gasses Up

By **MICHAEL NOBLE**
FRESH ENERGY

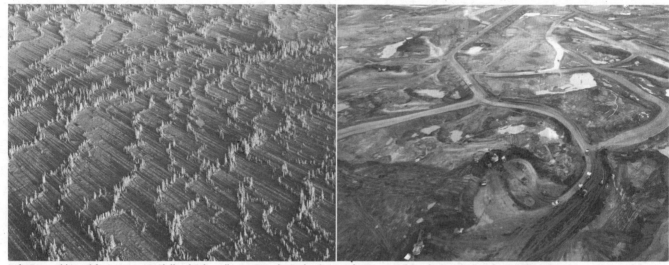

Left: Fen and boreal forest near McClelland Lake, Alberta, Canada. Right: Synacrude Aurora Oil Sands Mine, Alberta, Canada. Peter Essick

Ever wonder where your gasoline comes from? If you live in Minnesota, your gasoline mostly comes from unconventional oil sources like tar sands. These vast Canadian reserves of oil-soaked sands lie under 100 feet of virgin boreal forest in Alberta's Athabasca River basin. Oil companies and governments from Europe, China, Canada and Korea are spending $15 billion a year to extract oil from these tarry sands. Destruction of streams and peatlands by oil sands mining covers a vast geography. According to world-renowned water scientist David Schindler, "It probably wouldn't be a big concern if it were a small area, but of course, it's no longer a small area, and I predict it will disrupt the whole hydrology of the lower Athabasca system."

After moving the sandy oil in trucks the size of a three-story building, the sticky mess must be boiled with solvents and water using vast quantities of natural gas. One industry observer called it comparable to using caviar as fertilizer to grow turnips. The toxic effluent from washing the sand must be stored in vast holding ponds behind man-made earthen dams large enough to be seen from space.

By 2002, Canada had replaced Saudi Arabia and Mexico as the largest supplier of u.s. oil, and imports from Canada steadily grew to about one-fifth of u.s. oil consumption by 2008. To feed its addiction, the u.s. uses the equivalent of one supertanker of oil every four hours, according to Swedish oil expert Kjell Aleklett. That also drains about $1 billion of American wealth every day at current oil prices.

As global oil prices skyrocketed from 2000 to 2008, investment in Canada's tar sands grew so rapidly even the oil industry was shocked. Currently, oil pipeline developers like Enbridge are spending upwards of $30 billion on a network of pipelines to move dirty oil to new and expanded oil refineries on the Great Lakes, in the Mississippi River Valley and oil patch states like Texas, Louisiana and Oklahoma.

Do Midwesterners really want to embrace a huge new oil refining industry on our Great Lakes? Let's take stock of our dependence on oil. Better cars, better fuels, cars that run on electricity, strong transit infrastructure, high speed trains: modern technologies like these will put us on the road toward energy independence and a leadership position in clean power, the next major worldwide industry. Oil's role in our future is declining. Tar sands devastation—like the Gulf oil catastrophe—is a visible consequence of status quo oil use. America has what it takes to make the changes we need. Isn't it time we did?

ON THE WEB!

- The Pembina Institute: Oil Sands Watch, oilsandswatch.org
- The Dirty Oil Sands Network, dirtyoilsands.org

READ UP!

- *Tar Sands: Dirty Oil and the Future of a Continent*, by Andrew Nikiforuk, Greystone Books, 2009.
- *Why Your World Is About to Get a Whole Lot Smaller: Oil and the End of Globalization*, by Jeff Rubin, Random House, 2009.

ACT LOCALLY!

- Fresh Energy
  St. Paul, MM
  651-225-0878
  fresh-energy.org
- Sierra Club North Star Chapter
  Minneapolis, MN
  612-659-9124
  minnesota.sierraclub.org

You Can Help Make Hennepin a Cool County

Hennepin

Hennepin County is committed to an 80 percent reduction of greenhouse gas emissions from county operations by 2050 by:

- Increasing energy efficiency in buildings.
- Using renewable energy sources.
- Increasing fuel efficiency in our fleet and using alternative fuels.
- Utilizing new technologies as they become available to reduce or eliminate greenhouse gas emissions from standard operations.
- Leading efforts to improve transit and develop livable communities.
- Engaging employees to reduce their environmental impact.

10 ways to reduce the amount of greenhouse gas emissions you create

- Understand how you contribute greenhouse gas emissions. Take the Minnesota Energy Challenge at www.mnenergychallenge.org.
- Drive less: walk, bike, car pool or use transit instead of hopping in your car. Alter your driving habits and keep up on car maintenance.
- Use less energy for home heating and cooling: audit your home's energy consumption, turn down your thermostat, seal air leaks and keep up on maintenance.
- Use your refrigerator efficiently and purchase the most efficient model available.
- Save energy when using water: turn down your water heater, install a low-flow showerhead, wash your clothes in cold water and insulate your hot water heater.
- Install compact fluorescent light bulbs.
- Turn off and unplug appliances when they are not in use.
- Reduce, reuse and recycle as much as possible.
- Buy foods produced locally and in season.
- Visit *www.hennepin.us/coolcounty* for more information about reducing greenhouse gas emissions.

Hennepin

Hennepin County
Environmental Services
612-348-3777

www.hennepin.us/coolcounty

Hennepin County is a founding member of a coalition of counties across the United States that are taking action to eliminate the causes of global climate change.

In the Bad Old Days...

By **JEN GROEBNER**
MINNESOTA POLLUTION CONTROL AGENCY

Many older folks remember the days when smoke billowed out of the smokestacks that lined the Minneapolis and St. Paul skylines. Both large and small businesses produced unregulated air and water pollution 40 years ago, and this became the major focus of the newly-created MPCA. However, even at the time, agency staff recognized that the practices of individuals also added significant contributions, particularly in terms of waste disposal and vehicle emissions.

40 years ago, it was sadly routine for home and business owners to dump garbage and unwanted items in woods, wetlands and ditches, leaving ugly mysteries — often headline-making and sometimes toxic — for others to clean up 20 or 30 years later. Many containers of liquid wastes broke open and leached into the groundwater that Minnesotans used for drinking.

In cities, oil, paint and other polluting liquids were regularly dumped down drains and sewers, only to end up in rivers and lakes. Hazardous waste was casually stored and disposed of without regard for the danger it could pose, either immediately or in the future. Old, dirty, industrial sites were vacated and left too polluted for any further use, blighting cities and towns.

As late as 1976, 450 communities in Minnesota still had no or inadequate treatment of sewage and industrial waste. More than 40 percent of industries in the state did not treat their own wastes, but simply dumped them in rivers and lakes.

Before trash removal service was mandated, people often burned garbage in backyard burn barrels. Air quality in residential neighborhoods was occasionally smoky and unpleasant in the 1960s. Mrs. Walter Gehrke of Minneapolis wrote a letter to the Minneapolis Star, saying, "I would like to know what one ordinary individual can do to help herself from being gassed to death without wearing a gas mask...trash burns in our neighborhood, smoldering seven to eight hours at a time, making it impossible for

us to open our windows" (Letter to the Editor, July 21, 1965).

"Most backyard garbage-burning has ceased in the metro area, but it still takes place in rural areas," says the MPCA's Mark Rust. While Minnesota law banned burning industrial waste, garbage, and hazardous wastes, the law still allows farmers to conduct open burning if regularly scheduled trash pickup is not reasonably available. Rust says that as a result, in 2005, more than 45 percent of rural Minnesotans — less than half of whom are actually farmers — still burned their garbage, releasing a variety of toxic fumes into the air.

After the advent of catalytic converters in

the 1970s, gasoline in cars burned cleaner. Some drivers, though, removed the devices illegally, willing to trade cleaner air for what they perceived as better performance. The Minneapolis Tribune reported on February 26, 1967, that "Some car owners in the Twin Cities have disconnected anti-smog devices on their autos, apparently assuming the devices impair gas mileage and engine performance… one service manager received calls to disconnect the devices and had also seen devices that had been manually placed out of order."

It took years of hard work by citizens, local government, legislators and the MPCA to bring us to where we are today. Although we continue to have plenty of environmental work in front of us, we have made tremendous strides in cleaning up and preventing a great deal of pollution in Minnesota.

THEN

The Beginnings of Minnesota's Environmental Movement

By **NANCY MILLER**
MINNESOTA POLLUTION CONTROL AGENCY

In 1967, before the federal Clean Water Act or Clean Air Act and three years before the U.S. Environmental Protection Agency was established, the Minnesota Legislature created the Minnesota Pollution Control Agency. According to Sir Isaac Newton, for every action, there is an equal and opposite reaction. In this case, many actions over a long period built enough momentum for development of a state agency devoted to controlling pollution.

During the early years, Minnesota communities and businesses routinely dumped raw wastes into streams and lakes. In 1885, in order to control diseases spread through poor quality drinking water, the first legislation was passed to prevent pollution of rivers and other sources of drinking water. Responsibility for polluted state waters rested with the State Board of Health—later the Department of Health—for many years.

In 1945, because too many communities dumped raw sewage into lakes and rivers, the legislature authorized a new state Water Pollution Control Commission. One of the Commission's jobs was to encourage communities to build wastewater treatment plants to stop the flow of raw sewage into rivers and lakes.

In 1962, Rachel Carson's book *Silent Spring* outlined the dangers of pesticides such as DDT. The book raised the public's consciousness of the environment, prompted public outcry and, some say, set the national environmental movement in motion.

Environmentalists demanded not only protection of the natural world, but new regulations and punishment for those who broke them. As the environmental movement gained attention, national leaders, including Presidents John F. Kennedy and Lyndon Johnson, added environmental issues to their political agendas and legislative programs.

Close to home, 1962 was significant in Minnesota. Late that year, Minnesota witnessed

two of the most catastrophic oils spills in the history of the state. In December, sub-zero temperatures caused a pipeline break at Richards Oil in Savage. The ruptured line released a million gallons of oil into the Mississippi River. Shortly thereafter, a storage tank at the Honeymead plant in Mankato burst, releasing more than three million gallons of soy oil onto the ice of the Minnesota River. Oil from both spills slowly traveled downstream.

With the spring thaw, the tragic results were evident. Although Governor Rolvaag activated the National Guard to coordinate cleanup (a project rather quaintly known as Operation Save-a-Duck), and citizens volunteered to rescue and rehabilitate oil-covered ducks, it was not enough. The survival rate of oil-coated ducks was dismally small. Despite everyone's best efforts, more than 10,000 waterfowl and countless beaver, muskrats, turtles and fish died.

Because of this and other major environmental incidents during the next few years, the Minnesota Legislature finally created the Minnesota Pollution Control Agency in 1967. Its mission still today is to protect the air, land and waters of the state.

Minnesota's air, land and water are indeed cleaner today than they were 40 years ago, despite a population that grew from 3.5 million to 5.1 million, and corresponding growth in industry and transportation. The Twin Cities is one of only three major metropolitan areas in the country that today meets all federal ambient air quality standards. Minnesota is one of only 11 states to meet those same stringent standards statewide. In addition, compared to 1990 levels, mercury emissions from Minnesota sources have been reduced by 70 percent.

In 1967, we were ahead of the federal curve in recognizing and taking action to safeguard our environment. We're still ahead of the federal curve and continue to maintain our reputation as a national model of environmental protection.

NOW

Today's Environmental Challenges

By **LAURIE GUSTAFSON**
MINNESOTA POLLUTION CONTROL AGENCY

"The most obvious environmental issues we face today are those that challenge the entire planet," said Bill Sierks, MPCA manager for energy and climate change. "We've gone from solving environmental problems that states and communities could tackle to problems that require a regional or global approach."

Forty years ago, government used regulations to address smokestack industries, filthy rivers and lakes, and garbage piled in town dumps. These regulations have resulted in cleaner air, water and land. Today, we face different stresses on our environment—rising population, increased energy consumption, and changes in how we use land.

"Before, rules and technological fixes could address problems without requiring people to change their behavior," said Sierks. "Now we face problems, like air pollution from energy use, that require us to make behavior changes like how we drive."

Shifts in farming

Wayne Anderson is the agricultural liaison for the MPCA. He has worked for the MPCA for 34 years and has seen a dramatic shift from mostly family farms to larger, more industrial ones. "Forty years ago Minnesota had 100,000 farms with relatively few animals each. Today, we have about 30,000 feedlots, with about a thousand of those having more than a thousand animals."

Intensively-farmed animals produce a great deal of manure in one place, which must be managed if it is not to damage the environment.

"The technology of feedlots has changed, from a barn and open manure ponds where runoff was a major pollution issue to confined buildings with manure storage systems," Anderson said.

"Now, one focus is on how to get the most benefit from the manure, which is to get it onto the land in a way that minimizes odor by injecting into the soil or tilling within 24 hours of application."

Anderson added, "Producers are doing a better job at using the manure. It used to be considered waste. Now farmers are using the waste as fertilizer."

Pollution from all of us

It isn't all smokestacks and industry anymore. We are facing greater challenges now from nonpoint sources of pollution, meaning non-industrial but numerous sources, such as family yards, farms,

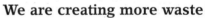

small businesses, vehicles and recreational activities. These sources individually produce small amounts of pollution, but when added together, they make big amounts.

According to the MPCA publication *Minnesota Environment 2005—How are we doing?* (pca.state.mn.us/publications/reports/mne-2005.html), "Minnesota's lake and stream quality ranges from very good in some parts of the state to very poor in others. Although Minnesota has assessed only a small portion of waters, many are unhealthy for aquatic life or unsafe for swimming and other water recreation. Many lakes and streams also have advisories limiting fish consumption because of unsafe mercury levels."

The original goal of the federal Clean Water Act was to ensure "fishable and swimmable" waters for all Americans. To address the nonpoint pollution challenge, the act was amended in 1987 to deal with polluted runoff from farm fields, roads, and residential sources.

We are creating more waste

While Minnesota's recycling rates are the second highest in the country, this is outpaced by increases in how much garbage per person we throw away. Studies show that much of our garbage has more value if it is recycled or composted than if it is landfilled or incinerated. Garbage represents wasted energy and natural resources and, when disposed of, creates air and water pollution.

New challenges require new approaches

"The top environmental problem we face is climate change," said Sierks. Wayne Anderson agrees that carbon and climate change are a priority. He acknowledged that this has not been much of an issue for the agricultural community, but he says it will be.

Both Sierks and Anderson agree that a broader, more global approach will be necessary to deal with nonpoint pollution and climate change.

"I'm working on the hypoxia issue in the Gulf of Mexico. It seems strange, but a lot of pollution in the Gulf of Mexico originates in midwestern states, including Minnesota, and travels down the Mississippi. In other words, in today's world, sources of pollution may be very far from where the problems are; the same is true for mercury pollution. Today's problems are bigger, global and more complex," said Anderson.

Headlines Then & Now

By **DAN OLSON**
MINNESOTA POLLUTION CONTROL AGENCY

TOP: **In 1995, research students near LeSueur found deformed frogs which led to research that is still being conducted today to find the source in the water that is causing these abnormalities.**
MIDDLE: **Inspectors with the Minnesota Pollution Control Agency, which has been regulating hazardous waste management and water permits for 47 years.** BOTTOM: **Man testing water: 40 years ago, oil, paint and other polluting and toxic liquids were dumped down drains and sewers ending up in our rivers and lakes.**

W e Minnesotans love our state. So when something happens that compromises the quality of our environment, it's news. Looking back at pollution stories that made headlines during the past four decades shows the many environmental problems we've overcome.

News articles about pollution have by no means disappeared, though. Nowadays, instead of stories about big business, we're just as likely to see stories about the role that individuals and communities play in preventing and reducing pollution.

"Lake Superior inundated with taconite tailings."

This dumping was discovered in the 1960s. These "taconite tailings" were potentially hazardous because of their similarity to asbestos fibers, which are known to cause cancer. By 1980 tailings were finally no longer being dumped into the lake.

"Toxic fog rolls in, residents roll out."

In late June 1992, three Burlington Northern liquid container cars derailed into the Nemadji River where it flows into Lake Superior. The resulting spill of the chemical benzene vaporized into a chemical fog that spread over Superior, Wisconsin and Duluth. More than 50,000 people were evacuated from both cities.

"Un-Golden Pond — frog stories leap to front page."

In August 1995, students studying wetlands near Le Sueur discovered large numbers of frogs with deformed, missing or extra legs. By the end of 1996, more than 175 reports of malformed frogs were received in two-thirds of the state's counties. Scientists continue to work on this issue in hopes of discovering what in the water is causing this problem.

"Point, nonpoint, what's the point?"

In the past 40 years, permitting processes have been developed that allow businesses and communities to build factories and wastewater treatment plants while keeping air and water pollution relatively low. Minnesota is now focusing on reducing "non-point" source pollution by supporting new partnerships with lake associations and landowners.

"Minnesota River gets an extreme makeover."

The idea that we're all part of the problem and all need to be part of the solution was captured in a challenge by Governor Arne Carlson as he stood on the banks of the Minnesota River in the early 1990s. He asked citizens to help make what many people considered the state's "dirtiest" river once again "fishable and swimmable" within 10 years. Since then, more farmers have set aside land in conservation programs and adopted best management practices to help prevent soil and nutrients from reaching the river. Communities are improving sewage treatment systems to reduce the dumping of bacteria into the river. Watershed groups are working on projects throughout the Minnesota River basin to reduce contaminants.

"Mighty Mississippi cleans up."

For much of the river's history since the settlement era, the Mighty Mississippi in Minnesota was a Mighty Mess, receiving untreated wastewater from every town, factory and home along its banks. In the 1980s, special funding was approved to separate the Twin Cities' combined storm and sanitary sewers to reduce sewage overflows during heavy rains. In 1996, the Twin Cities became one of the few metropolitan areas in the country to accomplish this goal. Recently, mayflies returned to the river after a long absence, a sign of improving river health.

"Everything old is new again."

Minnesota is one of the top recycling states, with a rate of 44 percent, just behind Oregon. This success is due to the Waste Management Act adopted in 1980. The bad news is that the amount of garbage each of us generates is rising. If this trend continues, the state's landfill capacity will be reached in about 10 years.

Solving the many environmental issues we face now and will face in the future will take time, thought and, yes, money. Solving them will also, more and more, require us to engage individual Minnesotans in taking charge of their own environmental attitudes, behaviors and practices.

Responding to a Violent Earth

By **JEFF BARTLETT**
DO IT GREEN! MINNESOTA

Minnehaha Falls, where dynamic geology and human activity interact. Wikimedia Commons

Our dynamic planet experiences change at all scales through processes ranging from gradual to violently destructive. Minnesota is about as far as possible from plate boundaries or other geologic hotspots, but we are still influenced by remote upheavals and, closer to home, our behavior can worsen the devastating power of natural hazards.

On the global scale, continental motions and molten rock cause widespread upheaval through earthquakes and volcanoes. Despite our distance from any geologic boundary, we will feel the effects of massive eruptions known as supervolcanoes. Every million years or so, for instance, a huge plume of energetic rock at Yellowstone National Park produces eruptions larger than we've ever noted in historic records. Minnesota lies downwind and within range of the ash cloud produced by prehistoric eruptions at Yellowstone. Our travel and communications could be disrupted much like Europe during recent Eyjafjallajökull eruptions in Iceland.

Our daily practices multiply the effects of local geologic processes. Southeastern Minnesota is home, for example, to rocks and landscapes that make sinkholes a hazard. Pollution of the atmosphere and the acid rain it produces greatly accelerate the dissolving of the rocks underlying the area, leading to increased sinkhole hazards.

The Land of 10,000 Lakes actually boasts more than that, but the number is rapidly dwindling due to the interplay of natural and human forces. The region began draining long ago when, with the removal of massive glaciers, the earth began a process of 'rebound' that has been lifting the land ever since the end of the last ice age. But development, farming and overuse of our groundwater supply have each taken a significant toll on the number of remaining lakes in our fair state.

Perhaps the most devastating of earth processes for the Midwest is the episodic flooding that occurs along our waterways. Even without human impact, streams flood frequently, but with unsound building practices and interruption of the natural water cycle, these events can be severe. 17 Minnesota floods were declared federal disasters just in the last 20 years, with the most recent affecting over two dozen counties. Conversion of wetlands to plowed fields, replacement of permeable land with pavement in urban areas, and overdevelopment in flood-prone areas may all intensify the damage caused by floods.

The flip side of this coin is that we now understand far more about the earth's forces and their effects. Preventive measures like smart land development practices will go far to mitigate the effects of geologic destruction on our lives and property. Future events from floods to faulting are inevitable, but we need not contribute to the destruction.

ON THE WEB!

- U.S. Geological Survey Flood information, usgs.gov/hazards/floods
- Flooding in Minnesota, dnr.state.mn.us/climate/floods
- Restoring Prairies Helps Reduce Flooding, by the Nature Conservancy, nature.org/wherewework/northamerica/states/minnesota/science/art26572.html
- Karst in Minnesota page, by the Minnesota Pollution Control Agency, pca.state.mn.us/index.php/water/water-types-and-programs/groundwater/about-groundwater/karst-in-minnesota.html

READ UP!

- *The Control of Nature*, by John McPhee, Farrar, Straus and Giroux, 1990.
- *Minnesota's Geology*, by Richard Ojakangas and Charles Matsch, University of Minnesota Press, 2001.

Our Faltering Fireflies

By **EVA LEWANDOWSKI**
DO IT GREEN! MINNESOTA

Usual firefly, *Pterotus obscuripennis*, with large antennae.

Fireflies have long been a source of wonder and entertainment for nature lovers. Also called lightning bugs because of their habit of flashing brightly, fireflies are found throughout the world. Regrettably, in the last decade people everywhere have reported drops in firefly populations. Here in Minnesota, where we have 15 species of the beautifully bioluminescent beetles, residents are also reporting fewer fireflies, especially in urban areas. While there is still no scientific proof of diminishing firefly populations, the wealth of anecdotal evidence has led researchers to begin studying the size and health of firefly populations worldwide.

If firefly populations truly are waning, many nature lovers suspect that, as with so many other species, human land use is behind the decline. Adult fireflies most often live in open areas like meadows and forest clearings, and their larvae require moist environments, such as riverbanks, leaf litter, and wetlands, where they burrow into the soil. Unfortunately, as human development increases and we drain wetlands, cut down woodlots, and convert riverbanks to front lawns to satisfy our desire for expansion, we are destroying prime firefly habitat. Those areas that do remain for fireflies to use are often sprayed with pesticides and other chemicals. Most insecticides are effective against all insects, and can be doubly harmful to fireflies because they can both kill the lightning bugs directly and eliminate the insects that serve as their food supply. It has also been suggested that light pollution could be interfering with the flashes used by males to attract mates, thus further damaging the firefly population. As more and more areas are overwhelmed by the light from streetlamps, 24-hour stores, and porch lights, fireflies may be finding it harder to see and distinguish mating flashes against the backdrop of human-created light.

Until scientists find solid evidence that firefly populations are on the decline and determine the cause or causes, concerned firefly lovers can only do their best to maintain firefly-friendly environments to host their populations. Keeping natural areas undeveloped, leaving litter and debris present in yards and parks, avoiding pesticide use, and using only a minimal amount of outdoor lighting are all good steps to take to augment firefly populations, as well as many other forms of wildlife. You can also join Firefly Watch, a joint effort between Boston's Museum of Science and university researchers that allows people across the country to track and report firefly sightings in their area. With so many concerned citizens here and abroad, we can hope that fireflies will one day return to the abundance of decades past.

ON THE WEB!

- Firefly Watch, mos.org/fireflywatch/
- MN DNR, dnr.state.mn.us
- Firefly, firefly.org

READ UP!

- *Fireflies, Honey, and Silk*, by Gilbert Waldbauer, University of California Press, 2009.
- *Beetles: A Field Guide to the Beetles of North America (Peterson Field Guides)*, by Richard White, Houghton Mifflin Harcourt, 1998.

Farm Fireflies

By **ELLEN TELANDER**,
Winsted Organic Farm

As children, my brother and I had different ideas of conservation. He'd collect the fireflies in our yard and then keep them stocked in a jar to watch at night. I'd find the jar and let them all go, making him mad. It was worth it, though, to see the fireflies light up and fly back into the darkness of the night.

Now as an adult, I've noticed something at our organic farm. We are surrounded by conventional farms that spray: on these farms around us, you won't see any fireflies. However, you look across to our farm and you see them everywhere. Most congregate where they can find cover. We have lots of fireflies in our prairie habitat areas, where we have allowed the grasses to grow long. The fireflies live in this type of cover and prefer these areas over the cut lawn areas.

WHAT YOU CAN DO:

- Provide firefly cover.
- Plant native grasses along fence lines and near trees.
- Encourage your neighbors to do the same, allowing "continuous coverage" to encourage other animal species to flourish too.

Small "Green" Steps Forward in the 2010 Minnesota Legislature

By **CHARLES BUCKMAN-ELLIS**
LEGISLATIVE CHAIR, SIERRA CLUB NORTH STAR CHAPTER

Students rally to move beyond coal. Peter Atkins

POLITICS, *n.*

...the conduct of public affairs for private advantage.

—by Ambrose Bierce,
The Devil's Dictionary

As a statewide, grassroots environmental organization, the Sierra Club North Star Chapter works alongside many allies to ensure that state policies reflect our environmental values, not private and short-sighted interests: fighting for action on global warming; defending Minnesota's laws from harmful rollbacks; continuing to work for our forests, wild lands, and waters; and supporting policies to increase transportation options and reduce our dependence on oil. In early 2010, we entered the State Capitol knowing that the climate of budget shortfalls and upcoming elections would likely mean a difficult year for environmental victories. But because Sierra Club members and concerned citizens got involved to make their voices heard, there were several bright spots and a few steps forward for our state's environment.

Maintaining Minnesota's Clean Energy Path — Nuclear and Coal Moratoria

This issue found environmental advocates in an unusual position: defending the status quo. Minnesota passed a moratorium on new nuclear reactors in 1994. Since then, nothing has changed, and still there is no solution for the permanent storage of high-level radioactive waste. Keeping the moratorium was an important win for all of us working for clean, renewable energy and concerned about nuclear waste.

The Next Generation Energy Act of 2007 established a moratorium on the use of new power from coal-fired power plants, until a comprehensive carbon reduction plan is in place statewide. This popular legislation was signed by the Governor, but was challenged this year. Environmental advocates spoke up to maintain this sensible policy, and legislators listened, maintaining our path to 21st century power sources like wind and solar.

Building Minnesota's Green Economy

With support from environmental and labor allies, legislation to enable a new local financing mechanism for renewable energy projects, called Property-Assessed Clean Energy loans (PACE), became law in Minnesota. It was another win for the next generation of clean energy.

Complete Streets

"Complete Streets" changes the street and road design process to make all users important in design decisions, to ensure accessibility for pedestrians, bicyclists and people with disabilities. The legislation passed, thanks to the organizing and advocacy efforts of the Minnesota Complete Streets Coalition, a large and diverse group of over 50 members. As state roads are redeveloped in your area, you can get involved to advocate for a safer design that increases transportation options.

Not Everything Came Up Green

It was a far-from-perfect session. Critical capital investments, including funding for transit infrastructure, were vetoed. Legislation to protect forests and wetlands from irresponsible ATV use, support "green" chemistry and reduce toxic chemical use, and protect Wild and Scenic Rivers from irresponsible development failed to advance. Only continued citizen involvement will ensure that we can protect and strengthen our environmental policies — to preserve our natural legacy for future generations.

It was not a bad year, considering the number of private actors seeking to find advantage in the public affairs of Minnesota.

ON THE WEB!

- Sierra Club North Star Chapter, northstar.sierraclub.org
- Minnesota Complete Streets Coalition, mncompletestreets.org
- Transit for Livable Communities, tlcminnesota.org
- Clean Water Action, cleanwateraction.org/mn
- Blue Green Alliance, bluegreenalliance.org
- Take Action Minnesota, takeactionminnesota.org
- Minnesota Environmental Partnership, mepartnership.org

READ UP!

- *Coming Clean: Breaking America's Addiction to Oil and Coal*, by Michael Brune, Sierra Club/Counterpoint, 2008.
- *Paper or Plastic: Searching for Solutions to an Overpackaged World*, by Daniel Imhoff, Sierra Club Books, 2005.

Minnesota Participates in the Climate Change Conference in Copenhagen

By **NICOLE ROM**
EXECUTIVE DIRECTOR, WILL STEGER FOUNDATION

Will Steger in Nyhavn, Copenhagen. Courtesy of Will Steger Foundation

As the Executive Director of the Will Steger Foundation, I was lucky enough to organize and lead a delegation of 12 youth from across the Midwest, along with staff and policy mentor support, to the United Nations Conference in Copenhagen (COP15). We were there to build U.S. awareness of climate policy and investment in strong participation in the conference; to highlight the unique role of the Midwest region since we are a key player in driving national climate policy, public opinion, and the renewable energy revolution; and to bring the U.S. youth voice, whose future is at stake, to the negotiations.

Why the Midwest?

The Midwest is poised to play a pivotal role in America's clean energy future because of its strong industrial base, its vast potential for generating power from wind and other renewable sources, and the crucial role of its Congressional delegations in shaping national energy policy. Because the region is a major emitter of greenhouse gases, it is

also positioned to contribute significantly to reducing these emissions — and to reap the economic and environmental benefits of doing so.

What was expected to happen at COP15?

Copenhagen hosted the 15th Conference of the Parties (COP15) to the United Nations Framework Convention on Climate Change (UNFCCC). The UNFCCC is an international environmental treaty that was agreed upon in 1992 at the United Nations Conference on Environment and Development, or "Earth Summit," in Rio de Janeiro, Brazil. The Parties to this treaty (that is, the countries that have formally endorsed it) have been holding annual meetings since 1995. There are now 194 Parties that have formally endorsed the UNFCCC — which is nearly all of the world's 203 sovereign states. Although the UNFCCC is technically considered a "treaty," it's most accurate to think of it as an "agreement to agree" to take action steps that prevent the worst

impacts of climate change. Nothing in the UNFCCC itself requires countries to take such action steps. That's why there have been fifteen UNFCCC conferences since 1995: the world still has a lot to do before it will have a global agreement that stands a chance of dealing adequately with the threat of climate change.

The Kyoto Protocol

The Kyoto Protocol, forged in 1997 in Kyoto, Japan, was the world's first and so far only attempt at a global agreement to address climate change. It calls for mandatory cuts in greenhouse gas emissions from developed countries, but exempts developing countries — including China and India, which are the world's first and fifth largest emitters of greenhouse gases despite their status as developing countries. Because of this, the U.S. has never ratified the Kyoto Protocol, which means that the binding emissions cuts accepted by every other developed country (except Australia, until it ratified the Protocol in 2007) do not apply here, although the U.S. is the world's second largest emitter of greenhouse gases after China.

The fact that three of the world's five largest emitters of greenhouse gases are not bound to cut their emissions under the Kyoto Protocol has made this agreement inadequate to deal with climate change — though it has led to meaningful emissions cuts in most developed countries that ratified it (with some important exceptions).

The Bali Road Map

In December 2007, at the 13th Conference of Parties to the UNFCCC in Bali, Indonesia, the countries of the world agreed on a plan for producing a new agreement that would work alongside and eventually replace the Kyoto Protocol. In particular, this "Bali

Road Map" called on parties to develop strategies to deal with five challenges:

1. Finding consensus on an overall "shared vision" for a post-Kyoto agreement;
2. Cutting greenhouse gas emissions, including those resulting from deforestation;
3. Adapting to those climate change impacts that are already guaranteed to occur as a result of past emissions;
4. Developing clean energy technologies, and transferring knowledge of these technologies to underdeveloped countries; and
5. Forging financial agreements among countries to pay for the efforts above.

Under the Bali Road Map, it was hoped that countries would agree on plans for "enhanced action" on these issues in 2008 and 2009, in time to roll the action plans together into a new international climate agreement by the end of the December 2009 conference in Copenhagen.

What actually happened at COP15?

The outcome of the conference was a three-page, non-binding "Copenhagen Accord" that provides the beginnings of an agreement to tackle climate change. The Accord was agreed to in the final 48 hours of the conference by heads of state from the United States, China, India, Brazil, and South Africa. The other countries assembled at the conference agreed to "take note" of the Accord, which is open to interpretation. The Copenhagen Accord is built on commitments to cut *overall* emissions by the United States and other developed countries, and commitments to cut *emissions*

intensity (emissions per unit of economic output) by India, China, and other developing countries.

What comes next?

Because the Copenhagen Accord is non-binding and because specific procedures remain to be agreed on, attention is now turning toward the 16th Conference of Parties (COP16), which will take place in November 2010 in Cancún, Mexico. Politically, it will be virtually impossible for the United States to make a binding commitment to any international agreement before the Senate passes energy and climate legislation. Such legislation will provide specific guidance for U.S. emissions cuts, Until the U.S. makes such a binding commitment, China and India are unlikely to do so.

Expedition Copenhagen

While in Copenhagen our delegation worked on a range of issues: interpreting high level policy discussions; participating in creative actions with youth from across the globe; and sharing our experiences with media and our peers in Copenhagen as well as back home in the Midwest. In addition to hosting a series of presentations and briefings over the course of the summit, Expedition Copenhagen team members met with government delegates and civil society from around the world.

While we were disappointed with the outcome of the Copenhagen Summit, what transpired there was incredibly important—for the first time U.S. climate leadership was at the table in a serious manner—from cabinet heads to President Obama arriving on the final day.

ON THE WEB!

- United Nations Framework Convention on Climate Change, unfccc.int/2860.php
- Will Steger Foundation videos and blogs from Copenhagen, willstegerfoundation.org/index.php/expedition-copenhagen-2009

READ UP!

- *Text of the Kyoto Protocol,* by the UNFCCC, 1997, unfccc.int/resource/docs/convkp/kpeng.pdf.
- *Greenhouse Gas Targets,* by the Committee on Stabilization Targets for Atmospheric Greenhouse Gas Concentrations, The National Academies Press, 2010, nap.edu/catalog/12877.html.

Minnesota Leaders in Copenhagen

- Institute for Agriculture & Trade Policy –12 staff, including Jim Harkness
- Fresh Energy – Michael Noble and Rick Fuentes
- University of Minnesota – Dr. Elizabeth Wilson
- MN Representative Kate Knuth
- MN Representative Jeremy Kali
- Great Plains Institute – Brad Crabtree and Rolf Nordstrom
- Will Steger Foundation – Will Steger, Nicole Rom, and twelve youth leaders
- City of Minneapolis
- City of Edina Energy & Environment Commission – Paul Thompson
- School of Environmental Studies – High School Youth Delegation
- St. John's University and the College of St. Benedict – Film students

The Expedition Copenhagen Team. Courtesy of Will Steger Foundation

Concerned about Offshore Drilling? Get Involved!

By **ANDREA SANCHEZ**
SIERRA CLUB ORGANIZER

North Star Sierra Club's June Rally in Response to the BP Oil Disaster. Amy Okaya

Despite the horrific images of the BP oil spill disaster as a result of offshore drilling gone awry, some still call the decision by President Obama to put a moratorium on offshore drilling rash. Oil-soaked wildlife. Wetlands that protect and improve water quality, store floodwaters, and act as an important barrier against storms—now hanging limp. It has proved impossible to clean these wetlands of their gooey new topcoat. Yet putting a moratorium on offshore drilling is rash?

There is no doubt that America has become reliant on oil. It powers most of our cars, brings food to grocery stores, gives us plastic and pesticides. Does this mean that we *need* oil? The answer is a loud, resounding "no". In today's world, with technology readily available, it seems laughable that we have not been willing to break away from oil. Supporters of the oil industry claim that a moratorium on oil drilling will lead to a loss of jobs. We must think of the bigger picture, and a new energy strategy would actually mean replacing outdated jobs as we build the 21st century clean energy jobs economy.

Continued reliance on oil means more drilling, and more drilling means more oil spills. The U.S. alone accounts for 880,000 gallons of oil spilled into the ocean each year. There is no safe way to conduct offshore drilling. Even BP, one of the most technologically advanced companies in the world, has been unable to implement standards for drilling safely.

While Minnesota is somewhat removed from the Gulf of Mexico, it is still being affected by the oil disaster. Many migratory birds from Minnesota have nesting grounds in the Gulf of Mexico, including the Common Loon, our state bird. Birds from all around the central region of the U.S. will not be returning from their migratory trip this winter. This disaster is a wake-up call. Jobs need not be lost by those working in the offshore oil industry or by communities affected by oil spills; the environment need not be destroyed. Everyone from the brilliant engineers to the brave people working on oil platforms can benefit greatly from a transition from dirty oil toward sustainable careers in renewable energy.

So what can Minnesota do to move us away from oil and stop new offshore drilling operations?
Personal decisions are the easiest way to go. Drive less, bike more. Choose products that are not petroleum-based. Opt for organic and locally grown food. But we can also organize for the policy changes we need to make the clean energy jobs economy a reality. Send messages to your elected officials to let them know that you support a clean energy future, and strong state and federal climate policies. To get more involved, find a local organization like the Sierra Club and volunteer your time with them. As we all do our part to reduce oil reliance, we can help save the planet.

ON THE WEB!

- Climate Crossroads blog, connect.sierraclub.org/Groups/Gulf_Oil_Disaster/blog
- Tar Sands: The Most Destructive Project on Earth, environmentaldefence.ca/reports/pdf/TarSands_TheReport.pdf
- Steps to reduce oil consumption, thedailygreen.com/environmental-news/latest/reduce-oil-consumption

ACT LOCALLY!

- Sierra Club
  Minneapolis, MN
  612-659-9124
  northstar.sierraclub.org
- Transit for Livable Communities
  St. Paul, MN
  tlcminnesota.org
  651-767-0298
- Fresh Energy
  St. Paul, MN
  651-225-0878

Sustainability of Family Life

By **SARA GROCHOWSKI**
DO IT GREEN! MINNESOTA

Busyness defines the lives of most Americans. For some, the focus of busyness is family. For others, it is career or social activities. Sometimes busyness results from a big event, like the catastrophic illness of a family member, but much of it builds from many seemingly inconsequential demands that collectively become overwhelming. Considering the demands on parents and families, it may seem as if the American family is facing greater challenges today than at any other time in history. American families seem to be besieged from all sides. Divorce rates are climbing; marriage is being postponed, if not rejected; fertility rates are falling; and increasing numbers of children are being raised only by their mothers, either because of divorce or because their parents were never married. In reading daily headlines, legislation routinely favors the worker over the parent, crime rates are rising, technology is creating a more impersonal environment and deadly diseases (e.g., cancer) are more widespread. The statistics seem to have changed significantly in the last ten to twenty years in all of these arenas, and it is true in many circumstances that we have a long way to go in preserving and sustaining the sanctity of family life. However, considering that social critics have pointed out a few centuries ago that children were little more than possessions or servants in their parents' eyes, families today are strong and will continue to grow.

A search through the Internet or any bookstore will lead to thousands of titles on parenting, from healthy eating to discipline to sleep. The amount of reading and research on any given topic is endless. Books, magazines and websites can all be useful in certain circumstances, but the most sustainable idea in creating a healthy family is to connect with your family. Healthy families make time for each other, time when they are only plugged in to each other and not cell phones or email accounts. Whether you are lying on the floor inside a carefully constructed fort, sitting next to your child while doing homework, or listening to your partner lament about the day, your mind is present. Our culture may define people by what they do, but families are defined by whether intense, gratifying relationships exist.

Parents and other caregivers are *extremely* important when it comes to modeling strong, healthy relationships for their children. They are considered to be a child's first teacher. In fact, it's been said that children pay more attention to what their parents *do* — rather than what they *say*. This is apparent in actions and speech between parents or caregivers as well as interactions between children. "More than ever, parents are seeking to offer their children every possible advantage, and research confirms the immense emotional, social and cognitive benefits to children from receiving one-on-one, unstructured time with their parents," said Barbara Nicholson, author and Co-founder of Attachment Parenting International. "Today's busy schedules can be quite an obstacle for families seeking quality time."

Families today are continually trying to find balance and this involves ensuring that everyone's needs — not just the child's — are recognized, validated, and met to the greatest extent possible. In an ideal world, every family member's needs are met all the time, everyone is happy and healthy, and the family is perfectly in balance. In the real world, nobody's family life is perfectly balanced all the time. It is not unusual for parents to feel out of balance at times.

The concept of the traditional family, where mothers are at home, fathers go to work every day and grandparents and extended family have a regular presence, does not exist the same as it did ten or twenty years ago and certainly not a few generations back. However, that does not mean that sustaining a loving, connected and healthy family cannot exist. Families are the bedrock of all societies. They can comprise anything from a small group to scores of individuals, and range from simple structures — such as a married couple and one child under one roof — to intricately complex, multigenerational combinations, living in one or more households. Invariably, as a society evolves, so does the family structure. With the modification of other factors — for example, life expectancy, or attitudes towards adoption — the impact on the family is telling.

With each generation, family life will change, parenting ideas will reformulate, and more publications will circulate but at the core of it all, healthy relationships will sustain a family regardless of life challenges. Use the articles in this section for ideas on making your family more healthy on all levels as well as those below and ↪➤

❧ *Sustainabile Family Life,* CONTINUED

know that even the most sustainable family unit is unbalanced at times, out of control, busy and very, very messy on many levels. When all else fails, use any of the ideas below.

- Do nothing
- Set priorities and be selective in what you do outside the home
- Go for a walk without a destination or time limit
- Put people before things
- Talk
- Keep promises
- Share family chores with age-appropriate jobs for each child
- Get out of the house
- Take time for yourself
- Set realistic goals
- Be creative in finding ways to spend couple time
- Ask for help
- Laugh
- Play
- Be affectionate
- Avoid overscheduling
- Develop family traditions
- Create family nights
- Have parent-child "dates"
- Take frequent deep breaths
- Maintain healthy eating habits
- Relax your standards

ON THE WEB!

- ✿ Attachment Parenting International, attachmentparenting.org
- ✿ Holistic Moms Network, holisticmoms.org
- ✿ Dr. Sears, askdrsears.com

READ UP!

- ✿ *Traits of a Healthy Family: Fifteen Traits Commonly Found in Healthy Families by Those Who Work with Them,* by Dolores Curran, Ballantine Books, 1990.
- ✿ *Natural Family Living,* by Peggy O'Mara, Pocket Books, 2000.

Healthy Snacks

By **KATRINA EDENFELD**
DO IT GREEN! MINNESOTA

Snacks don't have to come in boxes or bags! Here are some ideas for quick and easy foods that you won't mind serving between meals.

Ants on a Log variations: The "logs" can be any vegetable such as celery, bell pepper, carrot, zucchini, or cucumber, cut into sticks. The "bark" is a spreadable food: try hummus or other bean spread, cream cheese, peanut or other nut butter, tahini, cottage cheese, or yogurt cheese. Finally, the "ants" can be the traditional raisins, or try dried blueberries, sunflower seeds, sliced almonds, sesame seeds, or peanut halves. This snack can entertain kids for upwards of 30 minutes as they prepare their own food.

Roasted Chickpeas: Roast cooked or canned chickpeas, mixed with 1–3 tsp olive oil and a little salt, at 425° F for about 20–30 minutes. Observe closely to avoid burning.

Fruit Plate: Prepare an assortment of fruit for eating. Wash, core and slice apples, pears, plums, etc.; wash berries; peel kiwifruit. Place on a plate for all to share.

Vegetable Plate: Prepare raw vegetables for eating, such as carrots, cucumbers, green and red bell peppers, and red cabbage. Leftover steamed vegetables are also fair game. Optional: provide a dip, such as homemade ranch dressing or hummus.

Popcorn: Air-pop popcorn and add seasonings as desired. One of our favorites is olive oil, salt, and oregano.

Kale Chips: Wash kale and spin dry, rip from the thick stems and tear into uniform pieces. Mix with a small amount of olive oil and salt. Place in a single layer on an oiled baking sheet and bake at 350° F for about 10–15 minutes, until beginning to brown.

Homemade Trail Mix: Always an easy and portable option, try mixing various small foods together, such as granola, nuts, seeds, dried fruit, cereals, and even a few chocolate chips.

Hard-boiled Eggs: Kids may need help with peeling them, but they will love to use an egg slicer.

Chickpea Crackers: take a break from wheat and mix up these incredibly easy snacks: blog.fatfreevegan.com/2007/10/

Kids love to select and prepare their own foods. A vegetable plate and the fixings for a yogurt parfait allow them to create their own healthy snacks.

gluten-free-chickpea-crackers.html. Experiment with seasonings, and the nutritional yeast is optional.

Mini-Salad: Mix leftover beans, grains, and vegetables from the fridge. Top with olive oil, vinegar if desired, and salt/pepper.

Smoothies: Whirl fresh or frozen fruit with enough yogurt, milk, or water to blend. Leftover, cooked oatmeal will give dairy-free smoothies a creamy texture. Including a banana generally makes a sweeter smoothie.

Popsicles: While you're making smoothies, blend some extra and freeze it in popsicle molds.

Homemade Muffins, Healthy Cookies, Granola Bars: Bake and freeze for quick snacks. If you're adapting a recipe to make it healthier, try cutting the butter or oil and the sugar in half.

Snack Pizza (you can use prepared dough to make this a quicker project): Bake crust, spread with hummus, and top with cut-up vegetables.

Yogurt and Granola: use unsweetened plain yogurt; add a small spoon of healthy jam or some pureed berries for flavoring, or top with fresh, cut fruit.

ON THE WEB!

- ✿ More vegan snack recipes, chooseveg.com/vegan-snack-recipes.asp

Ten Toys that Don't Require Purchasing

By **KATRINA EDENFELD**
DO IT GREEN! MINNESOTA

A nature kit and other themed play items are easy to assemble from things already in your home.

Toys are everywhere—and nearly all of them made from plastics and imported from far away places. The easiest way to greener toys is hand-me-downs, whether from friends, relatives, or strangers who hold yard sales. However, a little creativity can produce toys from items already in your home, reducing clutter and the need to hand down more toys in the future—the items can be returned to their original purposes when play is completed.

Older toddlers and up

Pots and Pans Band: Pull out the earplugs as the kids parade through the house. Wooden spoons make great drumsticks.

Sorting Game: This engaged my child for much longer than I would have guessed. Mix dried beans of various types in a container and provide a muffin tin for sorting. This is a good exercise for developing dexterity.

Plastic Container Blocks: Turn the kids loose in the Tupperware cabinet. Lidded containers make excellent blocks for large-scale building. Try a skyscraper or an igloo!

Age 3+

Themed Play Boxes: Collect child-safe items for themes such as office (desk supplies, paper, an old badge or nameplate), veterinarian/doctor (Ace bandage, thermometer, scale, flashlight), or chef (empty boxes, canned foods from the pantry, measuring cups, spatula, pan).

Dress-up Box: I was very happy to finally find a use for random old cast-offs from my grandmother such as a lovely beaded bag, a mantilla, costume jewelry, and silk scarves. A box or laundry basket will keep dress-up items corralled.

Recycling Game: Collect clean recyclables in a box and pull it out on a random day for crafting. Make a castle or whatever else your heart desires from toilet paper tubes, plastic containers, small boxes, and newspaper. Kids love large boxes that come into your life and can spend hours decorating them as forts.

Beading: Disassemble and reuse costume jewelry beads to make customized, new pieces (for kids who won't put beads in their mouths).

Age 5+

Tools: Scavenge through the garage for safety hazards. Fun tools include a tape measure, measuring square, rubber mallet, and pliers. If the kids can handle them safely, add a screwdriver, small hammer, and a board in which you've started some nails or screws. Real tools are best used under observation.

Nature Kit: Save a few clear plastic containers with lids for bug observation. Add a magnifying glass, small notebook and pencil, some large tweezers, and the field guides that are sitting on your bookshelf. For extra fun, set up the tent that's been gathering dust as a backyard field station.

Play Village: For hours of fun in the summer, spend a few days collecting sticks, rocks, fallen bunches of leaves, acorns, etc. Sticks can be stacked to create houses for fairies or toads. Make tables, chairs, beds, etc. For more permanent structures, use glue.

ON THE WEB!

- Homemade toys for young children, robynsnest.com/homemade.htm
- Numerous activities for play and crafts, preschoolexpress.com
- Hours of fun for older kids, scitoys.com

READ UP!

- *Learn and Play the Green Way: Fun Activities with Reusable Materials*, by Rhoda Redleaf, Redleaf Press, 2008.
- *Do-It-Yourself Early Learning: Easy and Fun Activities and Toys from Everyday Home Center Materials*, by Jeff A. Johnson and Tasha Johnson, Redleaf Press, 2006.

ACT LOCALLY!

- Your Friends and Neighbors: put out the word when you're looking for a particular toy or are stumped about how to make something.
- Your Library: a fun, free place to play and check out books, music, and videos, as well as free museum passes. Some libraries have themed book bags with puppets or other toys.

Twenty Activities to Survive a Minnesota Winter

By **SARA GROCHOWSKI**
Do It Green! Minnesota

Let's face it: winter in Minnesota is cold! Whether you are a native or a transplant, the plunging temperatures and continual snowfall can be surprising come January. Hibernation is an alluring option, but not practical. The only way to survive the weather is to embrace it. And when you have run out of activities, pull out the list below of family winter recommendations and enjoy this time of year, without yard work or mosquitoes.

1. **Visit a museum.** Take advantage of the Museum Adventure Pass, which grants free admission to local area museums.

2. **Enjoy the weekly puppet show** October–March at In the Heart of the Beast puppet and mask theater and stay for the "Make and Take" workshop after. Prices are $2 for youth living in surrounding neighborhoods and $4 for others.

3. **Take a hike.** Find the closest park through the Three Rivers Park District and rent snowshoes for the family.

4. **Play games.** Warm milk for cocoa, make popcorn and pull out the board games. You will quickly find out who is the most competitive member of the family.

5. **Fly a kite.** Snow and ice is no excuse to store kites. When the ice is thick enough on your local lake and the wind is blowing from 5–25 mph, pull out the kite and enjoy the colors against the snowy backdrop.

6. **Put on a play.** Seriously… get into homemade costumes and act out a recently read picture book or viewed movie. Set up a video camera and watch it together after. If nothing else, it will be a good laugh.

7. **Build an igloo.** When properly constructed, the temperature inside an igloo will remain between 19° F and 61° F with just body heat, even if the temperature outside dips to −49° F. Search on wikiHow for detailed instructions; then recruit your family and neighbors to help. Have someone stay inside to routinely fuel everyone with hot chocolate and energy bars.

8. **Run the Minneapolis skyways.** Print off a map from minneapolis.org and let your children run and explore with you. (Note: this might not be the best activity during rush hour or weekday lunch times.)

9. **Participate in the St. Paul Winter Carnival medallion treasure hunt.** The first clue will be published in the mid-January edition of the St. Paul Pioneer Press.

10. **Host a neighborhood potluck.** Send out invitations with specifics on what to bring (e.g., appetizer, main dish, dessert) and reconnect with your neighbors.

11. **Schedule a babysitter and go on a date night.** Bring your partner for a romantic stroll through winter woods lit by candlelight at Richardson Nature Center for their annual Candlelight and Chocolate event during Valentine's weekend. Enjoy a dessert sampler plate and coffee or tea, live music and a crackling fire. This may not be a whole family activity but keeping the parents connected is always good for the family!

12. **Read new books.** Visit the Minneapolis downtown library. With the large windows and open spaces, you almost forget you are indoors.

13. **Enjoy the Woodlake Nature Center** Low Impact Scavenger Hunt.

14. **Eat at the Midtown Global Market**, an internationally-themed public market featuring fresh and prepared foods, restaurants, and a selection of ➤

Playing at the park does not always have to happen in the summer!

❧ *Winter Activities,* CONTINUED

arts and crafts from around the world.

15. **Volunteer.** Go to VolunteerMatch, type in your zip code and research the volunteer needs for your area.

16. **Bake and decorate cookies.** Then deliver bags to your neighbors.

17. **Set up an indoor spa.** Fill tubs with warm water and a few drops of essential oils. Soak feet in the tubs and give each other foot massages. Even the most reluctant teenager will not pass on a foot rub.

18. **Set up an indoor obstacle course** using equipment you have in the house or garage. Be creative. Use a timer to see how fast each family member can run through it.

19. **Create a family newsletter on your computer.** Give each family member an age appropriate job. Email the finished newsletter to family and friends.

20. **Play.** Turn off the phone, television and computer. Cover the clocks, have snacks on hand and give your children your undivided attention. Play does not have to be complicated nor organized and you will find that regardless of age, conversation during play happens naturally.

ON THE WEB!

* Museum Adventure Pass, melsa.org
* Three Rivers Park District, threeriversparks.org
* St. Paul Winter Carnival, winter-carnival.com
* Volunteer March, volunteermatch.org

ACT LOCALLY!

* In the Heart of the Beast Minneapolis, MN 612-721-2535 hobt.com

---

Diaper Free Babies!
By **KANDACE**
DIAPERFREEBABY

Human babies are born with an instinct to stay clean and with an awareness of elimination, which they display through body language and other nonverbal ways of communicating. Parents and caregivers who practice EC (infant potty training) do so for many reasons, one of them being that it is an environmentally friendly practice. 3.5 million tons of disposable diapers end up in the landfill each year. In addition, chemicals such as dioxin, which is a known carcinogen, are used to manufacturer conventional disposables. The second, more environmentally friendly, option is cloth. However, it still uses resources such as water for laundering, electricity or gas for the clothes dryer, detergent and the materials to make the diapers. Even part-time EC will greatly reduce the reliance on cloth or disposable diapers.

Some Basics of EC

* EC can be done full-time or part-time, and with or without diapers. EC enhances the communication between you and your child, and allows you to help your child eliminate into a receptacle until they are old enough to do it themselves. It is not forceful or coercive.

* Newborns communicate the need to eliminate differently from older infants or toddlers. Just before a pee, a newborn may squirm, grimace, fuss, or cry—or, before a bowel movement, grunt or breathe heavily. Newborns also tend to eliminate more frequently than older children. Infants in middle infancy may have more regular and predicable elimination patterns, and their ability to sit up makes it an ideal time to introduce a low potty.

* A common way to start is with an observation period. This is simply watching for signs that your baby is about to eliminate. This is best done without diapers, or with a coverless cloth diaper so that you can tell right away when the baby is eliminating. Watch for specific vocalizations, facial expressions, or movement.

* When you feel comfortable that it is time to start communicating with your baby regarding elimination needs, you will want to choose a time when you think the baby may need to eliminate. At this time, hold the baby securely over a receptacle and make a cueing sound ('psssss'). It may take time and practice for both you and baby to catch on to the communication. Also say your cue sound whenever you catch your baby eliminating.

* The ideal age to start is prior to 6 months old; however, EC can be started at any time.

* EC is compatible with all sorts of family lifestyles. It is best to ease into practicing EC very slowly and remain at this level until ready.

As with all parenting decisions, the most important factor for EC is to relax and remember that this is about the process, not the result.

DiaperFreeBaby of Minnesota is the local group of an international non-profit organization, dedicated to the awareness of Infant Potty Training or EC.

ON THE WEB!

* DiaperFreeBaby, diaperfreebaby.org
* Clean Earth … Happy Baby!, cleanearthhappybaby.org

READ UP!

* *The Diaper Free Baby,* by Christine Gross-Loh, Harper Paperbacks, 2007.
* *Infant Potty Training,* by Laurie Boucke, White-Boucke Publishing, 3rd edition, 2008.

ACT LOCALLY!

* Diaper Free Baby of Minnesota, groups.yahoo.com/group/ diaperfreebabyofmn

Cloth Choices for Covering Your Baby's Bum

By **MICHELLE KRUEGER**

On Mondays I wear black pumps to the office. On Saturdays I'm barefoot in my backyard, hanging 32 mostly off-white diapers on the clothesline. The grass scrunches under my feet and my crawling ten-month old is content climbing around the clothes basket. It feels vintage and oh-so-old-fashioned, but sometimes I want a connection to simpler living, something in contrast to my high-energy work week.

My experiment with cloth diapers started before the birth of our second baby girl as I researched late into the night the costs and benefits of cloth diapering. My husband moaned that it might get stinky.

"Are you forgetting the smell of the diaper genie?" I countered.

"We'll waste so much water." He hedged.

"Did you know how much water is wasted to *manufacture* disposables?"

Choosing Among Endless Cloth Diaper Options

Finally in agreement, my husband rigged up a diaper sprayer to our toilet and left the purchasing to me. That's where the *really* (ahem) stinky part started because options for cloth diapers are endless—which is great but can also be confusing. While many parents share a desire to be eco, budget or health conscious, we're all different in style, living arrangements and budget. Cloth diapers reflect this: from spendy organics in hip patterns to cost-effective white prefolds; pale baby pastel or bold crimson paired with orange; slick Velcro or trim snaps; elastic, fitted or squared; bamboo, wool or California organic cotton. Homemade, American made, imported, second-hand. Even if green living isn't the main reason for cloth diapering, disposables don't come close to the varieties of styles and colors, fabrics and patterns that have been created by the burgeoning cloth diaper trade. Etsy.com has artists who design diapers in designer paisleys, edgy skull and crossbones or adorable polka dots—fabrics Grandma couldn't have imagined drying in the sun for the neighbors to see.

While searching online, I found Sunshine Diapers, a web diaper store based in Florida, where I could rent a "test drive" set of 12 different brands of diapers in different styles and prices. I chose the set that would work from about three months on as well as a rental set for our newborn—19 ultra soft, ultra small Kissaluvs—the brand recommended to me by Peapods in St. Paul. They required leak-proof covers that I purchased from Pea Pods, where the store assistant said that Kissaluvs are her customer's personal favorite for young babies. This rental test drive option let us practice what fit our lifestyle, our finances and (excuse me, baby girl) my daughter's bum.

And speaking of bums, we decided on BumGenius, which had a fitted diaper that was going out of stock. To save money, I ordered 24 at a great discount from various online stores and paired them with five Thirsties covers. At $12 a cover, they tend to be a mid-range option. And because I love color, I found matching Thirsties diapers in pink, purple, pale green and blue at Linden Hills Natural Store in Minneapolis. Rounding out our diaper stash were all-in-ones by Dream-Eze—my personal Mercedes Benz that haven't lost their shine and still look brand new. Excellent for convenience with a unique snug fit, I bought three (they run almost $20 each) in a deep plummy purple, which look ador-

able under most baby dresses and fit best under slimmer pants (yes, skinny jeans have infiltrated baby clothing). While sweet as non-processed brown sugar, baby legs and bums come in sizes as varied as the cloth diapers available. So try one or two before committing to several.

Diaper Service Option

Not everyone can commit to cloth diapering along with cloth diaper *cleaning*. A local diaper service is a great fit for many families. When my friend Nicole was a law student expecting her quite unexpected little one, she and her husband (who himself was working 30 hours a week while finishing his Master's in Engineering) knew that schlepping diapers up the three flights of stairs between their apartment and the basement laundry wasn't what they'd envisioned when they'd dreamed about being green parents. But finding a diaper service that brought pre-folded diapers freshly laundered to their top step was a timesaving solution that kept their son in cloth for two years.

Make sure to ask the service if they will allow a trial run, what their drop-off guarantees are and how long they've been in business. Although many diaper services closed in 2008, soon thereafter several reasonably priced diaper services sprang up in the metro area, and most have been doing steady business the last few years despite the hardships of small operations. As the co-founder and owner of *Do Good Diapers*, Peter Allen noted, "Babies are pooping through the recession."

Diapering on a Budget

There is more than one way to cloth diaper your baby on a budget. If you prefer the higher end models, consider purchasing them used on Craigslist or diaperswappers.com. If you have time and elementary sewing skills, buy absorbent flannel or cotton, cut and hem them like our grandmothers once did or use a fitted diaper pattern. The lowest cost new diapers are prefolds—squares that fold into threes, stay put with a three-hook connector and fit under any type of leak-proof cover. Prefolds sound like complicated work but I've seen experienced mamas do the simple three-fold with one hand. Cutting down the purchase of wet wipes by using washcloths is another cost saver, unless you opt for the organic cloths I was swooning over until my midwife balked at the price, $16 for 3 cloths: "Sweetie, you can buy 20 washcloths for $1 or cut up an old towel."

Cleaning Your Diapers

Martha Stewart, cover your ears: Cloth diapering doesn't require folding, ironing or much tending. Right after a diaper is soiled, I spray mine with Earth Friendly Product's $3 "Everyday Odor and Stain Remover." In the wash, I use Charlie's Soap, which is safe on high-efficiency washers and requires only 1 T soap, along with 1 T of Oxyclean. Our diapers, diaper bag and washcloths come out of the dryer, into a diaper bag, up the stairs and are tipped full into the bin under our changing table. The diaper bag I carried them up in is wrapped into a $12 diaper pail, ready for more soiled ones. Dump and diaper, baby!

The steps it took me to walk our diaper genie to the garbage probably equals the extra few steps I now take onto the grass where, on a sunny weekend, you might find me hanging rows of baby bottoms on my urban clothesline to bounce in the breeze. It might be easier to use our dryer, but this summer ritual slows my hurried adult pace so I'm in better stride with my children. While she couldn't have imagined them in purple paisley, my grandma might have imagined us more simply, enjoying the summer breeze under a flapping of cloth.

ON THE WEB!

⚙ Diaperswappers.com
Great community to share tips and purchase used diapers,

⚙ Craigslist.com
Be prepared, good used diapers go fast in the Twin Cities market!

⚙ Etsy.com
Find cloth diaper patterns for as little as $3 and lots of new, homemade cloth diapers in any variety of colors, patterns and styles. Good source for wool soakers.

ACT LOCALLY!

Cloth Diapering Services

⚙ Do Good Diapers "We do all the gross stuff," dogooddiapers.com. *Weekly service runs $18-$24 a week. Special "Stripping Service" for home cloth diapering folks. This deep, professional clean is great for those with less than Cadillac washers or poor local water quality. (Chinook Book Coupon offers one week free!)*

⚙ All Things Diapers, allthingsdiapers.com *and on* Facebook Ham Lake, MN 763-439-1973 *3 day trial run, Includes face-to-face cloth diapering demo*

Cloth Diapering Stores

⚙ Linden Hills Natural Home Minneapolis, MN 612-279-2479 lindenhills.coop/naturalhome *Sells low cost pre-folds and lots of Thirsties brand covers and diapers in bright, happy baby colors. (Bring your Chinook Book coupon for $10 off a $50 purchase.) Also find Charlie's Soap at a great price.*

⚙ Peapods St. Paul, MN 651-695-5559 peapods.com *Best selection of Kissaluvs. Always a knowledgeable cloth diaper expert on hand to answer all your questions. Great resource for diaper bags for home and on the go bags. (Chinook Book Coupon—$5 off purchase of $25.)*

A Healthy Family Begins with a Healthy Home

By **PATTY BORN SELLY**
SMALL WONDERS LLC

When we think of creating and maintaining clean homes for healthy families, we often assume "the cleaner the better." But some products that seem helpful can actually be harmful. Did you know that some cleaning products are considered hazardous waste?

From the water we drink, to the foods we eat, to how we maintain our yards and clean our homes, we're exposed to chemicals in many ways. According to the EPA (Environmental Protection Agency), only a small fraction of the more than 75,000 registered chemicals have undergone complete testing for health concerns.

Because their physiology is still undergoing rapid development, children are especially susceptible to the negative effects of chemicals, but even if you don't have kids, it makes sense to reduce your chemical exposure.

What can we do to reduce the toxic chemicals in our homes?

In the bathroom:

- Use a fabric shower curtain instead of a vinyl one. A vinyl shower curtain or liner releases odors and chemical gases into your home. Use a shower curtain made of fabric instead, and wash it over and over for long-term reuse.
- Avoid chemical air fresheners. To freshen the air, open the windows or simmer a blend of essential oils in water. ❧➤

Non-Toxic Cleaning Recipes

Reprinted with permission from the MN Pollution Control Agency

ALL-PURPOSE CLEANER

¼ C white vinegar
2 tsp borax
3½ C hot water
20 drops essential oil
¼ C liquid dish soap

In a 32 oz. spray bottle, mix the vinegar, borax, and water thoroughly. Add essential oil if desired. Add dish soap last.

FLOOR CLEANER

1/8 C liquid soap
¼–½ C white vinegar or lemon juice
½ C herbal tea (peppermint has antibacterial properties)

Combine ingredients in pail with 3 gallons warm water. Swirl until it is sudsy. Rinse with 1 C vinegar in 3 gallons of cool water.

WOOD FLOOR CLEANER

Use ½ C vinegar per gallon of water. Wipe dry.

WOOD CLEANER

¼ C white vinegar
¼ C water
½ tsp liquid soap
A few drops olive oil

Combine the ingredients in a bowl, saturate sponge with the mixture, squeeze out the excess, and wash surfaces. The smell of vinegar will dissipate after a few hours.

CARPET SPOT REMOVER

Blot immediately. Sprinkle with baking soda, cornstarch, or borax and let dry. Wash with club soda and vacuum.

- A solution of straight vinegar is a safe, effective disinfectant and works to kill 99% of mold, germs and bacteria.

In the kitchen:
- A paste of baking soda and water makes a great, fume-free oven cleaner.
- To avoid the need for harsh cleansers and deodorizers, compost your food scraps instead of using a garbage disposal, which most often ends up in the landfill anyways. If odor is a problem and you do need to clean your disposal, use small pieces of lemon or lime rind.

In the playroom:
- Choose wooden or fabric toys instead of plastic. Many chemicals in plastic may have as-yet-unknown health effects on children's bodies.
- Buy local! Different countries have different manufacturing practices. Some chemicals that are banned in the U.S. are permitted in other countries.

In the laundry room:
- Avoid bleach. The fumes are harmful if inhaled, it is corrosive to skin and other surfaces, and it is harmful to our water supply. If whitening is desired, use oxygen cleaners, or mix Borax brand powder with your laundry soap.
- Fresh air is a great fabric softener! Try using a clothesline. Your clothes will smell fresh and feel soft, and you'll conserve energy and save money too.

In the entire home:
- Read labels, and avoid any products with the words "Caution," "Warning," "Danger," or "Poison."
- Buy fewer household chemicals! Save money and your family's health by making your own non-toxic cleaners using the handy recipes listed below.
- Remove carpet. Pollutants, dust, and other nasties can lodge down deep in the fibers of your carpets. Choose hardwood floors or low-pile rugs instead. Vacuum weekly.
- Remove your shoes at the door. Pollutants such as lead, arsenic, and pesticides may be found in soil and tracked into your home
- Houseplants make great, all-natural air purifiers. They can remove chemicals, fumes and other pollutants from the air.

Patty Born Selly is the mother of two young children. An environmental education consultant, she and her family live, work and play in Minneapolis. She may be contacted at patty@smallwondersmn.com.

ON THE WEB!

- Environmental Education Toolkit for Early Childhood Educators (contains activities that you can do as a family to reduce toxicity in the home), rethinkrecycling.com/ECFEtoolkit
- Indoor plants as air purifiers, plant-care.com/indoor-plants-clean-air-1.html

---

READ UP!

- *How to Grow Fresh Air,* by B.C. Wolverton, Penguin Books, 1997.
- *Better Basics for the Home,* by Annie Berthold-Bond, Three Rivers Press, 1999.

WINDOW CLEANER

¼ C white vinegar
½ tsp liquid soap or detergent
2 C water

Combine the ingredients in a spray bottle and shake to blend.

UNCLOG AND DEODORIZE DRAINS

Sprinkle a generous amount of baking soda in and around drain opening. Follow with a cup of white vinegar. Repeat if needed, and finally flush with very hot water.

TOILET BOWL CLEANER

Use Bon Ami cleaner with a non-scratching scrubber sponge.

SOFT SCRUBBER
for basin, tub and tile

½ C baking soda
Enough liquid soap or detergent to make frosting-like consistency
5 to 10 drops antibacterial essential oil

Place baking soda in bowl, and slowly pour in liquid soap, stirring continuously. Add essential oil. Scoop mixture onto sponge, wash surface, and rinse. Bon Ami is another option.

BACTERIA, MOLD, AND GERMS

A 5% solution of vinegar (such as you buy in the store) is effective for eliminating harmful bacteria, mold, and germs. Keep a spray bottle of vinegar in your bathrooms and kitchen.

Borax, non-chlorine bleach, and washing soda can be used by themselves as household cleaners and laundry products in accordance with label instructions. They can also be mixed with certain other products for certain uses. All of these products are harmful if swallowed. Washing soda is not the same as baking soda and should not be used in place of baking soda.

Make Your Own Craft Supplies

By **KATRINA EDENFELD**
DO IT GREEN! MINNESOTA

Homemade salt dough provides two doses of entertainment: first, in sculpting, and later, in painting.

What child of the 1970s doesn't remember dish detergent bubbles? Minnesota winters are an ideal time to experiment with recipes and satisfy creative urges with craft projects. A few simple steps can help you save money and reduce your crafting footprint by cooking up your own nontoxic craft supplies in the kitchen. As these materials contain no preservatives, observe carefully for signs of mold, and store in the refrigerator.

PLAY DOUGH

1 C flour
½ C salt
2 tsp cream of tartar
1 C water
2 T canola oil
food coloring

Mix dry ingredients and wet ingredients in separate bowls. Combine together in a small saucepan and stir over medium heat for several minutes until it forms a ball. Remove to a bowl and cool, then knead until smooth. Store in sealed container.

SALT DOUGH

1 C salt
2 C flour
¾ C to 1 C lukewarm water
1 T canola oil
food coloring (optional)

Mix ingredients together thoroughly, starting with ¾ C water and adding more gradually until it is a kneadable dough. Dough can be shaped by rolling and using cookie cutters, or used as a modeling clay. Place on an upside-down cooling rack and bake at the oven's lowest setting until thoroughly dry on both sides, or allow to air-dry. Paint after drying and cooling using tempera paints. Salt dough does not store well; make only enough for immediate use.

STAMP PAD

Household sponges can be used, but denser foam, available at fabric stores or from repurposed cushions or upholstery foam, will better coat your stamp. Cut a piece to size and place in a lidded container. Soak with tempera paint. Homemade stamps can be cut from a potato; for a more permanent stamp made from rubber bands, see frugalliving.about.com/od/frugalfun/ht/Rubber_Stamps.htm.

FINGER PAINTS

2 T sugar
⅓ C cornstarch
2 C cold water
¼ C clear liquid dish soap
food coloring

Mix sugar and cornstarch in a small saucepan, then slowly add water. Cook over low heat, stirring until the mixture becomes smooth and nearly transparent, about 5 minutes. After it has cooled, stir in dish soap. Divide between small containers and add food coloring as desired.

ON THE WEB!

- Recipes, art lessons and project ideas, kinderart.com
- Tips for crafting-impaired adults, fun.familyeducation.com/childrens-art-activities/crafts/32814.html
- Recipes that serve various crafting purposes, fun.familyeducation.com/crafts/toddler/37042.html

READ UP!

- *Mudworks: Creative Clay, Dough, and Modeling Experiences*, by MaryAnn F. Kohl, Bright Ring Publishing, 1989.
- *Art with Anything: 52 Weeks of Fun Using Everyday Stuff*, by MaryAnn F. Kohl, Gryphon House, 2010.

ACT LOCALLY!

- ArtStart ArtScraps, St. Paul, MN 651-698-2787, artstart.org
- Minneapolis Institute of Arts Minneapolis, MN 888-642-2787, artsmia.org
  See the calendar for Family Days

Cooking with Children

By **KATRINA EDENFELD**
DO IT GREEN! MINNESOTA

Cooking food is a rewarding, basic life skill that every individual should possess. What better time to start than as a child? Kids love to help and do the things that they see adults doing, even if it's just work to us. Even toddlers will have fun stirring, measuring, and helping as they develop motor skills and dexterity, learn math, and see how ingredients are transformed into meals. Children will learn that it can be simple, fun, and sociable to work together in the kitchen.

Consider the steps that go into a typical recipe: measure, add ingredients, stir, knead, grate, cut, clean up—any recipe can be adapted for our young—or not-so-young—helpers. Even the simplest meals, such as scrambled eggs, have opportunities for helpers (smashing the yolks is fun!). Adults should use their best judgment to determine when children are ready for potential hazards such as paring knives, graters, ovens, and stoves.

The most important thing to do when cooking with children is to relax. Relax about measuring, relax about mixing, and relax about the mess. Most recipes do not require extremely precise measurement, and any spills are easily taken care of after mixing. If you can relax when the spills happen, your helper might even want to help with cleanup!

HOMEMADE GRANOLA

Instead of buying cereal in a big bag and box, make your own in less time than it takes to wait in the grocery checkout. Cost comparison: You can make 2 large batches of granola from a 42-ounce oatmeal container, which runs about $2.50, the least that you'll pay for a one 15-ounce box of cereal. Taste comparison: No contest!

Kids can: measure, pour, stir, and spread.

6–8 C old fashioned rolled oats (use smaller quantity for sweeter granola)
1 T cinnamon

¼ C honey (can increase if desired, but this is enough)
¼ C canola oil (ditto)

Preheat oven to 300° F and oil two baking sheets. Mix the dry ingredients in a large bowl. Mix the wet ingredients and warm slightly in a pot or the microwave. Pour over the dry ingredients and mix well. Spread on the baking sheets. Stir after 20 minutes, and remove from the oven after 40 minutes. Let cool and store in a container in the refrigerator.

Optional additions:
½ C wheat germ: add at beginning with oats
coconut: add toward the end of baking time (look for unsweetened, preservative-free coconut in bulk at natural foods stores)
nuts and dried fruit: add after removing from the oven

HELPER'S DINNER: SALAD AND BREAD

Bread, Pretzels, Rolls, or Pizza Dough

Kneading and shaping dough is fun even for tiny hands! Allow about five hours from beginning to end for a loaf of bread. This basic dough can also be used for soft pretzels, rolls, or pizza.

Kids can: observe yeast action, measure, pour, knead, shape.

For 1 pound of dough (one loaf, about 12 rolls, or one 14-inch pizza crust), use:

1 C lukewarm water
2 tsp active dry or instant yeast
3 C flour (can substitute up to 1 C whole grain flour without significant changes; 100% whole grain dough becomes easier with experience)
1 T sugar or honey (optional)
1 tsp salt

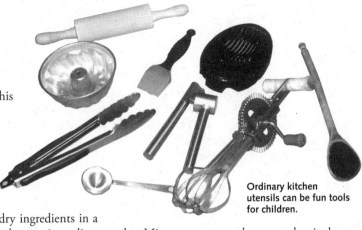
Ordinary kitchen utensils can be fun tools for children.

Mix yeast, sugar, and water and wait about 5 minutes to view yeast bloom (a learning moment). Stir in 2 C flour and mix thoroughly. Add more flour, slowly, until the dough is too thick to stir, then place it on a cutting board or in a large bowl to knead. Add flour slowly until dough is no longer extremely sticky, and then give it to your helper to finish the kneading. Pull, push, and turn your way around the dough. Form it into a ball, place in an oiled bowl, cover, and let rise in a warm place until doubled. Form into a loaf, either using a pan or freeform on a baking sheet. Allow the dough to rise a second time while preheating the oven to 450° F. Place bread in oven and after 10 minutes, reduce temperature to 350° F. Bake an additional 35 minutes. Smaller loaves can also be made and will require less baking time.

MAKE YOUR OWN SALAD

Kids love to make their own food—even when it's full of vegetables! Salad ingredients can be prepared ahead of time and refrigerated until dinner, making this a lightning-fast option for a busy afternoon.

Kids can: choose and wash vegetables; older children can assist in the chopping.

Lettuce
Vegetables: spinach, arugula, carrots, zucchini, celery, onion, bell pepper, squash, cucumber, jicama, cabbage. Some vegetables may be preferred when lightly steamed, such as kale or broccoli. ❧➤

Cooking with Children, CONTINUED

Fruit, fresh or dried
Nuts, sunflower, or pumpkin seeds if
   desired

Dressing options: Kids can shake a simple salad dressing ·in an unbreakable container—look for a vinaigrette or ranch in your favorite cookbook, and skip all the additives of purchased dressings.

Prepare the salad ingredients, placing each chopped vegetable in a separate container. Diners can assemble their own salads at the table. It is amazing how many vegetables can disappear in a meal like this!

ON THE WEB!

- Suggested activities by age, nhlbi.nih.gov/health/public/heart/obesity/wecan/downloads/cookwithchildren.pdf
- Articles about cooking with children, examiner.com/x-31662-Minneapolis-Cooking-With-Kids-Examiner

READ UP!

- *Salad People and More Real Recipes: A New Cookbook for Preschoolers and Up*, by Mollie Katzen, Tricycle Press, 2005.
- *Eat Fresh Food: Awesome Recipes for Teen Chefs*, by Rozanne Gold, Bloomsbury USA, 2009.

ACT LOCALLY!

- Whole Foods Markets
  Minneapolis, MN
  wholefoodsmarket.com/storesbeta/minneapolis/store-calendar/
  Check the calendar for kid-oriented cooking classes.
- Way Cool Cooking School
  Eden Prairie, MN
  951-949-6799
  waycoolcookingschool.com/content/view/91/49
  Classes for all ages—from parent & child to teens and adults

Summer camps and cooking parties:

- Kitchen Window, Minneapolis, MN
  Camps and Classes for Young Chefs
- Your friends!
- Form a Kids Cook group of your own.

Eating "Slow" for Dinner

By **SARA GROCHOWSKI**
DO IT GREEN! MINNESOTA

In certain countries and cultures, a meal can last for hours. People sit around a table, whole extended families gather, and they talk, eat and drink late into the evening. In the U.S., that just doesn't happen as often. The average American meal is eleven minutes long—with some breakfasts and lunches lasting barely two minutes. Even more surprising is that 19% of all meals and snacks are eaten in the car, according to a researcher at the Culinary Institute of America.

The Slow Food movement officially started in 1989 with the founding of Slow Food International to counteract fast food and fast life, the disappearance of local food traditions and people's dwindling interest in the food they eat, where it comes from, how it tastes and how our food choices affect the rest of the world. Slow Food is all about taking the time to savor the food we eat and the people we share it with. When our food is produced in a sustainable, responsible and conscientious manner, it is healthier for the environment and healthier for us. Family life can be busy, so the importance of eating slow is imperative both of each person's health and the health of the family unit.

Better nutrition and digestion

When you eat slowly, you give yourself a chance to taste the food and digest it well. The body uses enzymes and bacteria to break down food at various stages. There are enzymes in your saliva that begin the process. It is easier to break down smaller pieces of food than larger ones. Fully chewing your food keeps your digestive system from working overtime trying to break it down to a manageable size.

Better food choices

When you eat slowly, you end up tasting your food more. This is good because the more you pay attention to your foods, the more you will prefer natural, healthy foods. Most factory-produced foods are carefully designed by food engineers to taste great for the first three or so bites. After that the food begins to taste bland and uninteresting. You feel an urge to eat another cookie or potato chip after just a few chews. Natural foods, on the other hand, stay interesting as you chew them. A strawberry starts out with a burst of juice, but then stays interesting as you chew. Oranges, nuts and vegetables are the same.

Be more social

Eating can be a social event. Meals are a time when people gather and spend time together. Once the meal is over, everyone goes their separate ways. By taking more time at a meal, you'll be able to talk more with your friends and family, improve relationships and feel more connected.

Stop before you're full

It takes your stomach about 20 minutes to produce the hormones that tell your brain you are full. This process doesn't start until your stomach begins to stretch. If you slow down, you give yourself more time to feel full. This gives you a better chance of stopping before you "get stuffed."

ON THE WEB!

- Slow Food International, slowfood.com

READ UP!

- The Heavy Table e-magazine, heavytable.com
- *Renewing America's Food Traditions*, by Gary Paul Nabhan, Chelsea Green Publishing, 2008.

ACT LOCALLY!

- Slow Food Minnesota
  Minneapolis, MN
  slowfoodmn.org
- Institute for Agriculture and Trade Policy
  Minneapolis, MN, 612-870-0453
  iatp.org

Your Health: Slow and Steady Wins the Race

By **JILL GRUNEWALD**
HOLISTIC HEALTH COUNSELOR

There was a time in the not too distant past when choosing what to eat was simple. It entailed a jaunt to the garden or orchard and harvesting what was in season or venturing to the cellar for canned green beans or peaches. Meats were processed at the local butcher and cured for longevity. Maybe you traded raspberries for apples with a neighbor.

Until the proliferation of food processing, standardization, and packaging in the late 19th century, trading, foraging for, or growing your own food was a way of life for most Americans. People spent a great deal of time planting, tending livestock, harvesting, preparing, and preserving. It was a matter of survival and while undoubtedly stressful at times, the sunshine and physical activity that accompanied the procuring of your own whole, unadulterated foods lent itself to a natural lifestyle much different than what most of us experience today.

The Luxury of Convenience?

Nowadays, we have foods from numerous climates and cultures at our fingertips and aisles of ready-made meals and snacks proudly displayed in a kaleidoscope of packaging. Our choices are nothing short of staggering, yet things are more complicated. Sadly, much of what is in processed foods does not deserve to be called food. Add to this a dizzying array of choices and diet gurus touting "the way" and we're left overwhelmed with information and understandably confused about what to eat. According to Michael Pollan, author of *Food Rules*, "But for all the scientific and pseudoscientific food baggage we've taken on in recent years, we *still* don't know what we should be eating."

We're busy being busy, and for many folks food procurement and preparation have taken a backseat to our modern day priorities. We're working long hours. We're commuting long distances. Both parents work outside of the home. No wonder

we've become intoxicated with the post-World War II "heat it and eat it" culture. According to Marc David, visionary nutrition consultant and author of *The Slow Down Diet* and *Nourishing Wisdom*, "Many people are caught in a bind of what I call the one-minute eater. For these people, nourishment is secondary to taking care of business. Eating is no longer a basic need but a nuisance to be squeezed into the schedule."

Today, we're generally sicker, more stressed, and less physically fit than our forebears, and have transferred the food-on-demand mentality to healthcare. We don't have time to be sick, and there is always a well-intentioned doctor ready to write a prescription for what ails us. The problem is that many pharmaceuticals have serious side effects and most merely mask symptoms, instilling a false sense of security and leaving the inflammatory condition to lurk within. Not since the polio vaccine was developed in 1952 has modern ↪

medicine "cured" any ailment. It has arguably improved quality of life and perhaps extended life, but there exists no drug that cures any of our modern diseases.

They Don't Make 'Em Like They Used To

Most supermarket bread is not what bread used to be. It's full of high fructose corn syrup, a sweetener from corn that the body doesn't know how to digest, and contains highly processed grains, stripped of any nutritional integrity. Conventional meat isn't what meat used to be. It's full of growth hormones and antibiotics (from abused animals, but that's another story), which have been linked to early puberty and antibiotic resistance. Conventional produce is not what produce used to be. It's genetically modified, irradiated, prematurely harvested, and sprayed with chemical pesticides.

Herein lies our true health crisis. While indeed, there are folks who regularly eat fast and packaged foods, there are others who are eating what they believe to be whole foods, but the processing and adulteration these foods have undergone is compromising their health. Many are unaware of what our bigger, faster, cheaper food culture is doing to our collective well-being.

The devastating impact of processed convenience foods has contributed to overwhelming rates of degenerative disease, including obesity and Type II diabetes. I would argue that the processing of conventional, mass-produced meat, dairy, and produce has significantly contributed to this crisis. Add to this our modern stresses and a sedentary lifestyle, and we've got a recipe for an unhealthy society. According to Dr. Kara Parker of the Family Medical Center in Minneapolis, "Humans used to get up and go to bed with the sun and spend their days outside eating whole, fresh foods. Periods of stress were short. Today, stressors are constant: busy lifestyles, bad diets, lack of sleep."

How Did We Get Here?

When it comes to degenerative diseases, it should be understood that it takes a long time to become ill. What came about over time cannot be resolved overnight. The beautiful thing is that with a commitment to healing, patience, and informed food and lifestyle choices, most diseases are reversible. The body is an amazing machine, always seeking homeostasis and constantly looking to rebalance itself. With proper nutrients from clean, whole foods, adequate sleep, stress reduction, and the right exercise, what can happen is nothing less than miraculous. According to Dr. Joseph Mercola, also known as The Ultimate Wellness Game Changer, "What the drug industry and the FDA absolutely do not want you to learn is that healing foods, herbs, and supplements make virtually all pharmaceuticals obsolete."

A Grain of Hope

With the proliferation of recent films such as *King Corn, Fresh,* and *Food, Inc.*, and Michael Pollan's bestselling book *The Omnivore's Dilemma*, my sincere hope is that more people understand what has become of the food industry in this country. There is undoubtedly a local, organic, sustainable foods groundswell bubbling, and fortunately, Minnesota is leading the pack in many respects.

Since the early 1970s, we've made strides in a creating a healthier and more sustainable food system, but there is much work to be done. People have become increasingly concerned about how their food is grown and who grows it. In my estimation, it's nearing fever pitch and we're in for a food movement. Not a trend, but a much-needed movement. A recent Context Marketing ethical food study showed that 69% of us were willing to pay more for ethically produced food.

The recent downturn in the economy, while difficult, has encouraged many folks to get back to basics and back into their kitchens. People are growing gardens and preserving, young people are farming, more people are biking to work, vacations are spent simply enjoying the outdoors, the unemployed are finding time to get fit, and people are accepting their situations and eschewing their former high-stress lifestyles for something simpler. I'm convinced that the economy will turn around, but fortunately, the sustainable food and health movement is steamrolling forward.

What You Can Do:

- Buy locally grown foods and other locally produced products
- Grow a garden
- Take a cooking class
- Shop at your local farmers' market
- Take a food preservation class
- Join a community garden
- Bike to work
- Compost
- Become a member of and shop at your local cooperative grocery store
- Buy a share in a CSA (community supported agriculture)
- Do 10 minutes of deep breathing every day
- Say no to more things
- Get regular exercise that's right for your body
- Eat only whole, unprocessed grains
- Eat as much organic grains, produce, meat, and dairy as your budget will allow
- Dine at restaurants that feature local and sustainable foods
- Host a screening of the movie *Fresh*

ON THE WEB!

- Local Harvest, localharvest.org
- Eat Well Guide, eatwellguide.org

READ UP!

- *Food Rules,* by Michael Pollan, Penguin Books, 2009.
- *Nourishing Wisdom,* by Marc David, Bell Tower, 1991.

ACT LOCALLY!

- Weston A. Price Foundation Washington, DC 202-363-4394 westonaprice.org
- Minnesota Grown St. Paul, MN 651-201-6648 www3.mda.state.mn.us/mngrown

What Are Healing Gardens?

Used with permission from the **TAKING CHARGE OF YOUR HEALTH** *website, a consumer health resource created by the* CENTER FOR SPIRITUALITY & HEALING *and the* LIFE SCIENCE FOUNDATION. *For more information, please visit: takingcharge.csh.umn.edu.*

Why are some gardens called healing gardens, when it seems as though all gardens (and nature) are intrinsically appealing and beneficial to humans?

The term healing gardens is most often applied to green spaces in hospitals and other healthcare facilities that specifically aim to improve health outcomes. These gardens provide a place of refuge and promote healing in patients, families, and staff.

According to two leaders in this field, Clare Cooper Marcus and Marni Barnes, healing comes because the gardens promote:

- Relief from symptoms
- Stress reduction
- Improvement in overall sense of well-being and hopefulness

Any environment can promote healing, but gardens are particularly able to do so because humans are hard-wired to find nature engrossing and soothing.

Healing gardens differ somewhat from therapeutic landscapes, another term used in healthcare. Therapeutic landscapes or gardens are designed to meet the particular needs of a specific patient population. They often engage that population actively and deliberately. Healing gardens, on the other hand, generally aim for a more passive involvement and are designed to provide benefits to a diverse population with different needs.

What health benefits does viewing nature offer?

Nature provides a great distraction. Because we are genetically programmed to find nature engrossing, we are absorbed by nature scenes and distracted from our pain and discomfort.

Nature reduces stress and anxiety. One explanation for this is that nature provides a respite from the constant effort to screen out competing stimuli in our busy lives. Because humans find nature inherently engrossing, we don't have to make an effort

Marianna Padilla, Urban Gardening and Health Instructor, in her Minneapolis backyard.

to focus when presented with natural views. This reduces mental fatigue and refreshes the mind.

Another idea is that plants offer psychological comfort. As one researcher in this area says, "Plants take away some of the anxiety and tension of the immediate now by showing us that there are long, enduring patterns in life." Their growth is steady and progressive, not erratic.

While there are various theories why nature is so helpful, there is no variance in the outcomes. We know that viewing plants, flowers, water, and other nature elements reduces patient anxiety, even if the patients are very anxious.

The benefits of nature hold even for confirmed city dwellers. In a study of cardiac patients in New York who were shown various scenes, anxiety was reduced the most in those who saw a nature scene and heard a soundtrack of water, birds, and breezes.

In addition to the psychological benefits, reducing patient stress and anxiety has concrete physical benefits. This is nicely demonstrated in a study of patients who

underwent gallbladder surgery: half had a view of nature and half had a view of a wall. The half with the nature view tolerated pain better, slept better, reported less stress, and spent less time in a hospital.

Thus, it is no wonder that the Center for Health Design identifies nature as one of the key factors that reduces patient and staff stress and leads to better outcomes and staff satisfaction.

In addition, the Joint Commission for Accreditation of Hospitals (JCAHO) recommends that "Patients and visitors should have opportunities to connect with nature through outside spaces, plants, indoor atriums and views from windows."

Of course nature can benefit everyone, not just those in hospitals. One fascinating study reported that tenants in Chicago public housing who had trees around their buildings reported knowing more people, having stronger feelings of unity with neighbors, becoming more concerned with helping and supporting each other, and having stronger feelings of belonging than tenants in buildings without trees. The findings also showed less violence in buildings with tress than in those without trees.

Gardens provide distractions, reduce stress, and promote a sense of well-being. This leads to measurable psychological, physiological, and behavioral benefits, such as reduced anxiety, sadness, and other negative moods, lower blood pressure and improved immune function, and better compliance with treatment protocol.

ON THE WEB!

- Sustainable Urban Landscape Information Series, sustland.umn.edu/design/healinggardens.html
- Minnesota's Center for Spirituality and Healing, csh.umn.edu

Learn Stress Reduction Techniques

Used with permission from the **TAKING CHARGE OF YOUR HEALTH** *website,*
a consumer health resource created by the CENTER FOR SPIRITUALITY & HEALING *and the* LIFE SCIENCE FOUNDATION.
For more information, please visit: takingcharge.csh.umn.edu.

There are many ways to enhance your healthy behaviors and reduce your reliance on destructive habits. To start, learn how to turn off your body's "fight or flight" reflex through breathing, exercise, relaxation techniques, and mental or emotional reframing practices.

Realize that it takes practice to achieve ultimate benefit from any relaxation technique. Know also that your body can fight better when it is fit, so it's very important to eat well, get adequate rest, and exercise regularly.

Here are some simple stress-reducing strategies to help you on your quest for stress mastery:

Practice Mindful Relaxation

Mindful relaxation is an effective way to combat stress. With a little practice, you can learn how to shift into a relaxation mode. When done successfully, the relaxation response increases alpha brain wave activity; lowers blood pressure, pulse, respiration rate, metabolic rate, oxygen consumption, and anxiety; and produces a greater sense of well-being.

Over time, you will develop an ability to shift into a more relaxed state in the midst of stressful situations.

- Commit to an uninterrupted length of time each day to do your practice. You might begin with five minutes, and increase from there. Twenty minutes of relaxation once or twice a day is optimal.
- Choose a quiet place. Turn off the television, radio, computer, and telephone.
- Find a comfortable body position. You can sit or recline in a chair, or settle comfortably on the floor. Make sure you feel supported.
- Focus on the repetition of a word, sound, prayer, or your breath flowing in and out.
- Create a positive state of mind. While you may not always be able to block out worries or negative thoughts, don't attach to them. Let them float by like clouds in the sky.

Try Breathing Techniques

Another way to master stress is to be aware of your breathing. When people feel panicked or unconsciously stressed, they tend to take short, shallow gasps of air. The resulting lack of oxygen restricts blood flow and causes muscles to tense. By allowing more air to enter your body, you slow down your heart rate, lower your blood pressure, and break the stress cycle.

Try the following Two-Minute Relaxation breathing technique:
- Focus your attention on your breathing.

Take a few deep breaths, exhaling slowly.
- Mentally scan your body. Notice areas that feel tense or cramped. Quietly loosen them. Let go of as much tension as you can.
- Rotate your head in a smooth, circular motion once or twice, avoiding any movements that cause pain.
- Roll your shoulders forward and backward several times. Let all of your muscles completely relax.
- Recall a pleasant thought, event, or place.
- Take deep breaths and exhale slowly.

Use Imagery

Imagery exercises use creative imagination to "picture" scenarios that relax and heal. They can be done on your own, or with a facilitator guiding you, which is called *guided imagery.*

A common relaxation practice is to mentally picture yourself in a pleasant place that puts your mind and body at ease. For example, imagine yourself lying on a beach with the sun shining, listening to the waves. It is important to imagine a place that has a positive association for you (an ocean beach may not be a pleasant place for everyone).

Another use of imagery is when cancer patients imagine their healthy cells eating and destroying cancerous cells. Studies done with cancer patients show that the use of guided imagery markedly improves stress levels.

Add Body Exercises

Having awareness of where you store stress in your body is another important part of stress reduction. Learn how to release tension in your body by trying the following exercises.
- Body scan
- Progressive muscle relaxation (deliberately apply tension to certain muscle groups, and then stop the tension and turn your attention to noticing how the muscles relax as the tension flows away)
- Shoulder and neck relaxation

◆► *Stress Reduction,* CONTINUED

In addition, mindful movement practices such as yoga, tai chi, and qi gong are excellent for reducing body tension and stress and increasing flexibility and equanimity. These exercises are becoming increasingly popular and common, and are available at many local community centers, schools, and health clubs.

Consider Biofeedback

Biofeedback uses a measuring device to assess how relaxed you are and teach how to relax more effectively. Biofeedback equipment monitors systems of which you are not normally aware, such as blood pressure, pulse, temperature, and brain wave patterns. As you practice biofeedback, you develop the ability to change these systems (for example, lower your blood pressure).

You can try a simple biofeedback exercise on your own, using a thermometer as a guide. Hold a thermometer between your index finger and thumb, and note the temperature. Then, complete one of the relaxation techniques previously described.

After your session, measure your temperature again and see if it changes in response to the relaxation exercises.

If you are interested in further exploring biofeedback, consult with a psychologist or other health provider who works with it.

> ### ON THE WEB!
> ⚙ Minnesota's Center for Spirituality and Healing, csh.umn.edu

Your Body's Requirement for Iron

By **JENNETTE TURNER**
NATURAL FOODS EDUCATOR

I n my private practice counseling people on dietary issues, I see many vegetarians who are concerned about getting a balanced diet. And well they should be. Meat is a very nutrient-dense food; if you're not going to eat it, be sure you're getting those nutrients elsewhere. Meats are our best source of iron, so vegetarians need to make sure their diets are supplying them with adequate amounts of this important nutrient.

Iron deficiency is the most common nutritional deficiency in the U.S. for vegetarians and non-vegetarians alike. Men need about 9 milligrams (mg) per day, while women need 18 mg, and pregnant women need 27 mg. Younger children require about 10 mg per day. Lower iron levels can make you feel tired, unmotivated, and short on energy. Iron deficiency can also manifest as difficulty with cognitive tasks, shortened attention span, fatigue, apathy and sullenness. It can also affect the way your red blood cells function.

There are 2 kinds of iron: *heme iron* from animal foods and *non-heme iron* from plants. Non-heme iron isn't as easily absorbed as heme iron is: our bodies can only use around 15–20% of it. Heme iron is almost 90% absorbable. Vegetarian (non-heme) iron sources include legumes, molasses, beets, kale, raisins, sea vegetables and cooking with cast iron cookware. One thing you can do to increase absorption is consume these foods at a meal that also includes vitamin C-rich foods such as citrus fruits, tomatoes, bell peppers and

sauerkraut.

For people with low iron diets, including vegetarians, it's also important to limit caffeine, which can cut iron absorption by as much as 50%. This can be a vicious cycle: if you're low in iron you'll feel tired and maybe headachey, and want a cup of coffee or tea or a soft drink to perk you up, which then depletes you further, which makes you want more caffeine—and the cycle continues.

Attention should also be paid to the proper preparation for whole grains and legumes, as both of these wholesome foods can interfere with iron absorption. Whole grains and legumes contain an anti-nutrient called phytic acid that binds with iron, making it unusable. Soaking the grains and legumes for 8–24 hours before using them can neutralize the phytic acid. Traditional sourdough breads are phytic acid-free, too.

For soybeans, fermentation is the only way to neutralize the phytic acid they contain. Tempeh, miso, tamari and shoyu are all fermented soy products. Soy milk, tofu,

edamame, soy protein and all the imitation meats and dairy products made from soy contain ample phytic acid and should be avoided. These pseudo-foods are harmful to the endocrine system, digestive system and thyroid, so you'll be much better off without them.

Iron is too important to risk deficiency. Make sure you're getting enough!

Jennette Turner is a natural foods educator in the Twin Cities. Information about her workplace classes, private consultations and her online meal planning service, Dinner with Jennette, can be found at www.jennette-turner.com.

> ### ON THE WEB!
> ⚙ eatwild.com
> ⚙ westonaprice.org
> ⚙ wholefarmcoop.com

> ### READ UP!
> ⚙ *Caffeine Blues,* by Stephen Cherniske, New York, 1998.
> ⚙ *Nourishing Traditions,* by Sally Fallon, San Diego, 1995.
> ⚙ *The Vegetarian Myth,* by Lierre Keith, Oakland, 2009.
> ⚙ *Full Moon Feast,* by Jessica Prentice, White River Junction, 2006.

The Place for Superfoods in Real Health

By **DEBORAH SAVRAN**

Reprinted with permission from themix.coop

W hat is it that raises a food from mere mortal status up to "superfood" status?

Must they be foreign or exotic-sounding, like goji berries, acai berries, spirulina, bee pollen, pomegranate, or noni juice? Is it compelling research studies that make the transformation occur? Is there any consistency in their definition? I can easily find a plethora of lists of the "top 10 superfoods" from various nutrition gurus, and these lists are quite varied, with none that I've found having the exact same foods listed. Of course, there are many more than 10 foods that can be considered to be the most beneficial for us, and one could argue that all brightly colored fruits and vegetables are superfoods.

It is also true that some foods are remarkably beneficial for overall health or for a particular condition. If all we do is focus on trying to consume a short list of the latest fad super foods in an otherwise unbalanced diet, the benefits will be limited. There may even be detriment if a single food is eaten in excessive quantities. For us to make our own transformation from dietary mediocrity to super-nourishment, the focus must be on incorporating into a balanced diet a wide variety of the most healthful foods that suit our individual needs. Will the Real Superfoods please Stand Up?

Every few months there seems to be a new food that is all the rage among those who believe, or want us to believe, that a single food can bring miraculous nutritional benefits to all. Marketing for these foods includes numerous health claims, with weight loss frequently being among them. Furthermore, these are often foods that are not available fresh but only in juiced, dried or powdered forms, and at high prices. Feel free to enjoy them for their health benefits, but it's also important to be educated about their use and consumption.

- Where did these foods come from?
- Have they been ethically harvested and traded?

- Are the health claims associated with them more a marketing ploy or are they based upon solid research from peer-reviewed journals or traditional knowledge?
- Are they being consumed in compensation for a generally unhealthy diet?

The appeal of these superfoods is surely based, in part, on nutritional truths. What they commonly do have is high levels of one or more valuable phytochemicals. Phytochemicals are naturally occurring, nonessential nutrients. They are relatively new discoveries in the world of food science. New phytochemicals are being discovered almost daily, and many are extremely beneficial nutrients in preventing cancers, reducing inflammation, lowering cholesterol and blood pressure, preventing heart disease, regulating metabolism, or preventing other degenerative and life-threatening diseases. Some examples of phytochemicals you may have heard of are polyphenols, carotenoids, phytoestrogens, flavonoids, and lignans, but we are only beginning to understand the thousands of phytochemicals and the complexities of how they protect and heal our bodies. Fortunately, phytochemicals are present in many familiar, fresh and

locally available foods, and not just those growing in distant lands. Perhaps these are our true superfoods, based both upon particular phytochemicals they may generously contain, and on the food itself as a whole—its flavors, its growing conditions, what we know about what it offers us and the mysteries it has yet to reveal.

Lists that propose the "top foods" often narrow down to select one super-member from a group of truly super foods, such as selecting broccoli out of the *Brassica* family. Rather than narrowing down to one top food in a group, I propose to expand out and reinforce that any food from these phytochemical-rich groups listed below improves our diet in ways we are only beginning to understand. Blueberries may be the most super of the berries (or at least have the most research about them) but all berries, including cranberries, raspberries, boysenberries, blackberries, strawberries, fresh or frozen, are rich in protective phytochemicals. Berries support healthy metabolism, since they are low in glycemic load. Toss them into smoothies, on salads, with cereal or on their own.

Dark Leafy Greens: lightly cooked spinach, kale, and chard are top members of this family and contain indoles, carotenoids, and isothiocyanates.

Cruciferous vegetables: broccoli, cauliflower, Brussels sprouts, and bok choy are particularly valuable foods in this family and are rich in flavonoids.

Orange and yellow fruits and vegetables: rich in carotenoids and flavonoids are pumpkins, carrots, sweet potatoes, cantaloupe, and nectarines. The phytochemicals in orange and yellow vegetables are best assimilated when lightly cooked.

Whole grains: contain phytochemicals such as lignans, phenolic acids and phytosterols. Best choices are brown rice, basmati rice, wild rice, oats, quinoa and barley.

Nuts and seeds: walnuts, almonds, flax seeds and hemp seeds are among the best. They are rich in lignans and essential fatty acids.

Oily fish: wild Alaskan sockeye salmon, herring and sardines provide essential omega-3 fatty acids and are highly anti-inflammatory foods.

Tea: green, oolong and white teas are rich in the anti-oxidant compounds catechins.

Legumes and beans: black and adzuki beans, and chickpeas and lentils are wonderful vegetarian sources of quality protein, are rich in soluble fiber, have a low glycemic load, and contain the valuable phytochemicals isoflavones and phytosterols.

Other foods not in these groups, but worthy of superfood mention due to bountiful phytochemical and vitamin and mineral content include pomegranates, grapes, oranges, apples, pears, cherries, beets, onions, garlic, sea vegetables, raw salad greens, Chinese mushrooms and dark chocolate.

Don't Stop There! What Is a Balanced Diet?

The definition of a balanced diet is multifaceted. It encompasses an understanding of nutrition and a practice of eating that can continually be enhanced, and includes:

- **A rainbow of foods of as many different colors** (natural colors, that is!) as possible each day. The brilliant hues of foods are the result of phytochemicals, so deeply colored foods offer us beauty and goodness in one.
- **Supplements:** not as substitutes for whole foods, but as insurance against potential gaps in our diet. Products such as noni juice, acai berry juice, or mangosteen are perhaps better defined as supplements than foods, and so if you choose to take them, think of them as supplements, rather than as a food serving.
- **Assimilation of nutrients**, and metabolism through mindful, slow eating, helping to turn on the parasympathetic (the "rest and digest") nervous system. This can also help with improved awareness of satiety and thus the avoidance of overeating.
- **Foods that have meaning** to us as individuals from our family's traditions and our cultural customs.
- **Avoiding as much as possible refined sugar**, white-flour products, non-traditional soy products, hydrogenated and partially hydrogenated oils and generic vegetable oils, highly processed food, artificial ingredients, high-fructose corn syrup, chemical additives, and preservatives.

If these guidelines for a balanced diet are followed, even without any knowledge of phytochemicals and individual components of foods, the results will still promote vibrant health. Once you are committed to eating a truly balanced diet, then fine-tune it by educating yourself to be sure you are regularly including food from groups that have been found to be the very best at promoting health. Go the distance and learn tasty and enjoyable ways to cook and creatively incorporate these truly super gifts from the Earth effectively and easily, so that they can become an integral part of your diet and a vibrantly healthy lifestyle.

Deborah Savran is a naturopath and Maya Abdominal Massage practitioner. She is passionate about offering creative healing arts, including herbalism, energetic bodywork, sound healing, mindfulness practices, movement and nutrition, to support women in the journey to balance and wellness. She practices at Blooma, a yoga and wellness center.

ON THE WEB

- Dr. Andrew Weil's Anti-inflammatory Food Pyramid, drweil.com/drw/u/ART02995/Dr-Weil-Anti-inflammatory-Food-Pyramid.html
- U.S. Department of Agriculture Food Pyramid, mypyramid.gov
- Weston A. Price Foundation, westonaprice.org

READ UP!

- *Power Foods*, by Stephanie Beling, Harper Collins, 1997.
- *The Slow Down Diet*, by Mark David, Healing Arts Press, 2005.
- *The Encyclopedia of Healing Foods*, by Michael Murray, and Joseph Pizzorno, Atria Books, 2005.
- *SuperFoods HealthStyle*, by Steven Pratt and Kathy Matthews, Harper Collins, 2006.
- *Superfoods Rx*, by Steven Pratt and Kathy Matthews, Harper Collins, 2004.
- *Eating Well for Optimal Health*, by Andrew Weil, Random House, 2000.

Managing Eco-Anxiety

By **AARON VEHLING**

What can recycling a pop can or buying a compact fluorescent bulb really do? What's the point when there are up four million gallons of oil spilling into the Gulf of Mexico on a daily basis? What does it matter when the oceans' "dead zones" are growing and the rainforests are shrinking?

It can be overwhelming to maintain a green lifestyle when it seems that our small contributions are no match for environmental disasters and slow deaths that humankind is perpetuating all over the world. So what's the solution? Give up because, well, we're so far into the abyss anyway?

"Sometimes I feel like my own little contributions don't matter," says Jennifer Valmer of Burnsville. "Why would I recycle paper or my pop bottles when I'm up against all these problems? Maybe I should just throw my pop can away because everyone else seems to."

Licensed clinical social worker and therapist Ellen Bilanow-Wilcock has some pithy advice for people like Valmer: keep it simple. "Take it one day at a time," Bilanow-Wilcock says, adding that you should focus using "this is what I can control today and what I can't control today. Allow yourself

to feel good about what you did do today." In addition, she says, you have to acknowledge that you are anxious in the first place. "Anyone who is seriously paying attention is going to feel overwhelmed," she says. "Validate that."

Author Jen Pleasants has written "Bag Green Guilt, Five Easy Steps: Turn Eco-Anxiety into Constructive Energy." The book analyzes the emotional spectrum of green living and offers a five-step program to provide a sense of calm. The steps are relatively simple: breathe, acknowledge and affirm, write, act and praise.

What Pleasants attempts, she says in the book, is not to provide yet another laundry list of material lifestyle changes that adhere to a certain "green" aesthetic. Her goal with those steps is to address the reader's state of mind. "I wanted to inspire readers to transform their feelings of guilt and anxiety into power and action," Pleasants writes.

Bilanow-Wilcock's advice reflects an agreement with Pleasants. Bilanow-Wilcock says that one major way to feel as if your small contributions matter is to act. "Donating time and energy can feel good," she says. "Joining some kind of movement or bigger group can give you more power, too." The

advantage to joining a group of people with a common set of goals, she adds, is the support system. It is an old adage in support groups and self-help books, but it rings true: you are not alone.

By sharpening your focus to your own microcosm, you may find that your own inner strength emanates outward. In her book, Pleasants quotes a monk who struggled with his own eco-anxiety: "When I was a young man, I wanted to change the world. I found it was difficult to change the world, so I tried to change my nation. When I found I couldn't change my nation, I began to focus on my town. I couldn't change the town and as an older man, I tried to change my family. Now, as an old man, I realize the only thing I can change is myself, and suddenly I realize that if long ago I had changed myself, I could have made an impact on my family. My family and I could have made an impact on our town.

"Their impact could have changed the nation and I could indeed have changed the world."

ON THE WEB!

- Eco-Anxiety, eco-anxiety.blogspot.com
- "Worried About Environmental Doom? Go see an eco-therapist," jscms.jrn.columbia.edu/cns/2007 -03-13/nobel-ecoanxiety.html
- Anxiety Disorder Association of America, Silver Spring, MD, 240-485-1001, adaa.org.

READ UP!

- *Bag Green Guilt, 5 Easy Steps: Turn Eco-Anxiety into Constructive Energy*, by Jen Pleasants, Show the Love Media LLC, 2009.
- *How to Turn Your Parents Green*, by James Russell and illustrated by Oivind Hovland, Naked Guides Ltd, 2007.

ACT LOCALLY

- List of Minnesota environmental organizations one could join to "act," eco-usa.net/orgs/mn.shtml

FROM GREECE TO ALBERT LEA, MINNESOTA

Using Blue Zone Principles to Achieve Health and Longevity

Used with permission from the **TAKING CHARGE OF YOUR HEALTH** *website, a consumer health resource created by the* CENTER FOR SPIRITUALITY & HEALING *and the* LIFE SCIENCE FOUNDATION. *For more information, please visit: takingcharge.csh.umn.edu.*

If you haven't yet heard of the Blue Zones, it's likely you live in an area as remote and isolated as the five areas worldwide now identified for health and longevity. Coined by Minnesota explorer/researcher Dan Buettner in his bestselling book *The Blue Zones: Lessons for Living Longer From People Who've Lived the Longest,* Blue Zones are well-defined geographic areas where people experience exceptional longevity and where a high proportion live well into their nineties. Scientists and demographers have classified these longevity hotspots by having common healthy traits and life practices that result in higher-than-normal longevity.

Blue Zones have been identified in Sardinia, Italy; Okinawa, Japan; Loma Linda, California; the Nicoyan Peninsula of Costa Rica; and, most recently, Ikaria, Greece. The people inhabiting Blue Zones share common lifestyle characteristics that contribute to their longevity. For example, among the lifestyle characteristics shared among the Okinawa, Sardinia, and Loma Linda Blue Zones are: family is put ahead of other concerns, residents do not typically smoke, the majority of food consumed is derived

from plants, moderate physical activity is an inseparable part of life, people of all ages are socially active and integrated into their communities, and legumes are commonly consumed.

Dr. Georgiou, a well-know physician leader with a passion for simplifying the healthcare system, was quick to point out that while the Blue Zones team seek answers to sustained health and longevity, much of the work is anthropological research, gleaning insights and behaviors practiced by a population as a whole—and are consistent with data from other Blue Zones. "We don't want to encourage people to move to the five corners of the earth in order to live longer," says Georgiou. "Yet we do want to share lessons learned about how you can incorporate many simple and easy ways to add years to your life, and life to your years."

Meanwhile, a bit closer to home, AARP and the United Health Foundation have announced an effort to create a Blue Zone in Albert Lea, Minnesota. On May 14, 2009, hundreds of the city's residents pledged their support for the AARP/Blue Zones Vital-

ity Project to create "America's Healthiest Hometown." The project marks the first attempt to make over an entire town using Blue Zone principles. "Albert Lea residents will learn that by making a few simple changes to the way we live and the way we think, we can vastly improve our health and actually stack the deck in our favor to live longer, more vibrant lives," said Buettner.

Albert Lea was selected to be the hub of this innovative, research-backed 10-month pilot project designed to improve the health and life expectancy of the city's residents. The goal is to add up to 10,000 years of life to residents through various environmental and individual changes. Four areas critical to health and longevity have been identified as part of the project: Community Environment; Social Networks; Improving Habits; and Sense of Purpose.

"I'm a big fan of the Blue Zones work," said Center senior fellow, Richard Leider. "I'm also glad to see that 'purpose' has been recognized for the important factor that it is in impacting health and aging." Leider, who leads the Center's *Working on Purpose* workshops throughout the year, also led a series of free workshops for 1,500 Albert Lea residents as part of the project.

PUT FAMILY AHEAD OF OTHER CONCERNS

MAKE PHYSICAL ACTIVITY AN INSEPARABLE PART OF LIFE

NO SMOKING

CONSUME MORE PLANT-DERIVED FOODS

PEOPLE OF ALL AGES ARE SOCIALLY ACTIVE

EAT LEGUMES

ON THE WEB

- AARP, aarpmagazine.org/health /vitality_project
- Blue zones, bluezones.com
- Minnesota's Center for Spirituality and Healing, csh.umn.edu

How Communities Changed

Reproduced courtesy of **COMMUNITYGROUP.CO.UK** —
How To Unite Your Community

Mike Koolman

L isten to the older generations: many of them say there's no sense of community the way there was when they were young. They're probably right, since communities have changed with each generation during the last two decades, although not necessarily in a bad way. The grinding poverty and terrible conditions that characterized some neighborhoods have disappeared, and that can only be a good thing. For example, you won't find houses these days without bathrooms and indoor plumbing. Yet our elders are right in the sense that there is no longer the idea of people being bound together by the place they live. However, it might not be as bad as they imagine, as other types of communities have changed and grown.

What Changed Communities

In one word, it was redevelopment that changed everything. When the idea of owning your own house became the norm, it also became a major factor. As property values increased, people sold their houses and moved into what they saw as better neighborhoods—whether for improved schools for their kids or a host of other reasons. This gave rise to a more mobile population that didn't put down roots in a community the way their ancestors had

done. There was no longer a sense of belonging, and people knew fewer of their neighbors.

Modern Communities

Modern communities still tend to be more transient—just look at the number of 'For Sale' and 'Sold' signs on the houses on your street as an example. Some communities, especially in larger cities, rotate through in a constant stream.

Different Communities

In a lot of ways, community these days is less about where we live, and more about other things in our lives. It can be school, a place of worship, a pub, a team, even global communities that have sprung up thanks to the Internet—sometimes these types of communities remain far more constant than the places we live. Communities grow up around all of them, and they're all equally valid. As humans, we make communities around ourselves, it's our natural instinct. So, even though it might seem as if we've lost our sense of community, we haven't really. It's just changed. Look deeper and you'll find that it's as solid as it ever was—it just exists in different ways now.

Coldwater Spring: America's First Green Museum

By **SUSU JEFFREY**

Coldwater Spring is over 10,000 years old and the last natural spring in Hennepin County. The Creek and waterfall empties into sandstone bedrock over 451 million years old. At the top of the bluff where the spring flows out of bedrock fractures, the limestone is 438 million years old. Everything after that time was scraped south by glaciers, which is why we don't have native earthworms.

Mni Owe Sni (Dakota: water-spring-cold), located above the confluence of the Minnesota and Mississippi rivers, was a traditional gathering place for Upper Mississippi Indian peoples including Dakota, Anishinabe, Ho Chunk, Iowa, Sauk and Fox (within historic memory). Particularly blessed by water and considered sacred was the 2.5-mile stretch from what is now called Minnehaha Falls through Coldwater to the *b'dota*, the meeting of waters or confluence. Coldwater became the "Birthplace of Minnesota" when army troops camped around the spring from 1820–23 and mined limestone bluffs to build Fort Snelling. Pioneers arrived and built cabins at Camp Coldwater

to service the fort with meat, trade goods, whiskey, translators, guides, women and missionaries. Coldwater furnished water to the fort from 1820–1920.

From the 1880s to 1950 "Coldwater Park" was labeled on area maps. The Bureau of Mines established a Cold War facility to research metallurgy and mining on 27 acres around Coldwater from 1950–95. In 1988 the U.S. Congress established the Mississippi National River and Recreation Area

(MNRRA) under the National Park Service, a 72-mile long spaghetti-shaped parcel of critical habitat along the great river from Dayton to below Hastings.

Friends of Coldwater envisions Coldwater Park as an 80-acre urban wilderness from the top of the gorge to the river, America's first Green Museum—a place where the land is the legacy. Coldwater still flows at about 80,000 gallons a day.

The best thing for people to do to protect and preserve Coldwater is to come to Coldwater, to feed the spirit of this last sacred spring in our area. On Fridays from about 2:30 to 4:00 PM, Friends of Coldwater staff the site for people with questions but mostly because it is a beautiful, peaceful place to be. We can show you where and how to gather spring water. We also host a monthly Full Moon Walk at 7:00 PM on the day of the full moon.

Friends of Coldwater also keeps in touch with the National Park Service and promotes any public meeting where Coldwater issues are being discussed and decided. It will be at least 20 years before the scars from the Bureau of Mines days at Coldwater fade and the to-be-planted burr oak and prairie savanna plants settle in and thrive.

ON THE WEB!

- Friends of Coldwater, friendsofcoldwater.org
- Mississippi National Recreational Area, National Park Service, nps.gov/miss
- History of Camp Coldwater, www.tc.umn.edu/~white067

Environmental Education in Minnesota

By **COLLEEN SCHOENECKER**
MINNESOTA POLLUTION CONTROL AGENCY

What is environmental education?

The field of environmental education (EE) began to take shape in the 1970s as the international community gathered to address worldwide environmental problems. Out of these meetings came two landmark documents—the Belgrade Charter (UNESCOUNEP, 1976) and the Tbilisi Declaration (UNESCO, 1978)—which laid the foundation for EE. The Belgrade Charter was adopted by a United Nations conference, and provides a widely accepted goal statement for environmental education:

The goal of environmental education is to develop a world population that is aware of and concerned about, the environment and its associated problems, and which has the knowledge, skills, attitudes, motivations, and commitment to work individually and collectively toward solutions of current problems and the prevention of new ones.

Building on the Belgrade Charter, the Tbilisi Declaration established three broad goals for environmental education. These goals provide the foundation for much of what has been done in the field since 1978:

- To foster clear awareness of and concern about economic, social, political, and ecological interdependence in urban and rural areas;
- To provide every person with opportunities to acquire the knowledge, values, attitudes, commitment, and skills needed to protect and improve the environment; and
- To create new patterns of behavior of individuals, groups, and society as a whole toward the environment.

As EE has evolved, these principles have been researched, critiqued, revisited, and expanded, and still stand today as the backbone of environmental education.

EE in Minnesota

The emergence and evolution of EE in Minnesota parallels the national and international EE movement. In 1971, by executive order, Governor Wendell Anderson established the Minnesota Environmental Education Council. This group conducted a study that resulted in the first Minnesota state plan for environmental education which was published in 1972. The state plan was written to offer guidance and direction for educators, the EE community, and government as they work towards the state's environmental education goals.

Minnesota has revised its EE state plan four times since 1972. Today, *A GreenPrint for Minnesota: State Plan For Environmental Education, Third Edition* is a ten year plan (2008–2018) that serves as the guiding document for EE in Minnesota. The *GreenPrint Third Edition* and the three state plans before it have all been written to help educators bring their audiences closer to the state goals for environmental education. Because of the evolving nature of environmental education, *GreenPrint Third Edition* recommends that environmental educators target their programs and plans

toward achieving environmental literacy for all Minnesotans.

In 1992 a grassroots movement began to further grow and complement Minnesota's EE community. Several EE professionals gathered at the state EE conference and formed the Minnesota Association for Environmental Education (MAEE), a nonprofit professional organization. The mission of MAEE is to support and strengthen environmental education throughout the state. As a professional association, MAEE continues today to assist and support the work of individuals engaged in EE and to represent the EE community on relevant issues and legislation.

Environmental Education Resources

Minnesota is a national leader in environmental education and offers a number of resources:

Minnesota Association for Environmental Education (MAEE)
MAEE is a professional organization that supports and strengthens environmental education throughout Minnesota. MAEE also represents the EE community on relevant issues and legislation.

SEEK: Sharing Environmental Education Knowledge
SEEK stands for Sharing Environmental Education Knowledge and is Minnesota's online home of environmental education (EE) resources. SEEK is a partnership of roughly 150 organizations that represent a wide variety of environmental educators in Minnesota and includes zoos, aquariums, schools, colleges, government agencies, nature centers, businesses, and non-profit organizations. In addition to sharing Partner resources, SEEK also houses Minnesota's cornerstone EE documents, legislation, and resources.

A GreenPrint for Minnesota: State Plan for Environmental Education, Third Edition (2008)
A GreenPrint for Minnesota: State Plan for Environmental Education, *Third Edition* is the state plan for environmental education for 2008-2018. It was developed by the Environmental Education Advisory Board and supporting staff with input from the environmental education community. It is designed to serve those who educate, provide funds, develop programs, support efforts, and set policies that affect environmental education in Minnesota.

Environmental Literacy Scope and Sequence (2002)
The Environmental Literacy Scope and Sequence is a tool for educators that provides a systems approach to environmental education in Minnesota for pre-kindergarten through adult learners. It describes key concepts about the interaction of natural and social systems and a sequence in which they are to be taught. It also discusses benchmarks, standards, and applications for using the Scope and Sequence.

Natural Wonders: A Guide to Early Childhood for Environmental Educators (2002)
This guide is the culmination of a two-year project of the Minnesota Early Childhood Environmental Education Consortium. It was written especially for naturalists and environmental educators who are interested in learning more about how and why young children think and act. The guidelines offered here will help educators design developmentally appropriate EE programs and activities.

HOW CAN I GET INVOLVED?
If you are interested in learning more about environmental education in Minnesota and staying informed with the EE community, you can:

- Become a member of MAEE (naaee.org/maee/MembersArea.htm)
- Sign up for the SEEK Bulletin (seek.state.mn.us — click Stay Informed!)
- Explore the SEEK Calendar to find EE events for educators, individuals and families (seek.state.mn.us/calendar.cfm)
- Visit the EE Destinations section in SEEK's Regional Pages (seek.state.mn.us/region_detail. cfm?region=Metro#destinations)

Placemaking: Designing a Garden for the Community

The following information was adapted from "Placemaking: Designing for Community" (gardeningmatters.org/events/2010fair/placemaking.pdf)

By **SHANNON MCWALTERS**
GARDENING MATTERS

The benefits of a community garden are countless. From increasing a sense of community ownership and pride, building community leaders and stewards, and teaching youth where food comes from, to even bringing together multiple generations of people, community gardens can provide a vital element to any neighborhood or community. Designing for a community involves understanding five important steps.

#1: Follow some basic community gardening ethics
- Design for low waste.
- Design for integrated soil management — grow biomass for mulch through on-site composting. Think about crop rotation and crops that fix nitrogen in the off-season.
- Design for sustainability — use recycled materials or local materials. Avoid importing soils and materials.
- Design for water management systems.
- Design for sun access.
- Design for native planting.
- Design for biodiversity — community gardens can be a part of a city-wide network of native animal habitat. Plant species and design infrastructure to encourage this.

Designing with these basic ethical factors will assist in creating beautiful spaces for positive neighborly connections while contributing to the safety, security, and ➻

➥ *Placemaking,* CONTINUED

sustainability of your community garden.

#2: Determine needs and wants

It is an essential starting point for community gardeners to clarify their aims and objectives before commencing on a more detailed planning and design process. An established planning group including diverse community members is essential to this brainstorming process.

#3: Analyze current conditions

To get a better understanding of what's going on at and around the site, follow these steps of thoughtful observation based on the natural landscape features to understand the existing physical conditions of your garden site and community:

- Obtain a base map of the site. Make a few copies and write on the maps. In Minneapolis, Google Maps and the Hennepin County Property Tax Website are invaluable resources.
- Measure your site and make a to-scale site map. A 100' tape measure is helpful in this endeavor.

- Conduct a site analysis—design for the specifics of sites, clients, and cultures. Who lives near the site? What are their gardening needs? Indicate existing features such as pathways, trees, streets, buildings, and fencing to name just a few. Is there a school or elderly home near the site? What languages are spoken nearby? These are just some of the things to think about.

See the "sidebar" below for extensive tools and templates on site analysis for community gardens.

#4: Consider design characteristics and principles

First it is important to consider the characteristics of the spatial functions/elements you will be using in your garden for the planning of the growing spaces, paths, border, or structures.

Applying these design principles to your desired garden features will create a space that is not only beautiful but can represent the many cultural and natural characteristics of your community.

FORM is the shape of any element that you are putting in your garden.

COLOR is found throughout all seasons, in all planting materials, and in all manufactured building materials.

SCALE is the relative size difference when deciding where to place elements in your garden.

TEXTURE is an experience through sight or touch that can add mood or emotion to a garden.

SCENT can be experienced through flowers, fruits, vegetables, and herbs. Place along garden edges or along walkways.

#5: Tools

Choose the logistical systems that support your community's goals and reflect the needs and resources available. Community organizers, landscape designers, and planners can assist in this process. See the Resources section to contact planning assistance.

National and Local Community Gardening Resources

The following resources provide a national and local look at the community gardening movement including current events, classes, workshops, planning assistance, and potential funding ideas:

American Community Gardening Asscociation (ACGA)
Columbus, Ohio. A bi-national nonprofit membership organization of professionals, volunteers and supporters of community greening in urban and rural communities.
communitygarden.org

Gardening Matters
Minneapolis, MN. A local non-profit, Gardening Matters provides training and resources to support community gardeners in achieving community gardens that are successful and sustainable.
gardeningmatters.org
info@gardeningmatters.org
612-492-8964

Planning Assistance
The following links provide planning materials including worksheets and templates to guide you through a 5-step planning and design process with great sections on site analysis:

Gardening Matters: "Twin Cities Community Garden Start-up Guide." The Community Garden Start-Up Guide provides step-by-step instructions with worksheets to help groups get

started in developing a successful community garden.
gardeningmatters.org/resources/startupguide.pdf

City of Sydney
"Getting Started in Community Gardening".
cityofsydney.nsw.gov.au/Environment/documents/CommunityGardens.pdf

Good Reads As You Move through the Design Process
The following books are less planning guides, but instead tell the stories through a multilayered exploration of community gardening in our urban environment:

Seedfolks, by Paul Fleischman, Joanna Cotler Books, 1997.

Greening the City Streets: The Story of Community Gardens, by Barbara A. Huff, Clarion Books, 1990.

Mapping Assistance
Hennepin County Property Tax Website:
www16.co.hennepin.mn.us/pins/addrsrch.jsp

Downtown Community Garden Blog
Includes planning steps and how-to information.
gardendowntowndsm.com

The Transition Movement: Building Resilience in Uncertain Times

By **LOUIS D. ALEMAYEHU AND JONATHAN S. BUCKI**

For generations, people have recognized that the industrial growth economy is destructive and ultimately will engage in its own catabolic demise. Long before the 1972 seminal work *Limits to Growth* modeled the consequences of finite resources supplies and increasing world population, our indigenous brothers and sisters understood the implications of a culture and a lifestyle disconnected from the fundamental rules of nature: "When all the trees have been cut down, when all the animals have been hunted, when all the waters are polluted, when all the air is unsafe to breathe, only then will you discover you cannot eat money."

The need to adapt to emerging conditions is gaining hold of our collective consciousness. Peak oil, climate instability and economic collapse have all increased our awareness of the need to transition our communities and our enterprises to the concrete limits and emergent uncertainties we face.

If permaculture is a reconnection with our species' indigenous wisdom about living on the earth, the Transition Movement is a reconnection with traditional wisdom about living with each other. The Transition Movement is about empowering, involving mutual help at the most local levels. Rob Hopkins, a permaculturist who wrote the Transition Handbook, initiated the Transition Movement from his work on an Energy Descent Action Plan for a small town in the UK. He drew from the work and wisdom of many to come to the understanding of the need to make conscious choices about how we adapt.

The international Transition Movement is comprised of loosely allied grassroots community initiatives. Transition Initiatives seek to engage their communities in homegrown products, education, and action to increase local self-reliance and resilience. We succeed by using local assets and capacities, and respecting the deep patterns of nature and diverse cultures in their place.

Locally, we have a long legacy of many cultural groups working to heal and rebuild our communities after the oil-fueled trauma of the last several hundred years. In addition, new initiatives are taking hold focusing on building resilience, raising awareness, re-skilling for the emergent economy and planning for uncertain times with much less cheap energy. There is opportunity in change, and in transitioning, there is much potential for reconnection to the things we really care about.

Profoundly aware of the cultural nature of our predicament, Transition Initiatives works to create a fulfilling and inspiring local way of life that can withstand the shocks of rapidly shifting global systems and heal the trauma of these times. Many warned us of the dangers of the path we were on. Many have felt left outside of the larger environmental and sustainability movements. An effective transition will mean making authentic community with our neighbors, who reflect the human diversity of this planet. The Transition Movement seeks to be wildly inclusive, not an exclusive path with the answers, but rather a locally rooted, complex adaptation to a series of complex predicaments.

Transition Resources

ON THE WEB!

- **transitiontc.org**
  Local links and resources helping to support transitioning our communities to our lower-energy future.
- **transitionus.org**
  Capacity-building resources to support leaders developing transition initiatives.
- **transitionnetwork.org**
  Information about the international transition movement.
- **sharingindigenouswisdom.org**
  Conference proceedings from 2004 at the College of Menominee Nation, developing a vision of sustainability that allows for the preservation of indigenous lands, sovereignty and culture.
- **indigenous-permaculture.com**
  Building food security using traditional wisdom and affordable strategies. Inspired by indigenous people's understanding of how to live in place.

READ UP!

- *Transition Handbook,* by Rob Hopkins (blog: transitionculture.org).
- *Land & Power: Sustainable Agriculture and African Americans,* by Sustainable Agriculture Research and Education, U.S. Department of Agriculture.
- *Muddling to Frugality,* by Warren Johnson.
- *Long Descent,* by John Michael Greer (blog: thearchdruidreport.blogspot.com).
- *Depletion Abundance,* by Sharon Astyk (blog: scienceblogs.com/casaubonsbook/).
- *Reinventing Collapse,* by Dmitry Orlov (blog: cluborlov.blogspot.com).

Paint the Pavement

By **JUN-LI WANG**
PAINT THE PAVEMENT

Neighbors wave after completing 30-some turtles on Van Buren between Asbury and Simpson in St. Paul. Photos by Jun-Li Wang

Four seasons design in Macalester-Groveland on Griggs between Stanford and Wellesley.

What better way to build community than by doing something creative? While potlucks and ice cream socials with your neighbors serve a crucial purpose (you all get to know one another), carrying out a tangible project together is even more empowering (you all learn to work together).

Paint the Pavement (PtP) is a program established in 2006 that promotes community building and "placemaking" through creating neighborhood art. Our primary focus is in St. Paul, Minnesota, where we support groups of neighbors to organize to create their own public mural on low-traffic residential streets. Neighbors come together, gather support, create a design, petition for approval by the City of St. Paul, fundraise to buy supplies, and hold a "paint day" to create and celebrate their own community square. Other cities have different guidelines and options for residents to paint public areas — contact your local official for more information.

With Paint the Pavement, you build community by learning how to organize together, share responsibilities, work with all ages and backgrounds, create a shared commons, build a local identity, animate public spaces, paint a gorgeous mural, and even slow traffic! A stronger community — where people have organized together to make an artful design, collect signatures, figure out how to raise money, and sweat under the hot sun while painting — is a community that is more networked, more supportive, more safe, and more fun. A village at its best!

If doing a painted street is too daunting at first — or you aren't allowed (yet) in your city — start small and organize the neighbors to try something like painting artful property numbers, or boulevard chairs and benches (scavenged, of course). Build on the experience of organizing for this smaller project, and the enthusiasm and sense of accomplishment by everyone to take on painting your street!

To get started, see the website — it has more details than you could ever need — full instructions, tip sheets, worksheets, sample flyers, and a photo gallery of projects in St. Paul. Good luck!

The original idea for "Paint the Pavement" came from reading an article in YES! Magazine about neighbors in Portland, Oregon who painted their streets to create public square-type spaces on their own blocks. The St. Paul program is modeled after Portland's.

ON THE WEB!

- Paint the Pavement, paintthepavement.org
- Traffic Tamers, tools to tame traffic, traffictamers.com
- City Repair (Portland, OR), cityrepair.org

READ UP!

- *How to Turn a Place Around*, by Kathleen Madden, Project for Public Spaces, 2000.
- *Street Reclaiming*, by David Engwicht, New Society Publishers, 1999.
- *Mental Speed Bumps*, by David Engwicht, Envirobook, 2005.
- *The Great Neighborhood Book*, Jay Walljasper & Project for Public Spaces, New Society Publishers, 2007.

Organics Recycling — Give Back to Nature

By **ALISA RECKINGER**
HENNEPIN COUNTY

Whether at a school, church, or business, establishing an organics recycling program is a great way to reduce the amount of trash disposed of by your organization and reinvigorate your recycling program. Organics include all food waste and non-recyclable or food-soiled paper products and can make up approximately 25 percent of what we throw away.

Take the following steps when setting up an organics program:

- Meet with key staff who will be involved with the program. Consider people from all levels of your organization, including custodians and building maintenance, top-level management, food service, and so forth.
- Establish a budget and determine what resources you will need. Organics programs usually require an initial investment for setup and promotion of the program, but they can pay for themselves by reducing your garbage disposal fees.
- Find a hauler that offers organics recycling (refer to the resources below).
- Choose areas where organics will be collected. To make organics collection effective, evaluate where organic waste is generated in your organization, e.g., kitchens, dining areas, bathrooms, etc.
- Evaluate how your organization generates garbage, recycling and organic waste, and think about how you can reduce the amount of garbage generated. At large events and at regular meals or meetings, look for ways to avoid disposables and/or make sure that food is served in compostable or recyclable containers.
- Set goals in your organization for how much organic waste you will collect and how much trash you will reduce.
- Develop educational and promotional materials. Communicate how the program will work and what goals your organization has set. Let people know what they can do to help you achieve your goals.

- Obtain and place collection containers. Make containers available in kitchens, cafeterias and other locations where organic waste is generated. Set up waste stations with containers for recycling, organic waste and trash. Make sure all containers — for trash, recycling and organics — are clearly labeled.
- Spend some time educating people about the organics program. During events or meals, monitor waste containers to help people figure out in which container their waste belongs. Monitors should educate and encourage sorting while offering minimal assistance so that the organic program can eventually operate with little or no supervision.
- Evaluate your program. How much organics have you collected? Have you met your goals?
- Publicize and celebrate your successes.

Another option for recycling organics is to compost at your facility. You could involve members in constructing and maintaining compost bins, and the finished compost could be used on landscaping projects around your facility.

ON THE WEB!

- Hennepin County organics, hennepin.us. *Search:* "organics"
- RethinkRecycling.com, rethinkrecycling.com/how-keep-food-waste-out-garbage
- EPA food waste information www.epa.gov/wastes/conserve/materials/organics/food

READ UP!

- Biocycle Magazine, jgpress.com/biocycle.htm

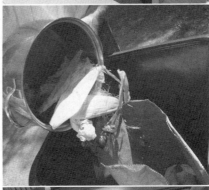

TOP: **Set up waste stations with containers for recycling, organics and trash all in one location. Make sure containers are clearly labeled.** MIDDLE: **Set up organics containers where food waste and compostable paper products are generated by your organization, such as in the kitchen.** BOTTOM: **Organic waste includes food waste and non-recyclable or food-soiled paper products.**
Courtesy of Hennepin County

Building a Community in Your Neighborhood

By **DO IT GREEN! MINNESOTA**

Kory Badertscher and Philipp Muessig crossing spatulas across the fence between their homes on which they've built the grilling station.

Building and maintaining a community in your neighborhood works only if the efforts are people-powered. Check out the ideas below or be creative and determine what works in your area.

- Drink your morning coffee on the front porch.
- Go for a walk; greet people you pass
- Buy local products
- Get to know your mail carrier
- Host a neighborhood potluck
- Build a garden in the front yard
- Pick up litter
- Shovel a neighbor's sidewalk
- Support neighborhood schools and organizations
- Start a neighborhood newsletter
- Buy from lemonade stands
- Visit the local library
- Take action to fix neighborhood infrastructure
- Form a neighborhood exercise club
- Plant a tree
- Clean up after your animals
- Start a neighborhood barter system
- Join a carpool
- Create a neighborhood vegetable garden
- Start a housewarming team to greet new neighbors

ON THE WEB!

- Syracuse Cultural Workers, syracuseculturalworkers.com
- Neighborhood Goods, neighborhoodgoods.net

READ UP!

- *Livable Neighborhoods: A Program to Make Life Better on the Street Where You Live*, by David Gershon, Empowerment Institute, 2008.

Random Acts of Kindness

By **MICAELA PRESTON**
AUTHOR OF *Practically Green: Your Guide to EcoFriendly Decision Making*

Have you ever had someone go out of their way to open a door for you, surprise you by picking up the tab for lunch or shovel your sidewalk after a big snow... or something equally unexpected? If you have (and I bet you have!), then you've experienced a **random act of kindness**.

Last June was Random Acts of Kindness Month in my neighborhood in South Minneapolis. We kept tabs of our daily RAKS (random acts of kindness) and let ✐➤

Keeping Community During the Frigid Months

By **SARA GROCHOWSKI**
DO IT GREEN! MINNESOTA

Springtime in Minnesota means waiting for the snow to melt, analyzing when the last thaw will happen and slowly emerging from hibernation. It can also often mean "re-meeting" the neighbors… the ones you saw raking leaves in October and, after the first snowfall, wondered if they relocated to warmer weather. Chances are, your neighbors may have thought the same about you. Winter can be harsh in Minnesota but keeping and building community with your neighbors can be just as vital to your health.

- **Host a neighborhood potluck.** Send out invitations with specifics on what to bring (such as appetizer, main dish, dessert) and reconnect with your neighbors.

- **Bake and decorate cookies.** Then deliver bags to your neighbors.

- **Create a neighborhood/block newsletter on your computer.** Give each neighbor an age appropriate job. Email or drop off the finished newsletter.

- **Shovel when your neighbors are out.**

- **Build an igloo in the front yard and gather the neighbors to help.** When properly constructed, the temperature inside an igloo will remain between 19° F and 61° F with just body heat, even if the temperature outside dips to −49° F. Search on wikiHow for detailed instructions, then recruit your family and neighbors to help. Have someone stay inside to routinely fuel everyone with hot chocolate and energy bars.

- **Organize a winter block party** either outside or have each participant host a snack in their home and go door to door visiting and eating.

- **Work with your local community center** and organize a day of winter olympics. Games could be indoor or

The Hawkins family and friends skating on the rink they constructed in their front yard.

outdoor. Use your imagination to plan the games.

- **Be creative.** Even the smallest gestures can create a communal feel in your area.

ON THE WEB!

- How to build an igloo, wikihow.com/Build-an-Igloo

---

our neighborhood association know about them. For each and every RAK, a flower was put up on the window of the neighborhood association office. The whole front was covered with flowers!

And what an amazing way to build community! With very little effort, we can make our community a nicer place to live. Most interesting for me was to notice that I tend to dismiss the little things that I do as not a big deal or not worthy of counting as a RAK. But they *are* important! Imagine a world without random acts of kindness. Not very nice, eh? And now that I'm paying attention, I'm finding that it's fun to go out of my way to do them.

Here are a few examples of RAKs that anyone can do:
- Open a door for someone.
- Give a helping hand when you see someone carrying a lot of stuff.
- Cook the favorite breakfast of someone you live with.
- Leave anonymous thank you notes to teachers.
- Give someone a shoulder rub.
- Pay for a cup of coffee for the person behind you in line.
- Invite a friend to the movies or dinner.
- Say I LOVE YOU.
- Leave a book you have already finished somewhere for someone else to read.

- Drop off a toy or game at a homeless shelter.
- Send someone a small gift anonymously.
- Drop off flowers at your friend or neighbor's house.
- Weed your neighbor's garden.
- Shovel for a neighbor in need.

The list goes on and on… **Have you committed a random act of kindness today?**

ON THE WEB!

- Micaela Preston's blog: Mindful Momma, mindfulmomma.com

A Green Development Pattern is Now a Financial Necessity

By **CHARLES MAROHN**
STRONG TOWNS

Strong Towns is a non-profit organization that is helping to change the way cities and neighborhoods are being built. The key insight that the Strong Towns movement provides is simple: it costs more financially to sustain our current development pattern than it generates in financial return.

At the beginning of the automobile era, America made huge investments in the interstate highway system. These investments paid off with new growth, large economic returns and a higher standard of living. By 1950, we were growing rapidly. Our debt was shrinking and America stood as the unrivaled economic power of the world.

Under the guise of "*if a little is good, more must be better,*" we continued to expand this development pattern throughout the following decades. Federal, state and local governments poured trillions of dollars—first in cash, then eventually shifting to borrowed funds—into the expansion of highways, sewers and other infrastructure systems. Each investment saw diminishing returns as we exchanged near-term financial growth for long-term financial liabilities.

Over time, naturalists grew to oppose the inefficient waste of land and the fragmenting of habitats. Sociologists fretted about the lack of community and the isolating nature of the new growth pattern. Medical experts pointed out the rising levels of obesity and other health problems inherent in a commuting lifestyle. Environmentalists talked about the high levels of resource consumption needed to sustain suburban life. Some national defense advocates even pointed out the high cost of oil dependency this lifestyle created. The term "sprawl" was coined by the growing number of people who found fault with America's homogeneous approach to growth.

While these realizations were important, they failed to slow our collective quest for the "American Dream." Only now, when we are faced with the hard reality that we literally cannot financially afford to live this way, are we coming to grips with what it all means.

Our cities and towns are now crumbling under mountains of debt and non-fundable maintenance liabilities. Roads, streets, sidewalks, sewers, and water pipes all need to be maintained. The near-term gains have been spent. The Ponzi scheme of growth has collapsed and the long-term liabilities are now looming.

Federal and state governments, whose policies have encouraged this pattern for decades, are being forced to walk away from local concerns due to their own fiscal constraints. This leaves local officials struggling alone.

The Strong Towns approach puts cities and towns on the right path to real prosperity. Instead of subsidizing one business to provide 25 jobs, cities have to work with 25 local businesses to add one new job to each. Instead of building the city park on cheap land outside of town, cities must improve the neighborhood park so its value will induce greater levels of private investment on existing blocks. Instead of spending money on wider roads to battle congestion, cities need to embrace mixed-use zoning, allowing the market to properly value living patterns that ultimately cost society less.

By focusing on "resiliency" instead of "growth," a Strong Towns development pattern ultimately looks more like the traditional neighborhoods we idealize on movie sets and less like the homogenous strip malls, big boxes and tract housing we have become familiar with.

With a Strong Towns approach, our towns and neighborhoods can become more financially secure and, in the process, become better places to live. You can find out more about Strong Towns on Facebook, Twitter and at **strongtowns.org**.

ON THE WEB:

- Strong Towns, strongtowns.org
- The Original Green, originalgreen.org
- The Creative Class, creativeclass.com
- NRDC Switchboard, switchboard.nrdc.org/blogs/kbenfield
- Smart Code Central, smartcodecentral.org

READ UP:

- *Suburban Nation: The Rise of Sprawl and the Decline of the American Dream,* by Andres Duany, Elizabeth Plater-Zyberk and Jeff Speck.
- *The Smart Growth Manual,* by Andres Duany, Jeff Speck and Mike Lydon.
- *Sprawl Repair Manual,* by Galina Tachieva.
- *The Original Green: Unlocking the Mystery of True Sustainability,* by Steve Mouzon.
- *The Great Reset: How New Ways of Living and Working Drive Post-Crash Prosperity,* by Richard Florida.

Businesses *Are* Going Green

By **MARK BLAISER**
EXECUTIVE DIRECTOR, MINNESOTA WASTE WISE

Historically, environmental initiatives have taken a backseat during difficult economic times. Not during this recession: consumers are still demanding "green" and, more importantly, companies large and small are realizing the economic benefits.

We live in a natural resource constrained world. Millions of people are entering the middle class as new, hungry consumers. With this higher demand for natural resources comes an increased cost, both financial and environmental. Innovation, resource efficiency, cradle-to-cradle, zero waste—these concepts and actions are leading forward-thinking businesses out of the recession and into the future.

Green is practical

Being environmentally sustainable as an organization is much more practical than many business leaders think. Much of the work lies in simply being less wasteful and controlling your supply chain. Minnesota businesses are catching on, and in many cases leading the way (e.g. Aveda, Marvin Windows, Great River Energy). Like other successful business strategies, having leadership effectively communicate sustainability is critical to uniform acceptance. It also allows for continuity with all environmental initiatives, avoiding the pitfall of "random acts of greenness."

Create a plan

Too often we hear the story of organizations wanting to "go green," but not knowing what steps to take. They lack a clear and concise strategy and cohesive company-wide vision. A department might decide to start printing all documents double-sided, only to discover the IT department will not purchase duplex-capable printers due to budget cuts from upper management. Or a department decides to start shutting down computers at night to save energy, missing critical IT updates done after business hours. Initiatives done in this manner are often implemented independently rather than as an organizational strategic plan.

With a clear, strategic environment sustainability plan obstacles like the ones mentioned above often become opportunities. Different departments begin to work together to create solutions. Employees bring practical ideas to the table. And what would traditionally cause tension between departments is suddenly viewed through a different lens. Departments begin to work together to create solutions with the understanding that environmental sustainability is no longer viewed as a separate component of the organization, but an integral part of day-to-day operations—part of the way business is done.

Taking that first step

Environmental sustainability protects our planet now and for future generations. It saves companies money. It's the right thing to do. So why are there still companies out there not recycling office paper? Change. They know how to make widgets or manage insurance policies, but they don't necessarily have the time or interest to invest in changing behaviors to better the environment.

What to do? Get some help. Hire a consultant. Create an internal green team—find the employee taking all her waste paper home at the end of the week to recycle it and appoint her as the leader. If the environment isn't really a concern for your company, the bottom-line and top-line returns on sustainability initiatives should be enough to convince any business leader to get started today.

Most importantly, create a strategic sustainability plan that becomes a long-term component of your company's culture. We've come a long way in the past ten to twenty years. Wal-Mart (yes, Wal-Mart), 3M, Securian Financial Group, and many of America's largest corporations have created sustainability plans. And like most trends with staying power, the businesses leading the way at the onset usually reap the most rewards in the long run.

Similar to the technology industry's rapid advancements (rotary phone to cordless phone to iPhone; typewriter to word processor to iPad), businesses that rapidly and continuously invent solutions to our environmental issues and incorporate sustainability as an ongoing business model will lead the way in environmental protection and shareholder profits. This is why many top businesses are betting that this wave of environmental awareness and green innovation is here to stay—even in tough economic times. After all, a sustainable business also means a company that stays around for many years to come.

ON THE WEB!

- Minnesota Waste Wise, mnwastewise.com
- GreenBiz.com: Business Voice of the Green Economy, greenbiz.com
- Minnesota Pollution Control Agency, reduce.org
- Natural Resource Defense Council, nrdc.org/greenbusiness

READ UP!

- *The Ecology of Commerce* by Paul Hawken, HarperCollins, 1994.

ecoEnvelopes — Reduce and Reuse

By **ANN DELAVERGNE**
FOUNDER, ECOENVELOPES

What is a simple way for each of us to help the environment in our everyday lives? Answer—Reusable envelopes for all your bills. Did you know that 87% of all households pay at least one bill by mail each month, according to the U.S. Post Office? If every bill you receive and paid by mail came in a reusable envelope—we could save energy, water, trees, carbon and pollutants. Each reusable envelope saves almost two cups of wastewater! And for every million reply envelopes eliminated? 123,989 gallons of water would be saved? We could reduce CO_2 by 36,986 pounds, save 23 tons of wood, and 249 million BTUs of energy would not be needed.

Reusable envelopes like ecoEnvelopes help the environment by reducing the amount of paper in the mail and using Forest Service Certified papers with recycled content from managed forests. If you pay your bill using an ecoEnvelope, the outer envelope is sent back to the company for recycling and there is virtually no envelope waste. Using an ecoEnvelope reduces the amount of paper used, it saves companies money and reduces our impact because paper is a natural fiber that is renewable and compostable. When considering the environment, think first about how to reduce, then how to reuse something, then how it can be recycled and made into something else. Do it green… in the mail.

How a reusable envelope works—after purchasing ecoEnvelopes

- Open using the perforated tear strip.
- Remove contents.
- When ready to reply put your return coupon in the envelope with the address showing through the window, the same as you currently do now.
- Seal the envelope on the bottom.
- Place your stamp in the upper-right corner of the envelope and mail. It's that simple.

ACT LOCALLY!

⚙ ecoEnvelopes, ecoenvelopes.com
651-231-1055

Do It Green! Directory

By **KATHARINE NEE**
DO IT GREEN! MINNESOTA

The **Do It Green! Directory** is comprised of green and sustainable businesses, organizations and artists throughout Greater Minnesota and Western Wisconsin. Do It Green! Minnesota is committed to promoting those who are truly green, so all listings are accepted by a review team and must meet two or more of the selection criteria listed at doitgreen.org.

Several members, both new and long-term answered the question: What is your green initiative? What do you, as a business, nonprofit, or artist, do to be green that others could emulate?

Kim Oedekovn of **reBAG-it** says she calculates how to use as much of the fabric for her bags as possible so there is very little waste. In terms of shipping, she looks for materials that have 30% or more post-consumer product.

Ruth Patton of **Fresh Energy** says transportation-wise they joined **HOURCAR** hybrid car rental as a company member. When they built out the office, they insisted on using environmentally friendly materials for the carpet, desks, and cubicle walls.

Alison Love Unzelman, the eco-artist behind **EcoBangle**, is always looking for materials she can reclaim or recycle. Everything she uses except paint or glue is recycled. A recycled object is the starting point for each piece of art.

Jeannie Piekos of **Bag-E-Wash** estimates that she has been involved with Do It Green! Minnesota for the last six years. She never buys packaging materials, but only reuses existing materials. Her labels are made from recycled materials and there is very little waste with any of her products.

Do It Green! Directory Membership listings start at just $35 a year. With potential benefits such as print ads, e-newsletter banner ads, and a free booth at the Green Gifts Fair, there are options to meet everyone's needs. Contact katharine@doitgreen.org to learn what level is right for you, or apply at doitgreen.org. Be sure to visit the directory to learn more about all of our excellent members: **doitgreen.org/directory**.

ON THE WEB!

⚙ doitgreen.org/directory
⚙ reBAG-it, reBAG-it.com
⚙ Fresh Energy, fresh-energy.org
⚙ Bag-E-Wash, bag-e-wash.com
⚙ EcoBangle, etsy.com/shop/EcoBangle
⚙ Hourcar, hourcar.org

Living Learning Center

THE FIRST LIVING BUILDING IN THE COUNTRY

As previously written by **ASHLEY DEROUSSE**
ECOLIFESTL.COM, ST. LOUIS, MO

Living Learning Center. Ashley, EcoLifeSTL.com

Washington University's Tyson Research Center acts as a living laboratory for ecology and environmental biology. During the summer, the Center houses a very active undergraduate research program. Last summer, Tyson received a grant that will allow it to play host to a high school internship program. This new grant program required Tyson Research Center to build a new facility to house it. The appointed architect, Dan Hellmuth, brought the idea of participating in the Living Building Challenge—and the Living Learning Center was born.

The Cascadia Region Green Building Council, one of three original chapters of the U.S. Green Building Council, created the Living Building Challenge a few years ago. The challenge encourages construction of a completely self-sustainable building. The first completed entry for the challenge was opened May 29, 2009 at Tyson Research Center.

Kevin Smith, an associate director at Tyson, said, "The Living Building Challenge suggests that even though everyone is comfortable with green sustainable buildings now, we can still do a lot better. There are much higher criteria that we can meet to constantly be pushing the limits of what we consider as green and sustainable. [Tyson] is an environmental research station, and so putting our money where our mouth is in terms of sustainability really appealed to us."

The Living Learning Center (LLC) had to meet stringent requirements in order to be in compliance with the Living Building Challenge. The building has to use zero net energy and zero net water. This means the building itself must produce all of the energy it uses. Water must be collected when it rains, filtered and stored at the facility. Other requirements set by the Green Building Council include the types of building materials used.

"There are two sets of requirements, really," said Smith. "There were 'red list' materials that could not be used in the building for the most part, PVC and lead for example. Also, the materials that could be used could only come from so far away, because of the carbon footprint created by all of the transportation."

The Building Council set distances for materials based on the material's density. Heavy materials such as metal had to be delivered from within 250 miles, wood 500 miles, and other materials could come from further away the lighter they were. Some alternatives were found for "red listed" materials, but they came from too far away. When this happened, Tyson would work with the Cascadia Region Green Building Council and file for an exemption. "A lot of this was a learning process, not only for us, but for the Green Building Council as well. They were relying on us to feel out a lot of these requirements to see how possible they were."

Tyson has met all of the requirements of the challenge so far. The features of the building are what make it so impressive. All of the exposed wood is manufactured from trees that come from around Tyson Research Center. The Center found trees that were invading other habitats and had to be removed, and also used trees that had already fallen.

The largest roof is slanted and covered in solar panels that produce the energy for the Living Learning Center. On a sunny day, the solar panels can produce 80 kilowatts of energy. This is enough energy to power 2½ houses a day. Because the LLC uses less energy than an average home, the excess energy is fed back into the grid, and the LLC is given credit from Ameren through a program called "net metering." This means that on a cloudy day when there is little solar energy being produced, the LLC can draw energy from the grid and continue to maintain zero net energy.

The slanted roof also aids in fulfilling the requirement of zero net water. Rainwater runs down the roof into a gutter system that collects the water, passes it through ⮑

➤ *Learning Center,* CONTINUED

4 different types of filters and then into an underground, 3,000-gallon storage tank. Then, as an extra requirement implemented by building inspectors, another filter on every faucet will eliminate any bacteria that could be remaining in the water. The LLC uses minimal amounts of water due to composting toilets, and landscaping that requires little watering. The 3,000-gallon tank could sustain the LLC for 60 days during a severe drought (zero inches of rainfall).

Landscaping around the building plays its part in sustainability, too—all of the plants are native to the area and require low maintenance and water, which reduces the carbon footprint necessary to sustain them. A rain garden collects runoff from one of the un-slanted roots. The water goes down a decorative "rain chain" and into the rain garden. The Living Learning Center even reduces runoff with the use of porous concrete. Rainwater that falls on the sidewalk permeates right through it and into the soil below.

Every piece of the LLC is designed to increase its sustainability and to make it more eco-friendly. From siding, energy usage, hyper-efficient zone-controlled air-conditioning, double-glazed windows, and composting toilets, the Living Learning Center can be used as an example for anyone who wants to create a greener living, learning, or working environment.

"The building as a system isn't separate from the environment, but integrated with the environment," said Smith. "It really fits with our mission."

If the Living Learning Center can maintain the requirements of the Living Building Challenge for one year, then this will be the first certified Living Building in the country. The building—used as classroom, office, research center, computer lab, and meeting space—will inspire anyone who walks inside to strive to include green-living in their day-to-day life.

ON THE WEB!

- ✿ EcoLife St. Louis, EcoLifeSTL.com
- ✿ International Living Building Institute, ilbi.org
- ✿ Tyson Research Center, tyson.wustl.edu
- ✿ Minnesota Green Building Coalition, usgbcmn.org
- ✿ Minnesota Green Star, mngreenstar.org

Locally Powering the Conversion to Electric Vehicles

By **ALEX DANOVITCH**
ReGo Electric Conversions

PLUG-IN
CONVERSIONS
FOR HYBRID CARS

Prius plug-in hybrid converted by ReGo Electric Conversions.
photo by Janell Vircks

Electric vehicles are finally coming, and this time it's for real. Investments in technology, policy shifts, rising fuel prices and awareness of global warming have brought us closer to the tipping point than ever before. Major car companies are releasing commercial versions of battery electric (BEV) and plug-in hybrid electric vehicles (PHEV) this year. And it's about time! 20% of our total carbon emissions are attributed to passenger vehicles and over 65% of U.S. oil consumption is used for transportation. Plus, electric vehicles drastically improve ➤

Career Networking in the *Local* Green Community

By **BARBARA PARKS**
Green Career Tracks

Local networking communities with shared green values are by far the best source of shared information about sustainable career and work opportunities. Being out in the community, learning and sharing information will put you on the frontline of emerging green technologies and business development in the local green economy.

In the Minneapolis/St. Paul area, you can tap into two green networking groups that have been established here for several years:

- EcoTuesday is a great networking group of eco-minded folks who meet on the 4th Tuesday of every month at different locations. The Minneapolis chapter, meeting since 2007, attracts a diverse group of sustainable business leaders involved in a wide variety of interests and fields. Visit: **ecotuesday.com**
- Another green networking opportunity can be found at Green Drinks gatherings. Join this green community to make some new connections and charge your eco-spirit. The organization is worldwide with a local chapter that meets regularly in the Metropolitan Area. Visit **greendrinks.com** ➤

air quality in our neighborhoods, eliminating harmful emissions by 96%.

Unfortunately, new cars alone are not the answer. There are over 900 million cars on the road today and experts predict that number to grow to two billion in the next decade. Most of these cars will stay on the road for 10–15 years. It took hybrid vehicles 10 years to get one percent of the market share, so even if we adopt electric vehicles much faster, there's still a long road of gas guzzling combustion engines ahead. The energy and resources that went into making the cars on the road today (think mining the metal, powering the process, transporting the product, etc.) account for more then 10% of the carbon emissions over their operating life. Given the embedded energy in these vehicles and their ongoing fuel consumption, converting existing cars must be part of any solution.

ReGo Electric Conversions, a local company, is embracing this opportunity to convert existing vehicles already on the road to next-generation electric cars. As a triple-bottom line business (valuing people, planet and profit), our mission is to provide reliable, cost-effective and accessible electric car conversions and services that benefit our community and the environment while building a strong local economy. We've successfully completed Minnesota's first two all-lithium battery conversion prototypes and continue to invest in research and development to improve electric vehicle performance in Minnesota's cold climate. Currently we offer services to convert existing hybrids to plug-in hybrids. This conversion gives you about 20–40 miles of electric driving range powered by local and potentially renewable energy. But we aren't stopping there; as new ideas become feasible and cost effective, ReGo is committed to bringing them to market. Learn more at the resources below.

ON THE WEB!

- ReGo Electric, regoelectric.com
- Minnesota Electric Auto Association, mneaa.com
- California Cars Initiative, calcars.org
- Plug in America, pluginamerica.org

READ UP!

- *Two Billion Cars: Driving Towards Sustainability,* by Gordon Sperling, Oxford University Press, 2009.
- *Stop Trashing the Climate,* stoptrashingtheclimate.org, Institute for Local Self Reliance, GAIA, Eco-Cycle, 2008.

ACT LOCALLY!

- Rego Electric Conversions
  Minneapolis, MN
  612-791-0263
  regoelectric.com

Other green networking groups have been meeting in Minneapolis and St. Paul in recent months, although they're not always visible to the public. **The key to scouting them out is to ask environmental professionals and eco-minded folks you meet what network groups they attend.** For newly formed green networking groups in the Twin Cities, check out LinkedIn and MeetUp groups. Other local networking sources include:

Nonprofit Networking

Explore volunteer opportunities at places like The Minnesota Project (**mnproject.org**) or Forum of Women in the Environmental Field (**fwef.org/employment**) and hook up with green nonprofits in the Twin Cities that align with your sustainability concerns and values. Even if you aren't interested in working in the non-profit world, you'll meet people who share your environmental and social justice concerns. Learn what they do, and more importantly, *whom* they know!

If you can't volunteer on an ongoing basis, find a way to participate in a one-time special event or conference planning; it's a great way to take a leadership role and rack up some project coordinator experience!

Professional Associations

Identify and research professional associations related to your green industry or field of interest with a chapter or home base in the Twin Cities. Most professional associations like Minnesota Renewal Energy Society (**mnrenewables.org**) or Net Impact (**netimpactminneapolis.org**) have well-informed members who are willing to share contact referrals, education resources, or information about local sustainability mandates and projects. You can usually attend one meeting as a first-time guest without paying a membership fee.

But do consider joining. Membership benefits often include:

- Direct exposure to green professionals, hiring authorities and business owners through participation in networking events and functions.
- Job boards and resume post or free listing on their website directory.
- Regular newsletters with up-to-date information on green industry or social justice issues and trends.
- Training and/or certification in green fields and industries.

Activist Groups

Seek out environmental or social justice meet-up groups, activist and other grassroots groups like Environmental Justice Advocates of Minnesota (**ejam.org**) or Healthy Legacy (**healthylegacy.org**) in the Minneapolis/St. Paul area. Learn their purpose statement, the issues they're concerned about, the people involved, and what they're trying to accomplish. (There's a certain amount of solidarity in working for the "cause." And greater access to environmental or social justice job possibilities!)

READ UP!

- *The Complete Idiot's Guide to Green Careers,* by Barbara Parks and Jody Helmer, Alpha, 2009.

ACT LOCALLY!

- Green Career Tracks
  Barbara Parks, Career Consultant
  612-822-0288
  barbara@greencareertracks.com
  greencareertracks.com

Getting to the "Soul" of Carbon Foodprinting

By **KIM BARTMANN**, RED STAG SUPPER CLUB
and **JIM KLEINSCHMIT**, INSTITUTE FOR AGRICULTURE AND TRADE POLICY

The Red Stag opened in 2007 as the first LEED-CI registered restaurant project in Minnesota.

In the fight against climate change, we are all (hopefully) beginning to scrutinize every area of our economy, work, and lifestyle for opportunities to reduce greenhouse gas (GHG) emissions. This includes our food system, which, just from the production and distribution side, is responsible for around 16% of U.S. total emissions.[1] In 2008 and again in 2009, the Red Stag restaurant in Minneapolis engaged in a process of measuring its carbon footprint using Green House Gas Protocol.

Carbon Foodprinting is the term for this "field to fork" climate assessment that encompasses the entire food production, consumption and disposal cycle. Such analyses can be very useful for farmers, retailers and "eaters" alike, but have their limits in assessing overall sustainability, as many aspects of what we would broadly call 'sustainable' farming are simply left out of the equation. So far, the Red Stag has not taken any steps significantly new to the operation because of this study, but we are learning a lot in the process.

Transportation remains the biggest challenge in the local food movement; and it accounts for the large majority of our restaurants carbon footprint.

Carbon foodprinting is most useful in identifying areas where there is excess energy use and waste, which results in water, soil, and air pollution. On the farm, the biggest chances to minimize GHG emissions are in reducing use of fossil fuels (for energy, but also for fertilizer and pesticides), reducing soil emissions and building soil organic matter by putting more carbon in the soil. For those parts of the food system in between the farm and the eater — including distributors, restaurants, and grocery stores — emission reductions largely involve increased energy efficiency, reduced transport and storage (especially refrigeration), and minimizing food waste.

Yet, perhaps the single most important opportunity for reducing global warming pollution from food lies with each of us. With up to 50% of food produced in the U.S. wasted each year, we can make a big difference by buying smarter (not too much and with minimal packaging and storage needs), and disposing responsibly, ideally through composting, which helps those nutrients return to the soil and produce new food, rather than producing GHGs in landfills.[2]

While the science is maturing, calculating GHG emissions from farming systems can be extremely difficult, especially with complex systems like sustainable farms. For example, assessing GHG emissions from rotationally-grazed cattle requires not only calculating emissions from the cattle, but also how their grazing contributes to the ability of the pasture to sequester carbon. Ironically, while such production systems are obviously more sustainable and less resource intensive than their conventional counterparts, the fact that grazing cattle appear to directly emit more GHGs than grain-fed cattle is being used to support claims that grass-fed is worse for the climate and environment. In reality, there are good reasons to assume that if you included the increased sequestration from well-managed pasture systems, grass-fed cattle are likely better for the climate than grain-fed beef, and are clearly better from a human and animal health, water quality and wildlife habitat perspective, but such a calculation is incredibly complicated, which has limited our "full" understanding of how global warming impacts grass-fed beef production.

Understanding the climate contributions of all parts of our lives and economy is critical for stopping global warming, and thankfully tools like carbon foodprints are emerging that can help farmers, consumers and businesses make better choices. But that said, carbon accounting is no silver bullet for assessing sustainability, and "carbon myopia" should not be used to deter us from considering other key sustainability attributes of our food and farming system. Truly understand- ➥

Small Biz: Reduce the Hail of Unwanted Mail!

By **ANGELA BOURDAGHS**
MINNESOTA POLLUTION CONTROL AGENCY

Carbon Foodprinting, CONTINUED

ing the overall sustainability footprint of your food requires that issues of health, water or soil quality, biodiversity, animal welfare and economic viability also be analyzed alongside GHG emissions.

---

[1] Weber and Matthews, "Food-Miles and the Relative Climate Impacts of Food Choices in the United States," pubs.acs.org/doi/full/10.1021/es702969f?cookieSet=1

[2] According to the EPA, food waste (including uneaten food and food preparation scraps) is the single-largest component of the waste stream by weight in the United States. Over 12 percent of the total municipal solid waste generated in American households was food scraps and less than three percent was recovered (epa.gov/wastes/conserve/materials/organics/food/fd-basic.htm)

ON THE WEB!

- Institute for Agriculture and Trade Policy, iatp.org

READ UP!

- *Food-Miles and the Relative Climate Impacts of Food Choices in the United States,* by Christopher L. Weber and H. Scott Matthews, 2008, pubs.acs.org.

ACT LOCALLY!

- Red Stag Supperclub Minneapolis, MN redstagsupperclub.com

When it comes to conserving resources and saving money, reducing paper waste trumps recycling. Businesses of all sizes can do well by doing the right thing. Consider the following two methods for reducing junk mail in the office:

Wheel and Spoke method

Employees save their unwanted mail individually, and then give it to someone (e.g. mailroom staff, intern, clerical) in charge of getting employees off mailers' lists. The "spokes" are the various employees funneling junk mail to the central person.

This method works well in a large office when there are many employees who might have the same problem mailer. The central person sorts by mailer, makes a list, and calls the problem mailers to say, for example, "I have 12 employees at the XYZ Corporation who need to be taken off your mailing list." Mail sent to employees who are no longer there—a common problem—should automatically be given to the central person for mailer notification. The Wheel and Spoke method is probably the most efficient for most businesses, if you have someone available to be the central person.

Individual method

With this method, individual employees are encouraged to get off mailing lists on their own. The company usually makes available a postcard that employees can send to mailers, requesting to get off lists.

The Individual approach does not require a central person like the Wheel and Spoke system, but there could be duplicate efforts from individual staff requesting to be removed from the same organization's list.

NOTE: Residential junk mail opt-outs don't work for businesses (unless it is a small home business). The residential system is not set up for businesses and most of the companies that you can opt-out of from residential websites do not contain common business junk mailers.

ON THE WEB!

- Ecological Mail Coalition, ecologicalmail.org
  Markets a free service to direct mailers by maintaining a database of the names and work addresses of former employees.
- Catalog choice, catalogchoice.org
  A free service for individuals and addresses who want to rid themselves of unwanted paper catalogs and advertising.

Winona, Minnesota

Winona is in a valley on the Mississippi River in southeastern Minnesota. It is a historic community of 27,000 people with a wealth of natural beauty and significant architecture. It is situated between the bluffs and the river, allowing for a variety of outdoor recreation.

Home to Wenonah Canoe, Winona hosts canoeing on the river and its backwaters as a favorite pastime. Hiking and mountain biking are popular bluff activities. The national wildlife refuge provides fisher people and birders abundant opportunities.

Winona's mayor, Jerry Miller, joined mayors from around the nation in endorsing the U.S. Conference of Mayors' Climate Protection Agreement and in promoting economic and environmental health throughout the City of Winona. Sustain Winona is a city-wide partnership between many local institutions.

Prairie Moon Nursery is known for restoring the natural prairie by supplying native plants and seeds for natural landscaping. Wildflower gardens and many of Winona's buildings are built with natural local limestone from locally-owned Biesanz Stone Company.

the local foods movement.

Sustain Winona Partnership
Community partners came together to create a consortium dedicated to addressing issues of sustainability across the entire community.

City Shade Project
City Shade is a public/private collaboration to reforest Winona sponsored by Sustain Winona. City Shade is designing a plan to substantially increase Winona's tree canopy, track tree cover, tree health, and species diversity across the City.

RECREATION

Upper Mississippi Wildlife Refuge
Refuge encompasses more than 240,000 acres of land and remains perhaps the most important corridor of fish and wildlife habitat in the central United States.

Levee Park
Walking path and boat docking with a view of the main channel of the Mississippi River.

Lake Park
Biking, walking path around two lakes. Canoeing, kayaking, and fishing on the lakes. Bandshell concerts, tennis courts and children's playground.

Latsch Island
Beach for swimming (no lifeguard) in the Mississippi River. Home to a unique community of people who live in boathouses on the backwaters of the Mississippi River.

Aghaming Park
1,950 acres of some of the best preserved floodplain forest in the country and a pristine destination for bird watching.

RECYCLING

Winona County Hazardous Waste Facility
Disposes of household hazardous waste. Accepts donations of paint and household products to be reused by Winona County residents.

Winona County provides curbside pickup of recyclable materials.

Habitat Restore
The Habitat ReStore is a building materials reuse and surplus center. Overstocked, discontinued or slightly damaged items as well as used materials and equipment will

Prairie Garden and Lake Winona.

FOOD

Bluff Country Co-op
bluff.coop
Sells naturally good food and the freshest ingredients for your table. Buys direct from the farmer whenever possible so shoppers can enjoy the freshest and least traveled products around.

Farmers Market
Foot of Main St.
winonafarmersmarket.com
Provides fresh, quality local produce and meat products for the public.

Blue Heron Coffeehouse
Promote good food that is local, seasonal and organically grown. Has a reputation for good food done well in a warm inviting space that appeals to people from a cross

section of the community.

Rochester Wholesale Fruit
Fresh fruit and vegetables, some local and organic products.

Wapasha Community Garden
Winona residents garden communally and raise their own organic produce. A hunger garden plot provides food for Winona's Food Shelf and Winona's Catholic Worker houses.

Community Supported Agriculture
Several area farms/gardens provide fresh, organic produce to consumers who make a financial pledge to support farmers.

Local Foods Forum and Expo
Designed to increase the production of foods grown in Winona County, and to expand the number of people involved in

be donated for resale to the public.

EDUCATION

Winona State University
Zipcar provides the freedom of car ownership—the ability to get off campus for errands, entertainment or road trips—without the cost and hassle of owning a car. All reservations include fuel, insurance, parking, roadside assistance and 180 free miles per day.

The Winona State University new ride board system includes a student ride board, student commuter ride board, faculty ride board, and a ride board for all members of the WSU community. It is the goal of the WSU Goes Green initiative and Student Senate to provide convenience for those who are traveling, and to reduce the carbon foot print of Winona State University by encouraging people to car pool.

Riverway Learning Community
Riverway Learning Community has five different gardening areas. Riverway students are included in all aspects of the growth cycle, including composting, garden space planning, planting, maintenance, harvesting, preserving and saving seeds.

Over the next five years, Riverway Learning Community hopes to farm, grow and prepare 50% of all cafeteria food on site. Their commercial kitchen allows them to prepare wholesome, organic foods on site. The garden program provides fresh produce and the poultry program has provided over 1000 lbs. of chicken this year.

ATTRACTIONS

Minnesota Marine Art Museum
The Minnesota Marine Art Museum is the product of vision, inspiration and generosity. The Museum features four galleries of world-class art and artifacts and is located in a unique building and picturesque setting on the banks of the Mississippi River.

In addition, there are over 60,000 native plants and grasses to stroll by and enjoy along the riverwalk.

Frozen River Film Festival
The Frozen River Film Festival identifies and offers programs that engage, educate and activate people to become involved in the world.

Hop on the Iron Range Sustainability Train

By **ARDY NURMI-WILBERG**
PROJECT DIRECTOR, IRON RANGE PARTNERSHIP FOR SUSTAINABILITY

At the Iron Range Earth Fest.

There's a movement afoot on Minnesota's Iron Range: a sustainability movement, evident in all the incredible projects from biomass generated electricity at the Virginia and Hibbing municipal power plants, to windmills on the mine dumps overlooking Minntac and the production of solar panels in Mountain Iron. The Range is buzzing about sustainability. For us on the east end of the Range, the acceptance of that movement is evident by the unprecedented success of Iron Range Earth Fest, the formation of the Iron Range Partnership for Sustainability, the publication of the "Everyday Guide to Sustainable Living on the Iron Range," and area youth participation in the Green Inventors Contest.

Iron Range Earth Fest is a celebration of local traditions and practical resources for sustainable living. The event offers opportunities to explore how we can all live more sustainably in our homes and communities,

our economy and our environment. Participants are invited to learn about new and existing technological approaches as well as rediscover some of our long-standing local traditions. We tap into the knowledge of cutting edge experts as well as our local indigenous knowledge through exhibits, speakers and vendors. Emphasis is placed on local products, local services, local foods, local traditions and our local wilderness.

Initially the Iron Range Partnership for Sustainability was formed to make it easier to list all the organizations presenting Earth Fest, but the group quickly realized that it could do much more to educate the Range about sustainability. So besides hosting the annual Iron Range Earth Fest, in 2010 the group created a non-profit corporation whose mission is to stimulate conversation and action for a sustainable future on the Iron Range. It's a grassroots organization with goals to encourage and provide educational opportunities, to become a

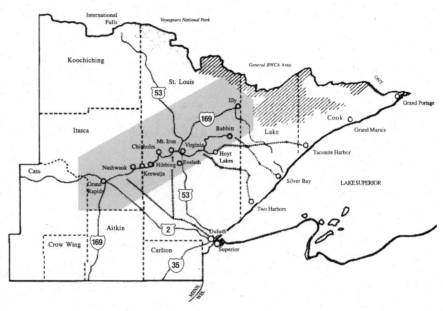

networking and information-sharing hub and to make sustainability an accepted core value on the Iron Range.

The "Everyday Guide to Sustainable Living on the Iron Range" is an annual resource guide published just in time for Earth Fest, with each edition exploring a different aspect of sustainability. The 2010 premiere copy focused on local sustainable food production complete with informative articles, stories about local farmers and a list of local food producers and farmers markets.

The Earth Fest Green Inventors Contest encourages Iron Range students to develop a green invention that can solve an environmental problem or make something more environmentally friendly. The first annual contest was held in 2010 with over 50 participants who came up with some remarkable inventions like composting cubes, a solar powered plant turner, the adjustable manplow and a lawnmower seed grower. Judging from the projects submitted, the future of the Iron Range is in very good hands.

The sustainability movement on the Iron Range is building momentum fast, like a train going downhill, and we're all just along for this incredible and exciting ride. Would you like to join us? Watch for our progress on the Earth Fest website at ironrangeearthfest.org or join us at the 3rd annual Iron Range Earth Fest on April 9, 2011.

Farmers markets are one of the oldest forms of marketing by small-scale farmers. From the Andes to Asia, growers and artisans all over the world gather to sell directly to the public. In the last decade farmers markets have become a preferred method for buying and delivering products for many consumers and farmers throughout the United States. Whether you live in or are visiting the Iron Range, support your local Farmers Market or grocery stores!

Cook Farmers Market
Summer hours 8 a.m.–1 p.m. Saturdays (starting late June or first weekend in July)
Contact: Missy Roach 218-969-6872

Ely Farmers Market
Tuesdays late May through September, 5:30-7:00 p.m.
Contact: Marcia Mahoney, marcialoon@hotmail.com

Embarrass Farmers Market
4th Saturday of each month 10-4:00 p.m.
Contact: Verna and Ron Sutton, 218- 984-2302

Grand Rapids Farmers Market
Wednesdays & Saturdays 8 a.m.–1 p.m. From May–October

Contact: Dawn, 218-697-2766

Hibbing Farmers Market
Tuesdays & Fridays, 8 a.m.–1:30 p.m.
Contact: Steve Yoder, 218-258-8959

Tower Farmers Market
Fridays 4 p.m.–6 p.m.
Contact: Janna Goerdt, fatchickenfarm@gmail.com

Virginia Farmers Market
Tues. & Fri. 11 a.m.–6 p.m. July–Oct.
Contact: Steve Yoder, 218-258-8959

Natural Harvest Food Cooperative
Virginia, MN
218-741-4663
natharv@mchsi.com
naturalharvestcoop.com

Sonja's Whole Foods Pantry at Evergreen Cottage
Ely, MN
218-365-2288
evergreencottage@frontiernet.net
elyevergreencottage.com/pantry.htm

COME JOIN THE MOVEMENT!

You can still catch the train:
- ❂ Iron Range Partnership for Sustainability, ironrangeearthfest.org
- ❂ Iron Range Earth Fest on Facebook, facebook.com/ironrangeearthfest